ON

HEROES, HERO-WORSHIP

AND

The Heroic in History

BY

THOMAS CARLYLE

CHICAGO

A. C. McCLURG AND COMPANY

1897

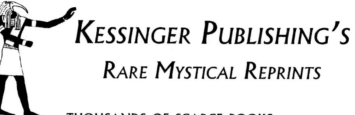

KESSINGER PUBLISHING'S
RARE MYSTICAL REPRINTS

THOUSANDS OF SCARCE BOOKS
ON THESE AND OTHER SUBJECTS:

Freemasonry * Akashic * Alchemy * Alternative Health * Ancient
Civilizations * Anthroposophy * Astrology * Astronomy * Aura *
Bible Study * Cabalah * Cartomancy * Chakras * Clairvoyance *
Comparative Religions * Divination * Druids * Eastern Thought *
Egyptology * Esoterism * Essenes * Etheric * ESP * Gnosticism *
Great White Brotherhood * Hermetics * Kabalah * Karma * Knights
Templar * Kundalini * Magic * Meditation * Mediumship * Mesmerism
* Metaphysics * Mithraism * Mystery Schools * Mysticism * Mythology
* Numerology * Occultism * Palmistry * Pantheism * Parapsychology
* Philosophy * Prosperity * Psychokinesis * Psychology * Pyramids *
Qabalah * Reincarnation * Rosicrucian * Sacred Geometry * Secret
Rituals * Secret Societies * Spiritism * Symbolism * Tarot * Telepathy
* Theosophy * Transcendentalism * Upanishads * Vedanta * Wisdom
* Yoga * *Plus Much More!*

DOWNLOAD A FREE CATALOG
AND
SEARCH OUR TITLES AT:

www.kessinger.net

CONTENTS.

HEROES, AND HERO-WORSHIP.

LECTURE I.

THE HERO AS DIVINITY. — ODIN: PAGANISM; SCANDINAVIAN MYTHOLOGY.

WE have undertaken to discourse here for a little on Great Men, their manner of appearance in our world's business, how they have shaped themselves in the world's history, what ideas men formed of them, what work they did; — on Heroes, namely, and on their reception and performance; what I call Hero-worship and the Heroic in human affairs. Too evidently this is a large topic; deserving quite another treatment than we can expect to give it at present. A large topic; indeed, an illimitable one; wide as Universal History itself. For, as I take it, Universal History, the history of what man has accomplished in this world, is at bottom the History of the Great Men who have worked here. They were the leaders of men, these great ones; the modellers, patterns, and in a wide sense creators, of whatsoever the general mass of men contrived to do or to attain; all things that we see standing accomplished in the world are properly the outer material result, the practical realization and embodiment, of Thoughts that dwelt in the Great Men sent into the world: the soul of the whole world's history, it may justly be considered, were the history of these. Too clearly it is a topic we shall do no justice to in this place!

One comfort is, that Great Men, taken up in any way, are profitable company. We cannot look, however imperfectly, upon a great man, without gaining something by him. He is the living light-fountain, which it is good and pleasant to be near. The light which enlightens, which has enlightened the darkness of the world; and this not as a kindled lamp only, but rather as a natural luminary shining by the gift of Heaven; a flowing light-fountain, as I say, of native original insight, of manhood and heroic nobleness; — in whose radiance all souls feel that it is well with them. On any terms whatsoever, you will not grudge to wander in such neighborhood for a while. These Six classes of Heroes, chosen out of widely-distant countries and epochs, and in mere external figure differing altogether, ought, if we look faithfully at them, to illustrate several things for us. Could we see *them* well, we should get some glimpses into the very marrow of the world's history. How happy could I but, in any measure, in such times as these, make manifest to you the meanings of Heroism; the divine relation (for I may well call it such) which in all times unites a Great Man to other men; and thus, as it were, not exhaust my subject, but so much as break ground on it! At all events, I must make the attempt.

It is well said, in every sense, that a man's religion is the chief fact with regard to him. A man's, or a nation of men's. By religion I do not mean here the church-creed which he professes, the articles of faith which he will sign and, in words or otherwise, assert; not this wholly, in many cases not this at all. We see men of all kinds of professed creeds attain to almost

all degrees of worth or worthlessness under each or
any of them. This is not what I call religion, this
profession and assertion; which is often only a profession and assertion from the outworks of the man,
from the mere argumentative region of him, if even so
deep as that. But the thing a man does practically
believe (and this is often enough *without* asserting it
even to himself, much less to others); the thing a man
does practically lay to heart, and know for certain,
concerning his vital relations to this mysterious Universe, and his duty and destiny there, that is in all
cases the primary thing for him, and creatively determines all the rest. That is his *religion;* or, it may be,
his mere scepticism and *no-religion:* the manner it is
in which he feels himself to be spiritually related to
the Unseen World or No-World; and I say, if you
tell me what that is, you tell me to a very great extent
what the man is, what the kind of things he will do is.
Of a man or of a nation we inquire, therefore, first of
all, What religion they had? Was it Heathenism, —
plurality of gods, mere sensuous representation of this
Mystery of Life, and for chief recognized element
therein Physical Force? Was it Christianism; faith
in an Invisible, not as real only, but as the only
reality; Time, through every meanest moment of it,
resting on Eternity; Pagan empire of Force displaced
by a nobler supremacy, that of Holiness? Was it
Scepticism, uncertainty and inquiry whether there was
an Unseen World, any Mystery of Life except a mad
one; — doubt as to all this, or perhaps unbelief and flat
denial? Answering of this question is giving us the
soul of the history of the man or nation. The thoughts
they had were the parents of the actions they did;
their feelings were parents of their thoughts: it was
the unseen and spiritual in them that determined the
outward and actual; — their religion, as I say, was the

great fact about them. In these Discourses, limited as we are, it will be good to direct our survey chiefly to that religious phasis of the matter. That once known well, all is known. We have chosen as the first Hero in our series, Odin the central figure of Scandinavian Paganism; an emblem to us of a most extensive province of things. Let us look for a little at the Hero as Divinity, the oldest primary form of Heroism.

Surely it seems a very strange-looking thing this Paganism; almost inconceivable to us in these days. A bewildering, inextricable jungle of delusions, confusions, falsehoods and absurdities, covering the whole field of Life! A thing that fills us with astonishment, almost, if it were possible, with incredulity, — for truly it is not easy to understand that sane men could ever calmly, with their eyes open, believe and live by such a set of doctrines. That men should have worshipped their poor fellow-man as a God, and not him only, but stocks and stones, and all manner of animate and inanimate objects; and fashioned for themselves such a distracted chaos of hallucinations by way of Theory of the Universe: all this looks like an incredible fable. Nevertheless it is a clear fact that they did it. Such hideous inextricable jungle of misworships, misbeliefs, men, made as we are, did actually hold by, and live at home in. This is strange. Yes, we may pause in sorrow and silence over the depths of darkness that are in man; if we rejoice in the heights of purer vision he has attained to. Such things were and are in man; in all men; in us too.

Some speculators have a short way of accounting for the Pagan religion: mere quackery, priestcraft, and dupery, say they; no sane man ever did believe it, — merely contrived to persuade other men, not worthy of the name of sane, to believe it! It will be often our duty to protest against this sort of hypothesis about men's doings and history; and I here, on the very threshold, protest against it in reference to Paganism, and to all other *isms* by which man has ever for a length of time striven to walk in this world. They have all had a truth in them, or men would not have taken them up. Quackery and dupery do abound; in religions, above all in the more advanced decaying stages of religions, they have fearfully abounded : but quackery was never the originating influence in such things; it was not the health and life of such things, but their disease, the sure precursor of their being about to die! Let us never forget this. It seems to me a most mournful hypothesis, that of quackery giving birth to any faith even in savage men. Quackery gives birth to nothing; gives death to all things.. We shall not see into the true heart of anything, if we look merely at the quackeries of it; if we do not reject the quackeries altogether; as mere diseases, corruptions, with which our and all men's sole duty is to have done with them, to sweep them out of our thoughts as out of our practice. Man everywhere is the born enemy of lies. I find Grand Lamaism itself to have a kind of truth in it. Read the candid, clear-sighted, rather sceptical Mr. Turner's " Account of his Embassy " to that country, and see. They have their belief, these poor Thibet people, that Providence sends down always an Incarnation of Himself into every generation. At bottom some belief in a kind of Pope! At bottom still better, belief that there is a *Greatest* Man; that *he* is discoverable; that, once discovered, we ought to treat him with an obedience which knows no bounds! This is the truth of Grand Lamaism; the " discoverability " is the only error here. The Thibet priests have methods of their own of discovering what Man is Greatest, fit to be supreme over them. Bad methods: but are they so much worse than our methods, — of understanding him to be always the eldest-born of a certain genealogy? Alas, it is a difficult thing to find good methods for! — 'We shall begin to have a chance of understanding Paganism, when we first admit that to its followers it was, at one time, earnestly true. Let us consider it very certain that men did believe in Paganism; men with open eyes, sound senses, men made altogether like ourselves; that we, had we been there, should have believed in it. Ask now, What Paganism could have been?

Another theory, somewhat more respectable, attributes such things to Allegory. It was a play of poetic minds, say these theorists; a shadowing-forth, in allegorical fable, in personification and visual form, of what such poetic minds had known and felt of this Universe. Which agrees, add they, with a primary law of human nature, still everywhere observably at work, though in less important things, That what a man feels intensely, he struggles to speak-out of him, to see represented before him in visual shape, and as if with a kind of life and historical reality in it. Now doubtless there is such a law, and it is one of the deepest in human nature; neither need we doubt that it did operate fundamentally in this business. The hypothesis which ascribes Paganism wholly or mostly to this agency, I call a little more respectable; but I cannot yet call it the true hypothesis. Think, would *we* believe and take with us as our life-guidance, an allegory, a poetic sport? Not sport but earnest is what we should require. It is a most earnest thing to be alive in this world; to die is not sport for a man. Man's life never was a sport to him; it was a stern reality, altogether a serious matter to be alive!

I find, therefore, that though these Allegory theorists

are on the way towards truth in this matter, they have not reached it either.. Pagan Religion is indeed an Allegory, a Symbol of what men felt and knew about the Universe; and all Religions are symbols of that, altering always as that alters : but it seems to me a radical perversion, and even *in*version, of the business, to put that forward as the origin and moving cause, when it was rather the result and termination. To get beautiful allegories, a perfect poetic symbol, was not the want of men; but to know what they were to believe about this Universe, what course they were to steer in it; what, in this mysterious Life of theirs, they had to hope and to fear, to do and to forbear doing. The " Pilgrim's Progress " is an Allegory, and a beautiful, just and serious one : but consider whether Bunyan's Allegory could have *preceded* the Faith it symbolizes! The Faith had to be already there, standing believed by everybody; — of which the Allegory could *then* become a shadow; and, with all its seriousness, we may say a *sportful* shadow, a mere play of the Fancy, in comparison with that awful Fact and scientific certainty which it poetically strives to emblem. The Allegory is the product of the certainty, not the producer of it; not in Bunyan's nor in any other case. For Paganism, therefore, we have still to inquire, Whence came that scientific certainty, the parent of such a bewildered heap of allegories, errors and confusions? How was it, what was it?.

Surely it were a foolish attempt to pretend "explaining," in this place, or in any place, such a phenomenon as that far-distant distracted cloudy imbroglio of Paganism, — more like a cloudfield than a distant continent of firm land and facts! It is no longer a reality, yet it was one. We ought to understand that this seeming cloudfield was once a reality; that not poetic allegory, least of all that dupery and deception was the origin of it. Men, I say, never did believe idle songs, never risked their soul's life on allegories: men in all times, especially in early earnest times, have had an instinct for detecting quacks, for detesting quacks. Let us try if, leaving out both the quack theory and the allegory one, and listening with affectionate attention to that far-off confused rumor of the Pagan ages, we cannot ascertain so much as this at least, That there was a kind of fact at the heart of them; that they too were not mendacious and distracted, but in their own poor way true and sane!

You remember that fancy of Plato's, of a man who had grown to maturity in some dark distance, and was brought on a sudden into the upper air to see the sun rise. What would his wonder be, his rapt astonishment at the sight we daily witness with indifference! With the free open sense of a child, yet with the ripe faculty of a man, his whole heart would be kindled by that sight, he would discern it well to be Godlike, his soul would fall down in worship before it. Now, just such a childlike greatness was in the primitive nations. The first Pagan Thinker among rude men, the first man that began to think, was precisely this child-man of Plato's. Simple, open as a child, yet with the depth and strength of a man. Nature had as yet no name to him; he had not yet united under a name the infinite variety of sights, sounds, shapes and motions, which we now collectively name Universe, Nature, or the like, — and so with a name dismiss it from us. To the wild deep-hearted man all was yet new, not veiled under names or formulas; it stood naked, flashing-in on him there, beautiful, awful, unspeakable. Nature was to this man, what to the Thinker and Prophet it forever is, *preter*natural. This green flowery rock-built earth, the trees, the mountains, rivers, many-sounding seas; — that great deep sea of azure that swims overhead; the winds sweeping through it; the black cloud fashioning itself together, now pouring out fire, now hail and rain; what *is* it? Ay, what? At bottom we do not yet know; we can never know at all. It is not by our superior insight that we escape the difficulty; it is by our superior levity, our inattention, our *want* of insight. It is by *not* thinking that we ceased to wonder at it. Hardened round us, encasing wholly every notion we form, is a wrappage of traditions, hearsays, mere *words*. We call that fire of the black thunder-cloud "electricity," and lecture learnedly about it, and grind the like of it out of glass and silk: but *what* is it? What made it? Whence comes it? Whither goes it? Science has done much for us; but it is a poor science that would hide from us the great deep sacred infinitude of Nescience, whither we can never penetrate, on which all science swims as a mere superficial film. This world, after all our science and sciences, is still a miracle; wonderful, inscrutable, *magical* and more, to whosoever will *think* of it.

That great mystery of TIME, were there no other: the illimitable, silent, never-resting thing called Time, rolling, rushing on, swift, silent, like an all-embracing ocean-tide, on which we and all the Universe swim like exhalations, like apparitions which *are*, and then *are not:* this is forever very literally a miracle; — a thing to strike us dumb, — for we have no word to speak about it. This Universe, ah me — what could the wild man know of it; what can we yet know? That it is a Force, and thousandfold Complexity of Forces; a Force which is *not we*. That is all; it is not we, it is altogether different from *us*. Force, Force, everywhere Force; we ourselves a mysterious Force in the centre of that. " There is not a leaf rotting on the

highway but has Force in it : how else could it rot ? "
Nay surely, to the Atheistic Thinker, if such a one
were possible, it must be a miracle too, this huge
illimitable whirlwind of force, which envelops us here ;
never-resting whirlwind, high as Immensity, old as
Eternity. What is it ? God's creation, the religious
people answer ; it is the Almighty God's ! Atheistic
science babbles poorly of it, with scientific nomenclatures, experiments and what-not, as if it were a poor
dead thing, to be bottled-up in Leyden jars and sold
over counters : but the natural sense of man, in all
times, if he will honestly apply his sense, proclaims it
to be a living thing, — ah, an unspeakable, godlike
thing ; towards which the best attitude for us, after
never so much science, is awe, devout prostration and
humility of soul ; worship if not in words, then in
silence.

But now I remark farther : What in such a time as
ours it requires a Prophet or Poet to teach us, namely,
the stripping-off of those poor undevout wrappages,
nomenclatures and scientific hearsays, — this, the
ancient earnest soul, as yet unencumbered with these
things, did for itself. The world, which is now divine
only to the gifted, was then divine to whosoever would
turn his eye upon it. He stood bare before it face to
face. "All was Godlike or God : " — Jean Paul still
finds it so ; the giant Jean Paul, who has power to
escape out of hearsays : but there then were no hearsays. Canopus shining-down over the desert, with its
blue diamond brightness (that wild blue spirit-like
brightness, far brighter than we ever witness here),
would pierce into the heart of the wild Ishmaelitish
man, whom it was guiding through the solitary waste
there. To his wild heart, with all feelings in it, with
no *speech* for any feeling, it might seem a little eye,
that Canopus, glancing-out on him from the great

deep Eternity ; revealing the inner Splendor to him. Cannot we understand how these men *worshipped* Canopus ; became what we call Sabeans, worshipping the stars ? Such is to me the secret of all forms of Paganism. Worship is transcendent wonder ; wonder for which there is now no limit or measure ; that is worship. To these primeval men, all things and everything they saw exist beside them were an emblem of the Godlike, of some God. .

And look what perennial fibre of truth was in that. To us also, through every star, through every blade of grass, is not a God made visible, if we will open our minds and eyes ? We do not worship in that way now : but is it not reckoned still a merit, proof of what we call a "poetic nature," that we recognize how every object has a divine beauty in it ; how every object still verily is " a window through which we may look into Infinitude itself " ? He that can discern the loveliness of things, we call him Poet, Painter, Man of Genius, gifted, lovable. These poor Sabeans did even what he does, — in their own fashion. That they did it, in what fashion soever, was a merit : better than what the entirely stupid man did, what the horse and camel did, — namely, nothing !

But now if all things whatsoever that we look upon are emblems to us of the Highest God, I add that more so than any of them is man such an emblem. You have heard of Saint Chrysostom's celebrated saying in reference to the Shekinah, or Ark of Testimony, visible Revelation of God, among the Hebrews : "The true Shekinah is Man !" Yes, it is even so : this is no vain phrase ; it is veritably so. The essence of our being, the mystery in us that calls itself " I," — ah, what words have we for such things ? — is a breath of Heaven ; the Highest Being reveals himself in man. This body, these faculties, this life of ours, is it

2

not all as a vesture for that Unnamed? "There is but one Temple in the Universe," says the devout Novalis, "and that is the Body of Man. Nothing is holier than that high form. Bending before men is a reverence done to this Revelation in the Flesh. We touch Heaven when we lay our hand on a human body!" This sounds much like a mere flourish of rhetoric; but it is not so. If well meditated, it will turn out to be a scientific fact; the expression, in such words as can be had, of the actual truth of the thing. *We* are the miracle of miracles, — the great inscrutable mystery of God. We cannot understand it, we know not how to speak of it; but we may feel and know, if we like, that it is verily so.

Well; these truths were once more readily felt than now. The young generations of the world, who had in them the freshness of young children, and yet the depth of earnest men, who did not think that they had finished-off all things in Heaven and Earth by merely giving them scientific names, but had to gaze direct at them there, with awe and wonder: they felt better what of divinity is in man and Nature; — they, without being mad, could *worship* Nature, and man more than anything else in Nature. Worship, that is, as I said above, admire without limit: this, in the full use of their faculties, with all sincerity of heart, they could do. I consider Hero-worship to be the grand modifying element in that ancient system of thought. What I called the perplexed jungle of Paganism sprang, we may say, out of many roots: every admiration, adoration of a star or natural object, was a root or fibre of a root; but Hero-worship is the deepest root of all; the tap-root, from which in a great degree all the rest were nourished and grown.

And now if worship even of a star had some meaning in it, how much more might that of a Hero! Worship of a Hero is transcendent admiration of a Great Man. I say great men are still admirable; I say there is, at bottom, nothing else admirable! No nobler feeling than this of admiration for one higher than himself dwells in the breast of man. It is to this hour, and at all hours, the vivifying influence in man's life. Religion I find stand upon it; not Paganism only, but far higher and truer religions, — all religion hitherto known. Hero-worship, heartfelt prostrate admiration, submission, burning, boundless, for a noblest godlike Form of Man, — is not that the germ of Christianity itself? The greatest of all Heroes is One — whom we do not name here! Let sacred silence meditate that sacred matter; you will find it the ultimate perfection of a principle extant throughout man's whole history on earth.

Or coming into lower, less *un*speakable provinces, is not all Loyalty akin to religious Faith also? • Faith is loyalty to some inspired Teacher, some spiritual Hero. And what therefore is loyalty proper, the life-breath of all society, but an effluence of Hero-worship, submissive admiration for the truly great? Society is founded on Hero-worship. All dignities of rank, on which human association rests, are what we may call a *Hero*archy (Government of Heroes), — or a Hierarchy, for it is "sacred" enough withal! The Duke means *Dux*, Leader; King is *Kön-ning, Kan-ning*, Man that *knows* or *cans*. Society everywhere is some representation, not *in*supportably inaccurate, of a graduated Worship of Heroes; — reverence and obedience done to men really great and wise. Not *in*supportably inaccurate, I say! They are all as bank-notes, these social dignitaries, all representing gold; — and several of them, alas, always are *forged* notes. We can do with some forged false notes; with a good many even; but not with all, or the most of them forged! No: there have to come revolutions then; cries of Democracy, Liberty and Equality, and I know not what: — the notes being all false, and no gold to be had for *them*, people take to crying in their despair that there is no gold, that there never was any! — "Gold," Hero-worship, *is* nevertheless, as it was always and everywhere, and cannot cease till man himself ceases.

I am well aware that in these days Hero-worship, the thing I call Hero-worship, professes to have gone out, and finally ceased. This, for reasons which it will be worth while some time to inquire into, is an age that as it were denies the existence of great men; denies the desirableness of great men. Show our critics a great man, a Luther for example, they begin to what they call "account" for him; not to worship him, but take the dimensions of him, — and bring him out to be a little kind of man! He was the "creature of the Time," they say; the Time called him forth, the Time did everything, he nothing — but what we the little critic could have done too! This seems to me but melancholy work. The Time call forth? Alas, we have known Times *call* loudly enough for their great man; but not find him when they called! He was not there; Providence had not sent him; the Time, *calling* its loudest, had to go down to confusion and wreck because he would not come when called.

For if we will think of it, no Time need have gone to ruin, could it have *found* a man great enough, a man wise and good enough: wisdom to discern truly what the Time wanted, valor to lead it on the right road thither; these are the salvation of any Time. But I liken common languid Times, with their unbelief, distress, perplexity, with their languid doubting characters and embarrassed circumstances, impotently crumbling-down into ever worse distress towards final ruin;—all this I liken to dry dead fuel, waiting for the lightning out of Heaven that shall kindle it. The great man, with his free force direct out of God's own hand, is the lightning. His word is the wise healing word which all can believe in. All blazes round him now, when he has once struck on it, into fire like his own. The dry mouldering sticks are thought to have called him forth. They did want him greatly; but as to calling him forth!— Those are critics of small vision, I think, who cry: " See, is it not the sticks that made the fire?" No sadder proof can be given by a man of his own littleness than disbelief in great men. There is no sadder symptom of a generation than such general blindness to the spiritual lightning, with faith only in the heap of barren dead fuel. It is the last consummation of unbelief. In all epochs of the world's history, we shall find the Great Man to have been the indispensable savior of his epoch;— the lightning, without which the fuel never would have burnt. The History of the World, I said already, was the Biography of Great Men.

Such small critics do what they can to promote unbelief and universal spiritual paralysis: but happily they cannot always completely succeed. In all times it is possible for a man to arise great enough to feel that they and their doctrines are chimeras and cobwebs. And what is notable, in no time whatever can they entirely eradicate out of living men's hearts a certain altogether peculiar reverence for Great Men; genuine admiration, loyalty, adoration, however dim and perverted it may be. Hero-worship endures forever while man endures. Boswell venerates his Johnson, right truly even in the Eighteenth century. The unbelieving French believe in their Voltaire; and burst-out round him into very curious Hero-worship, in that last act of his life when they " stifle him under roses." It has always seemed to me extremely curious this of Voltaire. Truly, if Christianity be the highest instance of Hero-worship, then we may find here in Voltaireism one of the lowest! He whose life was that of a kind of Antichrist, does again on this side exhibit a curious contrast. No people ever were so little prone to admire at all as those French of Voltaire. *Persiflage* was the character of their whole mind; adoration had nowhere a place in it. Yet see! The old man of Ferney comes up to Paris; an old, tottering, infirm man of eighty-four years. They feel that he too is a kind of Hero; that he has spent his life in opposing error and injustice, delivering Calases, unmasking hypocrites in high places; — in short that *he* too, though in a strange way, has fought like a valiant man. They feel withal that, if *persiflage* be the great thing, there never was such a *persifleur*. He is the realized ideal of every one of them; the thing they are all wanting to be; of all Frenchmen the most French. *He* is properly their god, — such god as they are fit for. Accordingly all persons, from the Queen Antoinette to the Douanier at the Porte St. Denis, do they not worship him? People of quality disguise themselves as tavern-waiters. The Maître de Poste, with a broad oath, orders his Postilion, "*Va bon train;* thou art driving M. de Voltaire." At Paris his carriage is "the nucleus of a comet, whose train fills whole streets." The ladies pluck a hair or two from his fur, to keep it as a sacred relic. There was nothing, highest, beautifullest, noblest in all France, that did not feel this man to be higher, beautifuller, nobler.

Yes, from Norse Odin to English Samuel Johnson, from the divine Founder of Christianity to the withered Pontiff of Encyclopedism, in all times and places, the Hero has been worshipped. It will ever be so. We all love great men; love, venerate and bow down submissive before great men : nay can we honestly bow down to anything else ? Ah, does not every true man feel that he is himself made higher by doing reverence to what is really above him ? No nobler or more blessed feeling dwells in man's heart. And to me it is very cheering to consider that no sceptical logic, or general triviality, insincerity and aridity of any Time and its influences can destroy this noble inborn loyalty and worship that is in man. In times of unbelief, which soon have to become times of revolution, much down-rushing, sorrowful decay and ruin is visible to everybody. For myself in these days, I seem to see in this indestructibility of Hero-worship the everlasting adamant lower than which the confused wreck of revolutionary things cannot fall. The confused wreck of things crumbling and even crashing and tumbling all round us in these revolutionary ages, will get down so far ; *no* farther. It is an eternal corner-stone, from which they can begin to build themselves up again. That man, in some sense or other, worships Heroes : that we all of us reverence and must ever reverence Great Men : this is, to me, the living rock amid all rushings-down whatsoever ; — the one fixed point in modern revolutionary history, otherwise as if bottomless and shoreless.

So much of truth, only under an ancient obsolete vesture, but the spirit of it still true, do I find in the Paganism, of old nations. Nature is still divine, the revelation of the workings of God ; the Hero is still worshipable : this, under poor cramped incipient forms, is what all Pagan religions have struggled, as they could, to set forth. I think Scandinavian Paganism, to us here, is more interesting than any other. It is, for one thing, the latest ; it continued in these regions of Europe till the eleventh century : eight-hundred years ago the Norwegians were still worshippers of Odin. It is interesting also as the creed of our fathers; the men whose blood still runs in our veins, whom doubtless we still resemble in so many ways. Strange: they did believe that, while we believe so differently. Let us look a little at this poor Norse creed, for many reasons. We have tolerable means to do it; for there is another point of interest in these Scandinavian mythologies: that they have been preserved so well.

In that strange island Iceland, — burst-up, the geologists say, by fire from the bottom of the sea; a wild land of barrenness and lava; swallowed many months of every year in black tempests, yet with a wild gleaming beauty in summer-time; towering up there, stern and grim, in the North Ocean; with its snow jokuls, roaring geysers, sulphur-pools and horrid volcanic chasms, like the waste chaotic battle-field of Frost and Fire; — where of all places we least looked for Literature or written memorials, the record of these things was written down. On the seaboard of this wild land is a rim of grassy country, where cattle can subsist, and men by means of them and of what the sea yields; and it seems they were poetic men these, men who had deep thoughts in them, and uttered musically their thoughts. Much would be lost, had Iceland not been burst-up from the sea, not been discovered by the Northmen! The old Norse Poets were many of them natives of Iceland.

Sæmund, one of the early Christian Priests there, who perhaps had a lingering fondness for Paganism, collected certain of their old Pagan songs, just about becoming obsolete then, — Poems or Chants of a mythic, prophetic, mostly all of a religious character: that is what Norse critics call the *Elder* or Poetic *Edda*. *Edda*, a word of uncertain etymology, is thought to signify *Ancestress*. Snorro Sturleson, an Iceland gentleman, an extremely notable personage, educated by this Sæmund's grandson, took in hand next, near a century afterwards, to put together, among several other books he wrote, a kind of Prose Synopsis of the whole Mythology; elucidated by new fragments of traditionary verse. A work constructed really with great ingenuity, native talent, what one might call unconscious art; altogether a perspicuous clear work, pleasant reading still: this is the *Younger* or Prose *Edda*. By these and the numerous other *Sagas*, mostly Icelandic, with the commentaries, Icelandic or not, which go on zealously in the North to this day, it is possible to gain some direct insight even yet; and see that old Norse system of Belief, as it were, face to face. Let us forget that it is erroneous Religion; let us look at it as old Thought, and try if we cannot sympathize with it somewhat.

The primary characteristic of this old Northland Mythology I find to be Impersonation of the visible workings of Nature. Earnest simple recognition of the workings of Physical Nature, as a thing wholly miraculous, stupendous and divine. What we now lecture of as Science, they wondered at, and fell down in awe before, as Religion. The dark hostile Powers of Nature they figure to themselves as "*Jötuns*," Giants, huge shaggy beings of a demonic character. Frost, Fire, Sea-tempest; these are Jötuns. The friendly Powers again, as Summer-heat, the Sun, are Gods. The empire of this Universe is divided between these two; they dwell apart, in perennial internecine feud. The Gods dwell above in Asgard, the Garden of the Asen, or Divinities; Jötunheim, a distant dark chaotic land, is the home of the Jötuns.

Curious all this: and not idle or inane, if we will look at the foundation of it! The power of *Fire*, or

Flame, for instance, which we designate by some trivial chemical name, thereby hiding from ourselves the essential character of wonder that dwells in it as in all things, is with these old Northmen, Loke, a most swift subtle *Demon*, of the brood of the Jötuns. The savages of the Ladrones Islands too (say some Spanish voyagers) thought Fire, which they never had seen before, was a devil or god, that bit you sharply when you touched it, and that lived upon dry wood. From us too no Chemistry, if it had not Stupidity to help it, would hide that Flame is a wonder. What *is* Flame? — *Frost* the old Norse Seer discerns to be a monstrous hoary Jötun, the Giant *Thrym*, *Hrym;* or *Rime*, the old word now nearly obsolete here, but still used in Scotland to signify hoar-frost. *Rime* was not then as now a dead chemical thing, but a living Jötun or Devil; the monstrous Jötun *Rime* drove home his Horses at night, sat " combing their manes," — which Horses were *Hail-Clouds*, or fleet *Frost-Winds*. His Cows — No, not his, but a kinsman's, the Giant Hymir's Cows are *Icebergs:* this Hymir " looks at the rocks " with his devil-eye, and they *split* in the glance of it.

Thunder was not then mere Electricity, vitreous or resinous; it was the God Donner (Thunder) or Thor, — God also of beneficent Summer-heat. The thunder was his wrath; the gathering of the black clouds is the drawing-down of Thor's angry brows; the fire-bolt bursting out of Heaven is the all-rending Hammer flung from the hand of Thor: he urges his loud chariot over the mountain-tops, — that is the peal; wrathful he " blows in his red beard," — that is the rustling storm-blast before the thunder begins. Balder again, the White God, the beautiful, the just and benignant (whom the early Christian Missionaries found to resemble Christ), is the Sun, — beautifullest of visible things; wondrous too, and divine still, after all our Astronomies and Almanacs! But perhaps the notablest god we hear tell-of is one of whom Grimm the German Etymologist finds trace: the God *Wünsch*, or Wish. The God *Wish;* who could give us all that we *wished!* Is not this the sincerest and yet rudest voice of the spirit of man? The *rudest* ideal that man ever formed; which still shows itself in the latest forms of our spiritual culture. Higher considerations have to teach us that the God *Wish* is not the true God.

Of the other Gods or Jötuns I will mention only for etymology's sake, that Sea-tempest is the Jötun *Aegir*, a very dangerous Jötun;—and now to this day, on our river Trent, as I learn, the Nottingham bargemen, when the River is in a certain flooded state (a kind of backwater, or eddying swirl it has, very dangerous to them), call it *Eager;* they cry out, " Have a care, there is the *Eager* coming!" Curious; that word surviving, like the peak of a submerged world! The *oldest* Nottingham bargemen had believed in the God Aegir. Indeed our English blood too in good part is Danish, Norse; or rather, at bottom, Danish and Norse and Saxon have no distinction, except a superficial one, — as of Heathen and Christian, or the like. But all over our Island we are mingled largely with Danes proper, — from the incessant invasions there were: and this, of course, in a greater proportion along the east coast; and greatest of all, as I find, in the North Country. From the Humber upwards, all over Scotland, the Speech of the common people is still in a singular degree Icelandic; its Germanism has still a peculiar Norse tinge. They too are " Normans," Northmen, — if that be any great beauty! —

Of the chief god, Odin, we shall speak by and by. Mark at present so much; what the essence of Scandinavian and indeed of all Paganism is: a recognition of the forces of Nature as godlike, stupendous, personal Agencies, — as Gods and Demons. Not inconceivable to us. It is the infant Thought of man opening itself, with awe and wonder, on this everstupendous Universe. To me there is in the Norse System something very genuine, very great and manlike. A broad simplicity, rusticity, so very different from the light gracefulness of the old Greek Paganism, distinguishes this Scandinavian System. It is Thought; the genuine Thought of deep, rude, earnest minds, fairly opened to the things about them; a faceto-face and heart-to-heart inspection of the things, — the first characteristic of all good Thought in all times. Not graceful lightness, half-sport, as in the Greek Paganism; a certain homely truthfulness and rustic strength, a great rude sincerity, discloses itself here. It is strange, after our beautiful Apollo statues and clear smiling mythuses, to come down upon the Norse Gods " brewing ale " to hold their feast with Aegir, the Sea-Jötun; sending out Thor to get the caldron for them in the Jötun country; Thor, after many adventures, clapping the pot on his head, like a huge hat, and walking off with it, — quite lost in it, the ears of the Pot reaching down to his heels ! A kind of vacant hugeness, large awkward gianthood, characterizes that Norse System; enormous force, as yet altogether untutored, stalking helpless with large uncertain strides. Consider only their primary mythus of the Creation. The Gods, having got the Giant Ymer slain, a giant made by " warm wind." and much confused work, out of the conflict of Frost and Fire, — determined on constructing a world with him. His blood made the Sea; his flesh was the Land, the Rocks his bones; of his eyebrows they formed Asgard their Gods'-dwelling; his skull was the great blue vault of Immensity, and the brains of it became the Clouds.

What a Hyper-Brobdignagian business! Untamed Thought, great, giant-like, enormous; to be tamed in due time into the compact greatness, not giantlike, but godlike and stronger than gianthood, of the Shakspeares, the Goethes! — Spiritually as well as bodily these men are our progenitors.

I like, too, that representation they have of the Tree Igdrasil. All Life is figured by them as a Tree. Igdrasil, the Ash-tree of Existence, has its roots deepdown in the kingdoms of Hela or Death; its trunk reaches up heaven-high, spreads its boughs over the whole Universe: it is the Tree of Existence. At the foot of it, in the Death-kingdom, sit Three *Nornas*, Fates, — the Past, Present, Future; watering its roots from the Sacred Well. Its "boughs," with their buddings and disleafings, — events, things suffered, things done, catastrophes, — stretch through all lands and times. Is not every leaf of it a biography, every fibre there an act or word? Its boughs are Histories of Nations. The rustle of it is the noise of Human Existence, onwards from of old. It grows there, the breath of Human Passion rustling through it; — or stormtost, the stormwind howling through it like the voice of all the gods. It is Igdrasil, the Tree of Existence. It is the past, the present, and the future; what was done, what is doing, what will be done; "the infinite conjugation of the verb *To do*." Considering how human things circulate, each inextricably in communion with all, how the word I speak to you today is borrowed, not from Ulfila the Mœsogoth only, but from all men since the first man began to speak, — I find no similitude so true as this of a Tree. Beautiful; altogether beautiful and great. The "*Machine* of the Universe," — alas, do but think of that in contrast!

Well, it is strange enough this old Norse view of Nature; different enough from what we believe of Nature. Whence it specially came, one would not like to be compelled to say very minutely! One thing we may say: It came from the thoughts of Norse men; — from the thought, above all, of the *first* Norse man who had an original power of thinking. The First Norse "man of genius," as we should call him! Innumerable men had passed by, across this Universe, with a dumb vague wonder, such as the very animals may feel; or with a painful, fruitlessly inquiring wonder, such as men only feel; — till the great Thinker came, the *original* man, the Seer; whose shaped spoken Thought awakes the slumbering capability of all into Thought. It is ever the way with the Thinker, the spiritual Hero. What he says, all men were not far from saying, were longing to say. The Thoughts of all start up, as from painful enchanted sleep, round his Thought; answering to it, Yes, even so! Joyful to men as the dawning of day from night; — *is* it not, indeed, the awakening for them from no-being into being, from death into life? We still honor such a man; call him Poet, Genius, and so forth: but to these wild men he was a very magician, a worker of miraculous unexpected blessing for them; a Prophet, a God! — Thought once awakened does not again slumber; unfolds itself into a System of Thought; grows, in man after man, generation after generation, — till its full stature is reached, and *such* System of Thought can grow no farther, but must give place to another.

For the Norse people, the Man now named Odin, and Chief Norse God, we fancy, was such a man. A Teacher, and Captain of soul and of body; a Hero, of worth *im*measurable; admiration for whom, transcending the known bounds, became adoration. Has he not the power of articulate Thinking; and many other powers, as yet miraculous? So, with boundless gratitude, would the rude Norse heart feel. Has he not solved for them the sphinx-enigma of this Universe; given assurance to them of their own destiny there? By him they know now what they have to do here, what to look for hereafter. Existence has become articulate, melodious by him; he first has made Life alive! — We may call this Odin, the origin of Norse Mythology: Odin, or whatever name the First Norse Thinker bore while he was a man among men. His view of the Universe once promulgated, a like view starts into being in all minds; grows, keeps ever growing, while it continues credible there. In all minds it lay written, but invisibly, as in sympathetic ink; at his word it starts into visibility in all. Nay, in every epoch of the world, the great event, parent of all others, is it not the arrival of a Thinker in the world! —

One other thing we must not forget; it will explain, a little, the confusion of these Norse Eddas. They are not one coherent System of Thought; but properly the *summation* of several successive systems. All this of the old Norse Belief which is flung-out for us, in one level of distance in the Edda, like a picture painted on the same canvas, does not at all stand so in the reality. It stands rather at all manner of distances and depths, of successive generations since the Belief first began. All Scandinavian thinkers, since the first of them, contributed to that Scandinavian System of Thought; in ever-new elaboration and addition, it is the combined work of them all. What history it had, how it changed from shape to shape, by one thinker's contribution after another, till it got to the full final shape we see it under in the *Edda*, no man will now ever know: *its* Councils of Trebisond, Councils of

Trent, Athanasiuses, Dantes, Luthers, are sunk without echo in the dark night! Only that it had such a history we can all know. Wheresoever a thinker appeared, there in the thing he thought-of was a contribution, accession, a change or revolution made. Alas, the grandest "revolution" of all, the one made by the man Odin himself, is not this too sunk for us like the rest! Of Odin what history? Strange rather to reflect that he *had* a history? That this Odin, in his wild Norse vesture, with his wild beard and eyes, his rude Norse speech and ways, was a man like us; with our sorrows, joys, with our limbs, features;—intrinsically all one as we: and did such a work! But the work, much of it, has perished; the worker, all to the name. "*Wednes*day," men will say tomorrow; Odin's day! Of Odin there exists no history; no document of it; no guess about it worth repeating.

Snorro indeed, in the quietest manner, almost in a brief business style, writes down, in his "Heimskringla," how Odin was a heroic Prince, in the Black-Sea region, with Twelve Peers, and a great people straitened for room. How he led these *Asen* (Asiatics) of his out of Asia; settled them in the North parts of Europe, by warlike conquest; invented Letters, Poetry and so forth,—and came by and by to be worshipped as Chief God by these Scandinavians, his Twelve Peers made into Twelve Sons of his own, Gods like himself; Snorro has no doubt of this. Saxo Grammaticus, a very curious Northman of that same century, is still more unhesitating; scruples not to find out a historical fact in every individual mythus, and writes it down as a terrestrial event in Denmark or elsewhere. Torfæus, learned and cautious, some centuries later, assigns by calculation a *date* for it: Odin, he says, came into Europe about the Year 70 before Christ. Of all which, as grounded on mere uncertainties, found to be untenable now, I need say nothing. Far, very far beyond the Year 70! Odin's date, adventures, whole terrestrial history, figure and environment are sunk from us forever into unknown thousands of years.

Nay Grimm, the German Antiquary, goes so far as to deny that any man Odin ever existed. He proves it by etymology. The word *Wuotan*, which is the original form of *Odin*, a word spread, as name of their chief Divinity, over all the Teutonic Nations everywhere; this word, which connects itself, according to Grimm, with the Latin *vadere*, with the English *wade* and suchlike, — means primarily *Movement*, Source of Movement, Power; and is the fit name of the highest god, not of any man. The word signifies Divinity, he says, among the old Saxon, German and all Teutonic Nations; the adjectives formed from it all signify *divine, supreme*, or something pertaining to the chief god. Like enough! We must bow to Grimm in matters etymological. Let us consider it fixed that *Wuotan* means *Wading*, force of *Movement*. And now still, what hinders it from being the name of a Heroic Man and *Mover*, as well as of a god? As for the adjectives, and words formed from it, — did not the Spaniards in their universal admiration for Lope, get into the habit of saying "a Lope flower," "a Lope *dama*," if the flower or woman were of surpassing beauty? Had this lasted, *Lope* would have grown, in Spain, to be an adjective signifying *godlike* also. Indeed, Adam Smith, in his "Essay on Language," surmises that all adjectives whatsoever were formed precisely in that way: some very green thing, chiefly notable for its greenness, got the appellative name *Green*, and then the next thing remarkable for that quality, a tree for instance, was named the *green* tree, — as we still say "the *steam* coach," "four-horse coach," or the like. All primary adjectives, according to Smith, were formed in this way; were at first substantives and things. We cannot annihilate a man for etymologies like that! Surely there was a First Teacher and Captain; surely there must have been an Odin, palpable to the sense at one time; no adjective, but a real Hero of flesh and blood! The voice of all tradition, history or echo of history, agrees with all that thought will teach one about it, to assure us of this.

How the man Odin came to be considered a *god,* the chief god? — that surely is a question which nobody would wish to dogmatize upon. I have said, his people knew no *limits* to their admiration of him; they had as yet no scale to measure admiration by. Fancy your own generous heart's-love of some greatest man expanding till it *transcended* all bounds, till it filled and overflowed the whole field of your thought! Or what if this man Odin, — since a great deep soul, with the afflatus and mysterious tide of vision and impulse rushing on him he knows not whence, is ever an enigma, a kind of terror and wonder to himself, — should have felt that perhaps *he* was divine; that *he* was some effluence of the "Wuotan," "*Movement,*" Supreme Power and Divinity, of whom to his rapt vision all Nature was the awful Flame-image; that some effluence of *Wuotan* dwelt here in him! He was not necessarily false; he was but mistaken, speaking the truest he knew. A great soul, any sincere soul, knows not *what* he is, — alternates between the highest height and the lowest depth; can, of all things, the least measure — Himself! What others take him for, and what he guesses that he may be; these two items strangely act on one another, help to determine one another. With all men rever-

ently admiring him; with his own wild soul full of
noble ardors and affections, of whirlwind chaotic
darkness and glorious new light; a divine Universe
bursting all into godlike beauty round him, and no
man to whom the like ever had befallen, what could
he think himself to be? "Wuotan?" All men
answered, "Wuotan!"—

And then consider what mere Time will do in such
cases; how if a man was great while living, he becomes tenfold greater when dead. What an enormous
camera-obscura magnifier is Tradition! How a thing
grows in the human Memory, in the human Imagination, when love, worship and all that lies in the human
Heart, is there to encourage it. And in the darkness,
in the entire ignorance; without date or document, no
book, no Arundel-marble; only here and there some
dumb monumental cairn. Why, in thirty or forty years,
were there no books, any great man would grow
mythic, the contemporaries who had seen him, being
once all dead. And in three-hundred years, and in
three-thousand years!— To attempt *theorizing* on such
matters would profit little: they are matters which re-
fuse to be *theoremed* and diagramed; which Logic
ought to know that she *cannot* speak of. Enough for
us to discern, far in the uttermost distance, some gleam
as of a small real light shining in the centre of that
enormous camera-obscura image; to discern that the
centre of it all was not a madness and nothing, but a
sanity and something.

This light, kindled in the great dark vortex of the
Norse mind, dark but living, waiting only for light;
this is to me the centre of the whole. How such light
will then shine out, and with wondrous thousandfold
expansion spread itself, in forms and colors, depends
not on *it*, so much as on the National Mind recipient
of it. The colors and forms of your light will be those

of the *cut-glass* it has to shine through. Curious to think how, for every man, any the truest fact is modelled by the nature of the man! I said, The earnest man, speaking to his brother men, must always have stated what seemed to him a *fact*, a real Appearance of Nature. But the way in which such Appearance or fact shaped itself, — what sort of *fact* it became for him, — was and is modified by his own laws of thinking; deep, subtle, but universal, ever-operating laws. The world of Nature, for every man, is the Fantasy of Himself: this world is the multiplex " Image of his own Dream." Who knows to what unnameable subtleties of spiritual law all these Pagan Fables owe their shape! The number *Twelve*, divisiblest of all, which could be halved, quartered, parted into three, into six, the most remarkable number, — this was enough to determine the *Signs of the Zodiac*, the number of Odin's *Sons*, and innumerable other Twelves. Any vague rumor of number had a tendency to settle itself into Twelve. So with regard to every other matter. And quite unconsciously too, — with no notion of building-up " Allegories "! But the fresh clear glance of those First Ages would be prompt in discerning the secret relations of things, and wholly open to obey these. Schiller finds in the *Cestus of Venus* an everlasting æsthetic truth as to the nature of all Beauty; curious : — but he is careful not to insinuate that the old Greek Mythists had any notion of lecturing about the " Philosophy of Criticism "! — On the whole, we must leave those boundless regions. Cannot we conceive that Odin was a reality? Error indeed, error enough: but sheer falsehood, idle fables, allegory aforethought, — we will not believe that our Fathers believed in these.

Odin's *Runes* are a significant feature of him. Runes, and the miracles of " magic " he worked by them, make a great feature in tradition. Runes are the Scandinavian Alphabet; suppose Odin to have been the Inventor of Letters, as well as "magic," among that people! It is the greatest invention man has ever made, this of marking-down the unseen thought that is in him by written characters. It is a kind of second speech, almost as miraculous as the first. You remember the astonishment and incredulity of Atahualpa the Peruvian King; how he made the Spanish Soldier who was guarding him scratch *Dios* on his thumb-nail, that he might try the next soldier with it, to ascertain whether such a miracle was possible. If Odin brought Letters among his people, he might work magic enough!

Writing by Runes has some air of being original among the Norsemen: not a Phœnician Alphabet, but a native Scandinavian one. Snorro tells us farther that Odin invented Poetry; the music of human speech, as well as that miraculous runic marking of it. Transport yourselves into the early childhood of nations; the first beautiful morning-light of our Europe, when all yet lay in fresh young radiance as of a great sunrise, and our Europe was first beginning to think, to be! Wonder, hope; infinite radiance of hope and wonder, as of a young child's thoughts, in the hearts of these strong men! Strong sons of Nature; and here was not only a wild Captain and Fighter; discerning with his wild flashing eyes what to do, with his wild lion-heart daring and doing it; but a Poet too, all that we mean by a Poet, Prophet, great devout Thinker and Inventor, — as the truly Great Man ever is. A Hero is a Hero at all points; in the soul and thought of him first of all. This Odin, in his rude semi-articulate way, had a word to speak. A great heart laid open to take in this great Universe, and man's Life here, and utter a great word about it. A

Hero, as I say, in his own rude manner; a wise, gifted, noble-hearted man. And now, if we still admire such a man beyond all others, what must these wild Norse souls, first awakened into thinking, have made of him! To them, as yet without names for it, he was noble and noblest; Hero, Prophet, God; *Wuotan,* the greatest of all. Thought is Thought, however it speak or spell itself. Intrinsically, I conjecture, this Odin must have been of the same sort of stuff as the greatest kind of men. A great thought in the wild deep heart of him! The rough words he articulated, are they not the rudimental roots of those English words we still use? He worked so, in that obscure element. But he was as a *light* kindled in it; a light of Intellect, rude nobleness of heart, the only kind of lights we have yet; a Hero, as I say: and he had to shine there, and make his obscure element a little lighter, — as is still the task of us all.

We will fancy him to be the Type Norseman; the finest Teuton whom that race had yet produced. The rude Norse heart burst-up into *boundless* admiration round him; into adoration. He is as a root of so many great things; the fruit of him is found growing, from deep thousands of years, over the whole field of Teutonic Life. Our own Wednesday, as I said, is it not still Odin's Day? Wednesbury, Wansborough, Wanstead, Wandsworth: Odin grew into England too, these are still leaves from that root! He was the Chief God to all the Teutonic Peoples; their Pattern Norseman; — in such way did *they* admire their Pattern Norseman; that was the fortune he had in the world.

Thus if the man Odin himself have vanished utterly, there is this huge Shadow of him which still projects itself over the whole History of his People. For this Odin once admitted to be God, we can understand well that the whole Scandinavian Scheme of Nature, or dim No-scheme, whatever it might before have been, would now begin to develop itself altogether differently, and grow thenceforth in a new manner. What this Odin saw into, and taught with his runes and his rhymes, the whole Teutonic People laid to heart and carried forward. His way of thought became their way of thought: — such, under new conditions, is the history of every great thinker still. In gigantic confused lineaments, like some enormous camera-obscura shadow thrown upwards from the dead deeps of the Past, and covering the whole Northern Heaven, is not that Scandinavian Mythology in some sort the Portraiture of this man Odin? The gigantic image of *his* natural face, legible or not legible there, expanded and confused in that manner! Ah, Thought, I say, is always Thought. No great man lives in vain. The History of the world is but the Biography of great men.

To me there is something very touching in this primeval figure of Heroism; in such artless, helpless, but hearty entire reception of a Hero by his fellow-men. Never so helpless in shape, it is the noblest of feelings, and a feeling in some shape or other perennial as man himself. If I could show in any measure, what I feel deeply for a long time now, That it is the vital element of manhood, the soul of man's history here in our world, — it would be the chief use of this discoursing at present. We do not now call our great men Gods, nor admire *without* limit; ah no, *with* limit enough! But if we have no great men, or do not admire at all, — that were a still worse case.

This poor Scandinavian Hero-worship, that whole Norse way of looking at the Universe, and adjusting oneself there, has an indestructible merit for us. A rude childlike way of recognizing the divineness of

Nature, the divineness of Man; most rude, yet heartfelt, robust, giantlike; betokening what a giant of a
man this child would yet grow to!— It was a truth,
and is none. Is it not as the half-dumb stifled voice
of the long-buried generations of our own Fathers,
calling out of the depths of ages to us, in whose veins
their blood still runs: "This then, this is what *we*
made of the world: this is all the image and notion we
could form to ourselves of this great mystery of a Life
and Universe. Despise it not. You are raised high
above it, to large free scope of vision; but you too are
not yet at the top. No, your notion too, so much enlarged, is but a partial, imperfect one; that matter is a
thing no man will ever, in time or out of time, comprehend; after thousands of years of ever-new expansion, man will find himself but struggling to comprehend
again a part of it: the thing is larger than man, not to
be comprehended by him; an Infinite thing!"

The essence of the Scandinavian, as indeed of all
Pagan Mythologies, we found to be recognition of the
divineness of Nature; sincere communion of man with
the mysterious invisible Powers visibly seen at work
in the world round him. This, I should say, is more
sincerely done in the Scandinavian than in any Mythology I know. Sincerity is the great characteristic of
it. Superior sincerity (far superior) consoles us for
the total want of old Grecian grace. Sincerity, I think,
is better than grace. I feel that these old Northmen
were looking into Nature with open eye and soul:
most earnest, honest; childlike, and yet manlike; with
a great-hearted simplicity and depth and freshness, in
a true, loving, admiring, unfearing way. A right
valiant, true old race of men. Such recognition of
Nature one finds to be the chief element of Paganism:
recognition of Man, and his Moral Duty, though this

too is not wanting, comes to be the chief element only in purer forms of religion. Here, indeed, is a great distinction and epoch in Human Beliefs; a great landmark in the religious development of Mankind. Man first puts himself in relation with Nature and her Powers, wonders and worships over those; not till a later epoch does he discern that all Power is Moral, that the grand point is the distinction for him of Good and Evil, of *Thou shalt* and *Thou shalt not.*

With regard to all these fabulous delineations in the *Edda*, I will remark, moreover, as indeed was already hinted, that most probably they must have been of much newer date; most probably, even from the first, were comparatively idle for the old Norsemen, and as it were a kind of Poetic sport. Allegory and Poetic Delineation, as I said above, cannot be religious Faith; the Faith itself must first be there, then Allegory enough will gather round it, as the fit body round its soul. The Norse Faith, I can well suppose, like other Faiths, was most active while it lay mainly in the silent state, and had not yet much to say about itself, still less to sing.

Among those shadowy *Edda* matters, amid all that fantastic congeries of assertions, and traditions, in their musical Mythologies, the main practical belief a man could have was probably not much more than this: of the *Valkyrs* and the *Hall of Odin;* of an inflexible *Destiny;* and that the one thing needful for a man was *to be brave.* The *Valkyrs* are Choosers of the Slain: a Destiny inexorable, which it is useless trying to bend or soften, has appointed who is to be slain; this was a fundamental point for the Norse believer; — as indeed it is for all earnest men everywhere, for a Mahomet, a Luther, for a Napoleon too. It lies at the basis this for every such man; it is the woof out of which his whole system of thought is woven. The *Valkyrs;* and then that these *Choosers* lead the brave to a heavenly *Hall of Odin;* only the base and slavish being thrust elsewhither, into the realms of Hela the Death-goddess : I take this to have been the soul of the whole Norse Belief. They understood in their heart that it was indispensable to be brave; that Odin would have no favor for them, but despise and thrust them out, if they were not brave. Consider too whether there is not something in this! It is an everlasting duty, valid in our day as in that, the duty of being brave. *Valor* is still *value.* The first duty for a man is still that of subduing *Fear.* We must get rid of Fear; we cannot act at all till then. A man's acts are slavish, not true but specious; his very thoughts are false, he thinks too as a slave and coward, till he have got Fear under his feet. Odin's creed, if we disentangle the real kernel of it, is true to this hour. A man shall and must be valiant; he must march forward, and quit himself like a man, — trusting imperturbably in the appointment and *choice* of the upper Powers; and, on the whole, not fear at all. Now and always, the completeness of his victory over Fear will determine how much of a man he is.

It is doubtless very savage that kind of valor of the old Northmen. Snorro tells us they thought it a shame and misery not to die in battle; and if natural death seemed to be coming on, they would cut wounds in their flesh, that Odin might receive them as warriors slain. Old kings, about to die, had their body laid into a ship; the ship sent forth, with sails set and slow fire burning it; that, once out at sea, it might blaze up in flame, and in such manner bury worthily the old hero, at once in the sky and in the ocean! Wild bloody valor; yet valor of its kind; better, I say, than none. In the old Sea-kings too, what an indomitable rugged energy! Silent, with closed lips, as I fancy them, unconscious that they were specially brave;

defying the wild ocean with its monsters, and all men and things; — progenitors of our own Blakes and Nelsons! No Homer sang these Norse Sea-kings; but Agamemnon's was a small audacity, and of small fruit in the world, to some of them; — to Hrolf's of Normandy, for instance! Hrolf, or Rollo Duke of Normandy, the wild Sea-king, has a share in governing England at this hour.

Nor was it altogether nothing, even that wild sea-roving and battling, through so many generations. It needed to be ascertained which was the *strongest* kind of men; who were to be ruler over whom. Among the Northland Sovereigns, too, I find some who got the title *Wood-cutter;* Forest-felling Kings. Much lies in that. I suppose at bottom many of them were forest-fellers as well as fighters, though the Skalds talk mainly of the latter, — misleading certain critics not a little; for no nation of men could ever live by fighting alone; there could not produce enough come out of that! I suppose the right good fighter was oftenest also the right good forest-feller, — the right good improver, discerner, doer and worker in every kind; for true valor, different enough from ferocity, is the basis of all. A more legitimate kind of valor that; showing itself against the untamed Forests and dark brute Powers of Nature, to conquer Nature for us. In the same direction have not we their descendants since carried it far? May such valor last forever with us!

That the man Odin, speaking with a Hero's voice and heart, as with an impressiveness out of Heaven, told his People the infinite importance of Valor, how man thereby became a god; and that his People, feeling a response to it in their own hearts, believed this message of his, and thought it a message out of Heaven, and him a Divinity for telling it them: this seems to me the primary seed-grain of the **Norse** Religion, from which all manner of mythologies, symbolic practices, speculations, allegories, songs and sagas would naturally grow.   Grow, — how strangely ! I called it a small light shining and shaping in the huge vortex of Norse darkness.   Yet the darkness itself was *alive;* consider that.   It was the eager inarticulate uninstructed Mind of the whole Norse People, longing only to become articulate, to go on articulating ever farther !   The living doctrine grows, grows ; — like a Banyan-tree ; the first *seed* is the essential thing : any branch strikes itself down into the earth, becomes a new root ; and so, in endless complexity, we have a whole wood, a whole jungle, one seed the parent of it all.   Was not the whole Norse Religion, accordingly, in some sense, what we called "the enormous shadow of this man's likeness" ? Critics trace some affinity in some Norse mythuses, of the Creation and suchlike, with those of the Hindoos. The Cow Adumbla, "licking the rime from the rocks," has a kind of Hindoo look.   A Hindoo Cow, transported into frosty countries.   Probably enough ; indeed we may say undoubtedly, these things will have a kindred with the remotest lands, with the earliest times.   Thought does not die, but only is changed. The first man that began to think in this Planet of ours, he was the beginner of all.   And then the second man, and the third man ; — nay, every true Thinker to this hour is a kind of Odin, teaches men *his* way of thought, spreads a shadow of his own likeness over sections of the History of the World.

Of the distinctive poetic character or merit of this Norse Mythology I have not room to speak ; nor does it concern us much.   Some wild Prophecies we have, as the *Völuspa* in the *Elder Edda;* of a rapt, earnest, sibylline sort.   But they were comparatively an idle adjunct of the matter, men who as it were but toyed with the matter, these later Skalds; and it is *their* songs chiefly that survive. In later centuries, I suppose, they would go on singing, poetically symbolizing, as our modern Painters paint, when it was no longer from the innermost heart, or not from the heart at all. This is everywhere to be well kept in mind.

Gray's fragments of Norse Lore, at any rate, will give one no notion of it; — any more than Pope will of Homer. It is no square-built gloomy palace of black ashlar marble, shrouded in awe and horror, as Gray gives it us: no; rough as the North rocks, as the Iceland deserts, it is; with a heartiness, homeliness, even a tint of good humor and robust mirth in the middle of these fearful things. The strong old Norse heart did not go upon theatrical sublimities; they had not time to tremble. I like much their robust simplicity; their veracity, directness of conception. Thor " draws down his brows " in a veritable Norse rage; "grasps his hammer till the *knuckles grow white.*" Beautiful traits of pity too, an honest pity. Balder "the white God " dies; the beautiful, benignant; he is the Sungod. They try all Nature for a remedy; but he is dead. Frigga, his mother, sends Hermoder to seek or see him: nine days and nine nights he rides through gloomy deep valleys, a labyrinth of gloom; arrives at the Bridge with its gold roof: the Keeper says, " Yes, Balder did pass here; but the Kingdom of the Dead is down yonder, far towards the North." Hermoder rides on; leaps Hellgate, Hela's gate; does see Balder, and speak with him: Balder cannot be delivered. Inexorable! Hela will not, for Odin or any God, give him up. The beautiful and gentle has to remain there. His Wife had volunteered to go with him, to die with him. They shall forever remain there. He sends his ring to Odin; Nanna his wife sends her *thimble* to Frigga, as a remembrance — Ah me!

For indeed Valor is the fountain of Pity too; — of Truth, and all that is great and good in man. The robust homely vigor of the Norse heart attaches one much, in these delineations. Is it not a trait of right honest strength, says Uhland, who has written a fine *Essay* on Thor, that the old Norse heart finds its friend in the Thunder-god? That it is not frightened away by his thunder; but finds that Summer-heat, the beautiful noble summer, must and will have thunder withal! The Norse heart *loves* this Thor and his hammer-bolt; sports with him. Thor is Summer-heat; the god of Peaceable Industry as well as Thunder. He is the Peasant's friend; his true henchman and attendant is Thialfi, *Manual Labor.* Thor himself engages in all manner of rough manual work, scorns no business for its plebeianism; is ever and anon travelling to the country of the Jötuns, harrying those chaotic Frost-monsters, subduing them, at least straitening and damaging them. There is a great broad humor in some of these things.

Thor, as we saw above, goes to Jötun-land, to seek Hymir's Caldron, that the Gods may brew beer. Hymir the huge Giant enters, his gray beard all full of hoar-frost; splits pillars with the very glance of his eye; Thor, after much rough tumult, snatches the Pot, claps it on his head; the "handles of it reach down to his heels." The Norse Skald has a kind of loving sport with Thor. This is the Hymir whose cattle, the critics have discovered, are Icebergs. Huge untutored Brobdignag genius, — needing only to be tamed-down; into Shakspeares, Dantes, Goethes! It is all gone now, that old Norse work, — Thor the Thunder-god changed into Jack the Giant-killer: but the mind that made it is here yet. How strangely things grow, and die, and do not die! There are twigs of that great world-tree of Norse Belief still curiously traceable. This poor Jack of the Nursery, with his miraculous shoes of swiftness, coat of darkness, sword of sharpness, he is one. *Hynde Etin*, and still more decisively *Red Etin of Ireland*, in the Scottish Ballads, these are both derived from Norseland; *Etin* is evidently a *Jötun*. Nay, Shakspeare's *Hamlet* is a twig too of this same world-tree; there seems no doubt of that. Hamlet, *Amleth*, I find, is really a mythic personage; and his Tragedy, of the poisoned Father, poisoned asleep by drops in his ear, and the rest, in a Norse mythus! Old Saxo, as his wont was, made it a Danish history; Shakspeare, out of Saxo, made it what we see. That is a twig of the world-tree that has *grown*, I think; — by nature or accident that one has grown!

In fact, these old Norse songs have a *truth* in them, an inward perennial truth and greatness, — as, indeed, all must have that can very long preserve itself by tradition alone. It is a greatness not of mere body and gigantic bulk, but a rude greatness of soul. There is a sublime uncomplaining melancholy traceable in these old hearts. A great free glance into the very deeps of thought. They seem to have seen, these brave old Northmen, what Meditation has taught all men in all ages, That this world is after all but a show, — a phenomenon or appearance, no real thing. All deep souls see into that, — the Hindoo Mythologist, the German Philosopher, — the Shakspeare, the earnest Thinker, wherever he may be:

"We are such stuff as dreams are made of!"

One of Thor's expeditions, to Utgard (the *Outer* Garden, central seat of Jötun-land), is remarkable in this respect. Thialfi was with him, and Loke. After

various adventures, they entered upon Giant-land;
wandered over plains, wild uncultivated places, among
stones and trees. At nightfall they noticed a house;
and as the door, which indeed formed one whole side
of the house, was open, they entered. It was a
simple habitation; one large hall, altogether empty.
They stayed there. Suddenly in the dead of the night
loud noises alarmed them. Thor grasped his hammer; stood in the door, prepared for fight. His companions within ran hither and thither in their terror,
seeking some outlet in that rude hall; they found a
little closet at last, and took refuge there. Neither
had Thor any battle: for, lo, in the morning it turned-
out that the noise had been only the *snoring* of a certain enormous but peaceable Giant, the Giant Skrymir,
who lay peaceably sleeping near by; and this that
they took for a house was merely his *Glove*, thrown
aside there; the door was the Glove-wrist; the little
closet they had fled into was the Thumb! Such a
glove; — I remark too that it had not fingers as ours
have, but only a thumb, and the rest undivided: a
most ancient, rustic glove.

Skrymir now carried their portmanteau all day;
Thor, however, had his own suspicions, did not like
the ways of Skrymir; determined at night to put an
end to him as he slept. Raising his hammer, he
struck down into the Giant's face a right thunderbolt
blow, of force to rend rocks. The Giant merely
awoke; rubbed his cheek, and said, Did a leaf fall?
Again Thor struck, so soon as Skrymir again slept;
a better blow than before; but the Giant only mur-
mured, Was that a grain of sand? Thor's third stroke
was with both his hands (the " knuckles white " I suppose), and seemed to dint deep into Skrymir's visage;
but he merely checked his snore, and remarked, There
must be sparrows roosting in this tree, I think ; what

is that they have dropt? — At the gate of Utgard, a place so high that you had to "strain your neck bending back to see the top of it," Skrymir went his ways. Thor and his companions were admitted; invited to take share in the games going on. To Thor, for his part, they handed a Drinking-horn; it was a common feat, they told him, to drink this dry at one draught. Long and fiercely, three times over, Thor drank; but made hardly any impression. He was a weak child, they told him: could he lift that Cat he saw there? Small as the feat seemed, Thor with his whole god-like strength could not; he bent-up the creature's back, could not raise its feet off the ground, could at the utmost raise one foot. Why, you are no man, said the Utgard people; there is an Old Woman that will wrestle you! Thor, heartily ashamed, seized this haggard Old Woman; but could not throw her.

And now, on their quitting Utgard, the chief Jötun, escorting them politely a little way, said to Thor: "You are beaten then; — yet be not so much ashamed; there was deception of appearance in it. That Horn you tried to drink was the *Sea;* you did make it ebb; but who could drink that, the bottomless! The Cat you would have lifted, — why, that is the *Midgard-snake*, the Great World-serpent, which, tail in mouth, girds and keeps-up the whole created world; had you torn that up, the world must have rushed to ruin! As for the Old Woman, she was *Time*, Old Age, Duration; with her what can wrestle? No man nor no god with her; gods or men, she prevails over all! And then those three strokes you struck, — look at these *three valleys;* your three strokes made these!" Thor looked at his attendant Jötun: it was Skrymir; — it was, say Norse critics, the old chaotic rocky *Earth* in person, and that glove-*house* was some Earth cavern! But Skrymir had vanished; Utgard with its

4

skyhigh gates, when Thor grasped his hammer to smite them, had gone to air; only the Giant's voice was heard mocking: " Better come no more to Jötun-heim ! " —

This is of the allegoric period, as we see, and half play, not of the prophetic and entirely devout : but as a mythus is there not real antique Norse gold in it? More true metal, rough from the Mimer-stithy, than in many a famed Greek Mythus *shaped* far better! A great broad Brobdignag grin of true humor is in this Skrymir; mirth resting on earnestness and sadness, as the rainbow on black tempest: only a right valiant heart is capable of that. It is the grim humor of our own Ben Jonson, rare old Ben; runs in the blood of us, I fancy; for one catches tones of it, under a still other shape, out of the American Backwoods.

That is also a very striking conception that of the *Ragnarök*, Consummation, or *Twilight of the Gods*. It is in the *Völuspa* Song; seemingly a very old, prophetic idea. The Gods and Jötuns, the divine Powers and the chaotic brute ones, after long contest and partial victory by the former, meet at last in universal world-embracing wrestle and duel; World-serpent against Thor, strength against strength; mutually extinctive; and ruin, " twilight " sinking into darkness, swallows the created Universe. The old Universe with its Gods is sunk; but it is not final death: there is to be a new Heaven and a new Earth; a higher supreme God, and Justice to reign among men. Curious: this law of mutation, which also is a law written in man's inmost thought, had been deciphered by these old earnest Thinkers in their rude style; and how, though all dies, and even gods die, yet all death is but a phœnix fire-death, and new-birth into the Greater and the Better! It is the fundamental Law of

Being for a creature made of Time, living in this Place of Hope. All earnest men have seen into it; may still see into it.

And now, connected with this, let us glance at the *last* mythus of the appearance of Thor; and end there. I fancy it to be the latest in date of all these fables; a sorrowing protest against the advance of Christianity, — set forth reproachfully by some Conservative Pagan. King Olaf has been harshly blamed for his over-zeal in introducing Christianity; surely I should have blamed him far more for an under-zeal in that! He paid dear enough for it; he died by the revolt of his Pagan people, in battle, in the year 1033, at Stickelstad, near that Drontheim, where the chief Cathedral of the North has now stood for many centuries, dedicated gratefully to his memory as *Saint* Olaf. The mythus about Thor is to this effect. King Olaf, the Christian Reform King, is sailing with fit escort along the shore of Norway, from haven to haven; dispensing justice, or doing other royal work: on leaving a certain haven, it is found that a stranger, of grave eyes and aspect, red beard, of stately robust figure, has stept in. The courtiers address him; his answers surprise by their pertinency and depth: at length he is brought to the King. The stranger's conversation here is not less remarkable, as they sail along the beautiful shore; but after some time, he addresses King Olaf thus: "Yes, King Olaf, it is all beautiful, with the sun shining on it there; green, fruitful, a right fair home for you; and many a sore day had Thor, many a wild fight with the rock Jötuns, before he could make it so. And now you seem minded to put away Thor. King Olaf, have a care!" said the stranger, drawing-down his brows; — and when they looked again, he was nowhere to be found. This is the last appearance of Thor on the stage of this world!

Do we not see well enough how the Fable might arise, without unveracity on the part of any one? It is the way most Gods have come to appear among men: thus, if in Pindar's time " Neptune was seen once at the Nemean Games," what was this Neptune too but a " stranger of noble grave aspect,"—*fit* to be " seen "! There is something pathetic, tragic for me in this last voice of Paganism. Thor is vanished, the whole Norse world has vanished; and will not return ever again. In like fashion to that pass away the highest things. All things that have been in this world, all things that are or will be in it, have to vanish: we have our sad farewell to give them.

That Norse Religion, a rude but earnest, sternly impressive *Consecration of Valor* (so we may define it), sufficed for these old valiant Northmen. Consecration of Valor is not a *bad* thing! We will take it for good, so far as it goes. Neither is there no use in *knowing* something about this old Paganism of our Fathers. Unconsciously, and combined with higher things, it is in *us* yet, that old Faith withal! To know it consciously, brings us into closer and clearer relation with the Past, — with our own possessions in the Past. For the whole Past, as I keep repeating, is the possession of the Present; the Past had always something *true*, and is a precious possession. In a different time, in a different place, it is always some other *side* of our common Human Nature that has been developing itself. The actual True is the *sum* of all these; not any one of them by itself constitutes what of Human Nature is hitherto developed. Better to know them all than misknow them. " To which of these Three Religions do you specially adhere? " inquires Meister of his Teacher. " To all the Three! " answers the other: " To all the Three; for they by their union first constitute the True Religion."

LECTURE II.

THE HERO AS PROPHET.—MAHOMET : ISLAM.

FROM the first rude times of Paganism among the Scandinavians in the North, we advance to a very different epoch of religion, among a very different people : Mahometanism among the Arabs. A great change ; what a change and progress is indicated here, in the universal condition and thoughts of men !

The Hero is not now regarded as a God among his fellow-men ; but as one God-inspired, as a Prophet. It is the second phasis of Hero-worship : the first or oldest, we may say, has passed away without return ; in the history of the world there will not again be any man, never so great, whom his fellow-men will take for a god. Nay we might rationally ask, Did any set of human beings ever really think the man they *saw* there standing beside them a god, the maker of this world ? Perhaps not : it was usually some man they remembered, or *had* seen. But neither can this any more be. The Great Man is not recognized henceforth as a god any more.

It was a rude gross error, that of counting the Great Man a god. Yet let us say that it is at all times difficult to know *what* he is, or how to account of him and receive him ! The most significant feature in the history of an epoch is the manner it has of welcoming a Great Man. Ever, to the true instincts of men, there is something godlike in him. Whether they shall take him to be a god, to be a prophet, or what they shall take him to be ? that is ever a grand question ; by their way of answering that, we shall see, as through a little window, into the very heart of these men's spiritual condition. For at bottom the Great Man, as he comes from the hand of Nature, is ever the same kind of thing : Odin, Luther, Johnson, Burns ; I hope to make it appear that these are all originally of one stuff ; that only by the world's reception of them, and the shapes they assume, are they so immeasurably diverse. The worship of Odin astonishes us, — to fall prostrate before the Great Man, into *deliquium* of love and wonder over him, and feel in their hearts that he was a denizen of the skies, a god ! This was imperfect enough : but to welcome, for example, a Burns as we did, was that what we can call perfect ? The most precious gift that Heaven can give to the Earth ; a man of " genius " as we call it ; the Soul of a Man actually sent down from the skies with a God's-message to us, — this we waste away as an idle artificial firework, sent to amuse us a little, and sink it into ashes, wreck and ineffectuality : *such* reception of a Great Man I do not call very perfect either ! Looking into the heart of the thing, one may perhaps call that of Burns a still uglier phenomenon, betokening still sadder imperfections in mankind's ways, than the Scandinavian method itself ! To fall into mere unreasoning *deliquium* of love and admiration, was not good ; but such unreasoning, nay irrational supercilious no-love at all is perhaps still worse ! It is a thing forever changing, this of Hero-worship : different in each age, difficult to do well in any age. Indeed, the heart of the whole business of the age, one may say, is to do it well.

We have chosen Mahomet not as the most eminent Prophet ; but as the one we are freest to speak of. He is by no means the truest of Prophets ; but I do esteem him a true one. Farther, as there is no danger of our becoming, any of us, Mahometans, I mean to say all the good of him I justly can. It is the way to get at his secret: let us try to understand what *he* meant with the world; what the world meant and means with him, will then be a more answerable question. Our current hypothesis about Mahomet, that he was a scheming Impostor, a Falsehood incarnate, that his religion is a mere mass of quackery and fatuity, begins really to be now untenable to any one. The lies, which well-meaning zeal has heaped round this man, are disgraceful to ourselves only. When Pococke inquired of Grotius, Where the proof was of that story of the pigeon, trained to pick peas from Mahomet's ear, and pass for an angel dictating to him? Grotius answered that there was no proof! It is really time to dismiss all that. The word this man spoke has been the life-guidance now of a hundred-and-eighty millions of men these twelve-hundred years. These hundred-and-eighty millions were made by God as well as we. A greater number of God's creatures believe in Mahomet's word at this hour than in any other word whatever. Are we to suppose that it was a miserable piece of spiritual legerdemain, this which so many creatures of the Almighty have lived by and died by? I, for my part, cannot form any such supposition. I will believe most things sooner than that. One would be entirely at a loss what to think of this world at all, if quackery so grew and were sanctioned here.

Alas, such theories are very lamentable. If we would attain to knowledge of anything in God's true Creation, let us disbelieve them wholly! They are the product of an Age of Scepticism; they indicate the saddest spiritual paralysis, and mere death-life of the souls of men: more godless theory, I think, was never promulgated in this Earth. A false man found a religion? Why, a false man cannot build a brick house! If he do not know and follow *truly* the properties of mortar, burnt clay and what else he works in, it is no house that he makes, but a rubbish heap. It will not stand for twelve centuries, to lodge a hundred-and-eighty millions; it will fall straightway. A man must conform himself to Nature's laws, *be* verily in communion with Nature and the truth of things, or Nature will answer him, No, not at all! Speciosities are specious — ah me! — a Cagliostro, many Cagliostros, prominent world-leaders, do prosper by their quackery, for a day. It is like a forged bank-note; they get it passed out of *their* worthless hands: others, not they, have to smart for it. Nature bursts-up in fire-flames, French Revolutions and suchlike, proclaiming with terrible veracity that forged notes are forged.

But of a Great Man especially, of him I will venture to assert that it is incredible he should have been other than true. It seems to me the primary foundation of him, and of all that can lie in him, this. No Mirabeau, Napoleon, Burns, Cromwell, no man adequate to do anything, but is first of all in right earnest about it; what I call a sincere man. I should say *sincerity*, a deep, great, genuine sincerity, is the first characteristic of all men in any way heroic. Not the sincerity that calls itself sincere; ah no, that is a very poor matter indeed; — a shallow braggart conscious sincerity; oftenest self-conceit mainly. The Great Man's sincerity is of the kind he cannot speak of, is not conscious of: nay, I suppose, he is conscious rather of *in*sincerity; for what man can walk accurately by the law of truth for one day? No, the Great Man does not boast himself sincere, far from that; perhaps does not ask himself if he is so: I would say rather, his sincerity does not depend on himself; he cannot help being sincere! The great Fact of existence is great to him. Fly as he will, he cannot get out of the awful presence of this Reality. His mind is so made; he is great by that, first of all. Fearful and wonderful, real as Life, real as Death, is this Universe to him. Though all men should forget its truth, and walk in a vain show, he cannot. At all moments the Flame-image glares-in upon him; undeniable, there, there!— I wish you to take this as my primary definition of a Great Man. A little man may have this, it is competent to all men that God has made: but a Great Man cannot be without it.

Such a man is what we call an *original* man; he comes to us at first-hand. A messenger he, sent from the Infinite Unknown with tidings to us. We may call him Poet, Prophet, God;— in one way or other, we all feel that the words he utters are as no other man's words. Direct from the Inner Fact of things; — he lives, and has to live, in daily communion with that. Hearsays cannot hide it from him; he is blind, homeless, miserable, following hearsays; *it* glares-in upon him. Really his utterances, are they not a kind of "revelation;"— what we must call such for want of some other name? It is from the heart of the world that he comes; he is portion of the primal reality of things. God has made many revelations: but this man too, has not God made him, the latest and newest of all? The "inspiration of the Almighty giveth *him* understanding:" we must listen before all to him.

This Mahomet, then, we will in no wise consider as an Inanity and Theatricality, a poor conscious ambitious schemer; we cannot conceive him so. The rude message he delivered was a real one withal; an earnest confused voice from the unknown Deep. The man's words were not false, nor his workings here below; no Inanity and Simulacrum; a fiery mass of

Life cast-up from the great bosom of Nature herself. To *kindle* the world; the world's Maker had ordered it so. Neither can the faults, imperfections, insincerities even, of Mahomet, if such were never so well proved against him, shake this primary fact about him.

On the whole, we make too much of faults; the details of the business hide the real centre of it. Faults? The greatest of faults, I should say, is to be conscious of none. Readers of the Bible above all, one would think, might know better. Who is called there "the man according to God's own heart,"? David, the Hebrew King, had fallen into sins enough; blackest crimes; there was no want of sins. And thereupon the unbelievers sneer and ask, Is this your man according to God's heart? The sneer, I must say, seems to me but a shallow one. What are faults, what are the outward details of a life; if the inner secret of it, the remorse, temptations, true, often-baffled, never-ended struggle of it, be forgotten? "It is not in man that walketh to direct his steps." Of all acts, is not, for a man, *repentance* the most divine? The deadliest sin, I say, were that same supercilious consciousness of no sin; — that is death; the heart so conscious is divorced from sincerity, humility and fact; is dead: it is "pure" as dead dry sand is pure. David's life and history, as written for us in those Psalms of his, I consider to be the truest emblem ever given of a man's moral progress and warfare here below. All earnest souls will ever discern in it the faithful struggle of an earnest human soul towards what is good and best. Struggle often baffled, sore baffled, down as into entire wreck; yet a struggle never ended; ever, with tears, repentance, true unconquerable purpose, begun anew. Poor human nature! Is not a man's walking, in truth, always that: "a succession of falls"? Man can do no other. In this wild element of a Life, he has to struggle onwards; now fallen, deep-abased; and ever, with tears, repentance, with bleeding heart, he has to rise again, struggle again still onwards. That his struggle *be* a faithful unconquerable one: that is the question of questions. We will put-up with many sad details, if the souls of it were true. Details by themselves will never teach us what it is. I believe we misestimate Mahomet's faults even as faults: but the secret of him will never be got by dwelling there. We will leave all this behind us; and assuring ourselves that he did mean some true thing, ask candidly what it was or might be.

These Arabs Mahomet was born among are certainly a notable people. Their country itself is notable; the fit habitation for such a race. Savage inaccessible rock-mountains, great grim deserts, alternating with beautiful strips of verdure: wherever water is, there is greenness, beauty; odoriferous balm-shrubs, date-trees, frankincense-trees. Consider that wide waste horizon of sand, empty, silent, like a sand-sea, dividing habitable place from habitable. You are all alone there, left alone with the Universe; by day a fierce sun blazing down on it with intolerable radiance; by night the great deep Heaven with its stars. Such a country is fit for a swift-handed, deep-hearted race of men. There is something most agile, active, and yet most meditative, enthusiastic in the Arab character. The Persians are called the French of the East; we will call the Arabs Oriental Italians. A gifted noble people; a people of wild strong feelings, and of iron restraint over these: the characteristic of nobleminded-ness, of genius. The wild Bedouin welcomes the stranger to his tent, as one having right to all that is there ; were it his worst enemy, he will slay his foal to treat him, will serve him with sacred hospitality for three days, will set him fairly on his way ; — and then, by another law as sacred, kill him if he can.   In words too, as in action.   They are not a loquacious people, taciturn rather ; but eloquent, gifted when they do speak.   An earnest, truthful kind of men.   They are, as we know, of Jewish kindred : but with that deadly terrible earnestness of the Jews they seem to combine something graceful, brilliant, which is not Jewish. They had " Poetic contests " among them before the time of Mahomet.   Sale says, at Ocadh, in the South of Arabia, there were yearly fairs, and there, when the merchandising was done, Poets sang for prizes : — the wild people gathered to hear that.

One Jewish quality these Arabs manifest ; the outcome of many or of all high qualities ; what we may call religiosity.   From of old they had been zealous worshippers, according to their light.   They worshipped the stars, as Sabeans ; worshipped many natural objects, — recognized them as symbols, immediate manifestations, of the Maker of Nature.   It was wrong ; and yet not wholly wrong.   All God's works are still in a sense symbols of God.   Do we not, as I urged, still account it a merit to recognize a certain inexhaustible significance, " poetic beauty " as we name it, in all natural objects whatsoever ?   A man is a poet, and honored, for doing that, and speaking or singing it, — a kind of diluted worship. They had many Prophets, these Arabs ; Teachers each to his tribe, each according to the light he had.   But indeed, have we not from of old the noblest of proofs, still palpable to every one of us, of what devoutness and noblemindedness had dwelt in these rustic thoughtful peoples ?   Biblical critics seem agreed that our own *Book of Job* was written in that region of the world. I call that, apart from all theories about it, one of the grandest things ever written with pen. One feels, indeed, as if it were not Hebrew; such a noble universality, different from noble patriotism or sectarianism, reigns in it. A noble Book; all men's Book! It is our first, oldest statement of the never-ending Problem, — man's destiny, and God's ways with him here in this earth. And all in such free flowing outlines; grand in its sincerity, in its simplicity; in its epic melody, and repose of reconcilement. There is the seeing eye, the mildly understanding heart. So *true* everyway; true eyesight and vision for all things; material things no less than spiritual : the Horse, — " Hast thou clothed his neck with *thunder ?* " — he " *laughs* at the shaking of the spear ! " Such living likenesses were never since drawn. Sublime sorrow, sublime reconciliation; oldest choral melody as of the heart of mankind; — so soft, and great; as the summer midnight, as the world with its seas and stars ! There is nothing written, I think, in the Bible or out of it, of equal literary merit. —

To the idolatrous Arabs one of the most ancient universal objects of worship was that Black Stone, still kept in the building called Caabah at Mecca. Diodorus Siculus mentions this Caabah in a way not to be mistaken, as the oldest, most honored temple in his time; that is, some half-century before our Era. Silvestre de Sacy says there is some likelihood that the Black Stone is an aerolite. In that case, some man might *see* it fall out of Heaven ! It stands now beside the Well Zemzem; the Caabah is built over both. A Well is in all places a beautiful affecting object, gushing out like life from the hard earth; — still more so in those hot dry countries, where it is the first condition of being. The Well Zemzem has its name from the bubbling sound of the waters, *zem-zem ;*

they think it is the Well which Hagar found with her little Ishmael in the wilderness: the aerolite and it have been sacred now, and had a Caabah over them, for thousands of years. A curious object, that Caabah! There it stands at this hour, in the black cloth-covering the Sultan sends it yearly; " twenty-seven cubits high; " with circuit, with double circuit of pillars, with festoon-rows of lamps and quaint ornaments: the lamps will be lighted again *this* night, — to glitter again under the stars. An authentic fragment of the oldest Past. It is the *Keblah* of all Moslem: from Delhi all onwards to Morocco, the eyes of innumerable praying men are turned towards *it*, five times, this day and all days: one of the notablest centres in the Habitation of Men.

It had been from the sacredness attached to this Caabah Stone and Hagar's Well, from the pilgrimings of all tribes of Arabs thither, that Mecca took its rise as a Town. A great town once, though much decayed now. It has no natural advantage for a town; stands in a sandy hollow amid bare barren hills, at a distance from the sea; its provisions, its very bread, have to be imported. But so many pilgrims needed lodgings: and then all places of pilgrimage do, from the first, become places of trade. The first day pilgrims meet, merchants have also met: where men see themselves assembled for one object, they find that they can accomplish other objects which depend on meeting together. Mecca became the Fair of all Arabia. And thereby indeed the chief staple and warehouse of whatever Commerce there was between the Indian and the Western countries, Syria, Egypt, even Italy. It had at one time a population of 100,000; buyers, forwarders of those Eastern and Western products; importers for their own behoof of provisions and corn. The government was a kind of irregular aristocratic republic, not without a touch of theocracy. Ten Men of a chief tribe, chosen in some rough way, were Governors of Mecca, and Keepers of the Caabah. The Koreish was the chief tribe in Mahomet's time; his own family was of that tribe. The rest of the Nation, fractioned and cut-asunder by deserts, lived under similar rude patriarchal governments by one or several : herdsmen, carriers, traders, generally robbers too; being oftenest at war one with another, or with all : held together by no open bond, if it were not this meeting at the Caabah, where all forms of Arab Idolatry assembled in common adoration; — held mainly by the *inward* indissoluble bond of a common blood and language. In this way had the Arabs lived for long ages, unnoticed by the world; a people of great qualities, unconsciously waiting for the day when they should become notable to all the world. Their Idolatries appear to have been in a tottering state; much was getting into confusion and fermentation among them. Obscure tidings of the most important Event ever transacted in this world, the Life and Death of the Divine Man in Judea, at once the symptom and cause of immeasurable change to all people in the world, had in the course of centuries reached into Arabia too; and could not but, of itself, have produced fermentation there.

It was among this Arab people, so circumstanced, in the year 570 of our Era, that the man Mahomet was born. He was of the family of Hashem, of the Koreish tribe as we said; though poor, connected with the chief persons of his country. Almost at his birth he lost his Father; at the age of six years his Mother too, a woman noted for her beauty, her worth and sense : he fell to the charge of his Grandfather, an old man, a hundred years old. A good old man : Mahomet's Father, Abdallah, had been his youngest favorite son. He saw in Mahomet, with his old life-worn eyes, a century old, the lost Abdallah come back again, all that was left of Abdallah.   He loved the little orphan Boy greatly; used to say, They must take care of that beautiful little Boy, nothing in their kindred was more precious than he.   At his death, while the boy was still but two years old, he left him in charge to Abu Thaleb the eldest of the Uncles, as to him that now was head of the house.   By this Uncle, a just and rational man as everything betokens, Mahomet was brought-up in the best Arab way.

Mahomet, as he grew up, accompanied his Uncle on trading journeys and suchlike; in his eighteenth year one finds him a fighter following his Uncle in war. But perhaps the most significant of all his journeys is one we find noted as of some years' earlier date: a journey to the Fairs of Syria.   The young man here first came in contact with a quite foreign world, — with one foreign element of endless moment to him: the Christian Religion.   I know not what to make of that "Sergius, the Nestorian Monk," whom Abu Thaleb and he are said to have lodged with; or how much any monk could have taught one still so young.   Probably enough it is greatly exaggerated, this of the Nestorian Monk.   Mahomet was only fourteen; had no language but his own : much in Syria must have been a strange unintelligible whirlpool to him.   But the eyes of the lad were open; glimpses of many things would doubtless be taken-in, and lie very enigmatic as yet, which were to ripen in a strange way into views, into beliefs and insights one day.   These journeys to Syria were probably the beginning of much to Mahomet.

One other circumstance we must not forget: that he had no school-learning; of the thing we call school-learning none at all.   The art of writing was but just introduced into Arabia; it seems to be the true opinion that Mahomet never could write !   Life in the Desert, with its experiences, was all his education. What of this infinite Universe he, from his dim place, with his own eyes and thoughts, could take in, so much and no more of it was he to know. Curious, if we will reflect on it, this of having no books. Except by what he could see for himself, or hear of by uncertain rumor of speech in the obscure Arabian Desert, he could know nothing. The wisdom that had been before him or at a distance from him in the world, was in a manner as good as not there for him. Of the great brother souls, flame-beacons through so many lands and times, no one directly communicates with this great soul. He is alone there, deep down in the bosom of the Wilderness; has to grow up so, — alone with Nature and his own Thoughts.

But, from an early age, he had been remarked as a thoughtful man. His companions named him "*Al Amin*, The Faithful." A man of truth and fidelity; true in what he did, in what he spake and thought. They noted that *he* always meant something. A man rather taciturn in speech; silent when there was nothing to be said; but pertinent, wise, sincere, when he did speak; always throwing light on the matter. This is the only sort of speech *worth* speaking! Through life we find him to have been regarded as an altogether solid, brotherly, genuine man. A serious, sincere character; yet amiable, cordial, companionable, jocose even; — a good laugh in him withal: there are men whose laugh is as untrue as anything about them; who cannot laugh. One hears of Mahomet's beauty: his fine sagacious honest face, brown florid complexion, beaming black eyes; — I somehow like too that vein on the brow, which swelled-up black when he was in anger: like the "*horse-shoe* vein" in Scott's "Redgauntlet." It was a kind of feature in the Hashem family, this black swelling vein in the brow; Mahomet

5

had it prominent, as would appear. A spontaneous, passionate, yet just, true-meaning man ! Full of wild faculty, fire and light; of wild worth, all uncultured; working out his life-task in the depths of the Desert there.

How he was placed with Kadijah, a rich Widow, as her Steward, and travelled in her business, again to the Fairs of Syria; how he managed all, as one can well understand, with fidelity, adroitness; how her gratitude, her regard for him grew: the story of their marriage is altogether a graceful intelligible one, as told us by the Arab authors. He was twenty-five ; she forty, though still beautiful. He seems to have lived in a most affectionate, peaceable, wholesome way with this wedded benefactress; loving her truly, and her alone. It goes greatly against the impostor theory, the fact that he lived in this entirely unexceptionable, entirely quiet and commonplace way, till the heat of his years was done. He was forty before he talked of any mission from Heaven. All his irregularities, real and supposed, date from after his fiftieth year, when the good Kadijah died. All his "ambition," seemingly, had been, hitherto, to live an honest life ; his "fame," the mere good opinion of neighbors that knew him, had been sufficient hitherto. Not till he was already getting old, the prurient heat of his life all burnt out, and *peace* growing to be the chief thing this world could give him, did he start on the "career of ambition ; " and, belying all his past character and existence, set-up as a wretched empty charlatan to acquire what he could now no longer enjoy ! For my share, I have no faith whatever in that.

Ah no: this deep-hearted Son of the Wilderness, with his beaming black eyes and open social deep soul, had other thoughts in him than ambition. A silent great soul; he was one of those who cannot *but* be in earnest; whom Nature herself has appointed to be sincere. While others walk in formulas and hear-says, contented enough to dwell there, this man could not screen himself in formulas; he was alone with his own soul and the reality of things. The great Mys-tery of Existence, as I said, glared-in upon him, with its terrors, with its splendors; no hearsays could hide that unspeakable fact, " Here am I ! " Such *sincerity*, as we named it, has in very truth something of divine. The word of such a man is a Voice direct from Nature's own Heart. Men do and must listen to that as to nothing else; — all else is wind in compar-ison. From of old, a thousand thoughts, in his pil-grimings and wanderings, had been in this man: What am I ? What *is* this unfathomable Thing I live in, which men name Universe? What is Life; what is Death? What am I to believe ? What am I to do? The grim rocks of Mount Hara, of Mount Sinai, the stern sandy solitudes answered not. The great Heaven rolling silent overhead, with its blue-glancing stars, answered not. There was no answer. The man's own soul, and what of God's inspiration dwelt there, had to answer !

It is the thing which all men have to ask them-selves; which we *too* have to ask, and answer. This wild man felt it to be of *infinite* moment; all other things of no moment whatever in comparison. The jargon of argumentative Greek Sects, vague tradi-tions of Jews, the stupid routine of Arab Idolatry: there was no answer in these. A Hero, as I repeat, has this first distinction, which indeed we may call first and last, the Alpha and Omega of his whole Heroism, That he looks through the shows of things into *things*. Use and wont, respectable hearsay, respectable formula: all these are good, or are not good. There is something behind and beyond all these, which all these must correspond with, be the image of, or they are — *Idolatries;* "bits of black wood pretending to be God;" to the earnest soul a mockery and abomination. Idolatries never so gilded, waited on by heads of the Koreish, will do nothing for this man. Though all men walk by them, what good is it? The great Reality stands glaring there upon *him.* He there has to answer it, or perish miserably. Now, even now, or else through all Eternity never! Answer it; *thou* must find an answer. Ambition? What could all Arabia do for this man; with the crown of Greek Heraclius, or Persian Chosroes, and all crowns in the earth; — what could they all do for him? It was not of the Earth he wanted to hear tell; it was of the Heaven above and of the Hell beneath. All crowns and sovereignties whatsoever, where would *they* in a few brief years be? To be Sheik of Mecca or Arabia, and have a bit of gilt wood put into your hand, — will that be one's salvation? I decidedly think, not. We will leave it altogether, this impostor hypothesis, as not credible; not very tolerable even, worthy chiefly of dismissal by us.

Mahomet had been wont to retire yearly, during the month Ramadhan, into solitude and silence; as indeed was the Arab custom; a praiseworthy custom, which such a man, above all, would find natural and useful. Communing with his own heart, in the silence of the mountains; himself silent; open to the "small still voices:" it was a right natural custom! Mahomet was in his fortieth year, when having withdrawn to a cavern in Mount Hara, near Mecca, during this Ramadhan, to pass the month in prayer, and meditation on those great questions, he one day told his wife Kadijah, who with his household was with him or near him this year, That by the unspeakable special favor of Heaven he had now found it all out; was in doubt and darkness no longer, but saw it all. That all these Idols and Formulas were nothing, miserable bits of wood; that there was One God in and over all; and we must leave all Idols, and look to Him. That God is great; and that there is nothing else great! He is the Reality. Wooden Idols are not real; He is real. He made us at first, sustains us yet; we and all things are but the shadow of Him; a transitory garment veiling the Eternal Splendor. "*Allah akbar*, God is great;"—and then also "*Islam*," That we must *submit* to God. That our whole strength lies in resigned submission to Him, whatsoever He do to us. For this world, and for the other! The thing He sends to us, were it death and worse than death, shall be good, shall be best; we resign ourselves to God. "If this be *Islam*," says Goethe, "do we not all live in *Islam?*" Yes, all of us that have any moral life; we all live so. It has ever been held the highest wisdom for a man not merely to submit to Necessity,—Necessity will make him submit,—but to know and believe well that the stern thing which Necessity had ordered was the wisest, the best, the thing wanted there. To cease his frantic pretension of scanning this great God's-World in his small fraction of a brain; to know that it *had* verily, though deep beyond his soundings, a Just Law, that the soul of it was good;—that his part in it was to conform to the Law of the Whole, and in devout silence follow that; not questioning it, obeying it as unquestionable.

I say, this is yet the only true morality known. A man is right and invincible, virtuous and on the road towards sure conquest, precisely while he joins himself to the great deep Law of the World, in spite of all superficial laws, temporary appearances, profit-and-loss calculations; he is victorious while he co-

operates with that great central Law, not victorious
otherwise : — and surely his first chance of co-operating with it, or getting into the course of it, is to know
with his whole soul that it *is;* that it is good, and
alone good ! This is the soul of Islam; it is properly
the soul of Christianity; — for Islam is definable as a
confused form of Christianity; had Christianity not
been, neither had it been. Christianity also com-
mands us, before all, to be resigned to God. We are
to take no counsel with flesh-and-blood; give ear to
no vain cavils, vain sorrows and wishes : to know that
we know nothing; that the worst and cruelest to our
eyes is not what it seems; that we have to receive
whatsoever befalls us as sent from God above, and
say, It is good and wise, God is great ! "Though He
slay me, yet will I trust in Him." Islam means in its
way Denial of Self, Annihilation of Self. This is yet
the highest Wisdom that Heaven has revealed to our
Earth.

Such light had come, as it could, to illuminate the
darkness of this wild Arab soul. A confused dazzling
splendor as of life and Heaven, in the great darkness
which threatened to be death : he called it revelation
and the angel Gabriel; — who of us yet can know
what to call it ? It is the "inspiration of the Almighty" that giveth us understanding. To *know;* to
get into the truth of anything, is ever a mystic act, —
of which the best Logics can but babble on the sur-
face. "Is not Belief the true god-announcing Miracle?" says Novalis. That Mahomet's whole soul,
set in flame with this grand Truth vouchsafed him,
should feel as if it were important and the only important thing, was very natural. That Providence had
unspeakably honored *him* by revealing it, saving him
from death and darkness; that he therefore was
bound to make known the same to all creatures : this

is what was meant by " Mahomet is the Prophet of God; " this too is not without its true meaning. —

The good Kadijah, we can fancy, listened to him with wonder, with doubt: at length she answered: Yes, it was *true* this that he said. One can fancy too the boundless gratitude of Mahomet; and how of all the kindnesses she had done him, this of believing the earnest struggling word he now spoke was the greatest. " It is certain," says Novalis, " my Conviction gains infinitely, the moment another soul will believe in it," It is a boundless favor. He never forgot this good Kadijah. Long afterwards, Ayesha his young favorite wife, a woman who indeed distinguished herself among the Moslem, by all manner of qualities, through her whole long life; this young brilliant Ayesha was, one day, questioning him: " Now am not I better than Kadijah? She was a widow; old, and had lost her looks: you love me better than you did her?" — " No, by Allah!" answered Mahomet: " No, by Allah! She believed in me when none else would believe. In the whole world I had but one friend, and she was that!" Seid, his Slave, also believed in him; these with his young Cousin Ali, Abu Thaleb's son, were his first converts.

He spoke of his Doctrine to this man and that; but the most treated it with ridicule, with indifference; in three years, I think, he had gained but thirteen followers. His progress was slow enough. His encouragement to go on, was altogether the usual encouragement that such a man in such a case meets. After some three years of small success, he invited forty of his chief kindred to an entertainment; and there stood-up and told them what his pretension was: that he had this thing to promulgate abroad to all men; that it was the highest thing, the one thing: which of them would second him in that? Amid the doubt and silence of all, young Ali, as yet a lad of sixteen, impatient of the silence, started-up, and exclaimed in passionate fierce language, That he would! The assembly, among whom was Abu Thaleb, Ali's Father, could not be unfriendly to Mahomet; yet the sight there, of one unlettered elderly man, with a lad of sixteen, deciding on such an enterprise against all mankind, appeared ridiculous to them; the assembly broke-up in laughter. Nevertheless it proved not a laughable thing; it was a very serious thing! As for this young Ali, one cannot but like him. A noble-minded creature, as he shows himself, now and always afterwards; full of affection, of fiery daring. Something chivalrous in him; brave as a lion; yet with a grace, a truth and affection worthy of Christian knighthood. He died by assassination in the Mosque at Bagdad; a death occasioned by his own generous fairness, confidence in the fairness of others: he said, If the wound proved not unto death, they must pardon the Assassin; but if it did, then they must slay him straightway, that so they two in the same hour might appear before God, and see which side of that quarrel was the just one!

Mahomet naturally gave offence to the Koreish, Keepers of the Caabah, superintendents of the Idols. One or two men of influence had joined him: the thing spread slowly, but it was spreading. Naturally he gave offence to everybody: Who is this that pretends to be wiser than we all; that rebukes us all, as mere fools and worshippers of wood! Abu Thaleb the good Uncle spoke with him: Could he not be silent about all that; believe it all for himself, and not trouble others, anger the chief men, endanger himself and them all, talking of it? Mahomet answered: If the Sun stood on his right hand and the Moon on his left, ordering him to hold his peace, he

could not obey! No: there was something in this
Truth he had got which was of Nature herself; equal
in rank to Sun, or Moon, or whatsoever thing Nature
had made. It would speak itself there, so long as the
Almighty allowed it, in spite of Sun and Moon, and
all Koreish and all men and things. It must do that,
and could do no other. Mahomet answered so; and,
they say, "burst into tears." Burst into tears: he felt
that Abu Thaleb was good to him; that the task he
had got was no soft, but a stern and great one.

He went on speaking to who would listen to him;
publishing his Doctrine among the pilgrims as they
came to Mecca; gaining adherents in this place and
that. Continual contradiction, hatred, open or secret
danger attended him. His powerful relations pro-
tected Mahomet himself; but by and by, on his own
advice, all his adherents had to quit Mecca, and seek
refuge in Abyssinia over the sea. The Koreish grew
ever angrier; laid plots, and swore oaths among them,
to put Mahomet to death with their own hands. Abu
Thaleb was dead, the good Kadijah was dead. Mahomet is not solicitous of sympathy from us; but his
outlook at this time was one of the dismallest. He
had to hide in caverns, escape in disguise; fly hither
and thither; homeless, in continual peril of his life.
More than once it seemed all-over with him; more
than once it turned on a straw, some rider's horse
taking fright or the like, whether Mahomet and his
Doctrine had not ended there, and not been heard of
at all. But it was not to end so.

In the thirteenth year of his mission, finding his
enemies all banded against him, forty sworn men, one
out of every tribe, waiting to take his life, and no
continuance possible at Mecca for him any longer,
Mahomet fled to the place then called Yathreb, where
he had gained some adherents; the place they now

call Medina, or "*Medinat al Nabi,* the City of the Prophet," from that circumstance. It lay some 200 miles off, through rocks and deserts; not without great difficulty, in such mood as we may fancy, he escaped thither, and found welcome. The whole East dates its era from this Flight, *Hegira* as they name it: the Year 1 of this Hegira is 622 of our Era, the fifty-third of Mahomet's life. He was now becoming an old man; his friends sinking round him one by one; his path desolate, encompassed with danger: unless he could find hope in his own heart, the outward face of things was but hopeless for him. It is so with all men in the like case. Hitherto Mahomet had professed to publish his Religion by the way of preaching and persuasion alone. But now, driven foully out of his native country, since unjust men had not only given no ear to his earnest Heaven's-message, the deep cry of his heart, but would not even let him live if he kept speaking it, — the wild Son of the Desert resolved to defend himself, like a man and Arab. If the Koreish will have it so, they shall have it. Tidings, felt to be of infinite moment to them and all men, they would not listen to these; would trample them down by sheer violence, steel and murder: well, let steel try it then! Ten years more this Mahomet had; all of fighting, of breathless impetuous toil and struggle; with what result we know.

Much has been said of Mahomet's propagating his Religion by the sword. It is no doubt far nobler what we have to boast of the Christian Religion, that it propagated itself peaceably in the way of preaching and conviction. Yet withal, if we take this for an argument of the truth or falsehood of a religion, there is a radical mistake in it. The sword indeed: but where will you get your sword! Every new opinion, at its starting, is precisely in a *minority of one.* In

one man's head alone, there it dwells as yet. One
man alone of the whole world believes it; there is one
man against all men. That *he* take a sword, and try
to propagate with that, will do little for him. You
must first get your sword! On the whole, a thing will
propagate itself as it can. We do not find, of the
Christian Religion either, that it always disdained the
sword, when once it had got one. Charlemagne's conversion of the Saxons was not by preaching. I care
little about the sword: I will allow a thing to struggle
for itself in this world, with any sword or tongue or
implement it has, or can lay hold of. We will let it
preach, and pamphleteer, and fight, and to the uttermost bestir itself, and do, beak and claws, whatsoever
is in it; very sure that it will, in the long-run, conquer
nothing which does not deserve to be conquered.
What is better than itself, it cannot put away, but
only what is worse. In this great Duel, Nature herself is umpire, and can do no wrong: the thing which
is deepest-rooted in Nature, what we call *truest*, that
thing and not the other will be found growing at last.

Here however, in reference to much that there is in
Mahomet and his success, we are to remember what
an umpire Nature is; what a greatness, composure of
depth and tolerance there is in her. You take wheat
to cast into the Earth's bosom: your wheat may be
mixed with chaff, chopped straw, barn-sweepings, dust
and all imaginable rubbish; no matter: you cast it
into the kind just Earth; she grows the wheat, — the
whole rubbish she silently absorbs, shrouds *it* in, says
nothing of the rubbish. The yellow wheat is growing
there; the good Earth is silent about all the rest, —
has silently turned all the rest to some benefit too, and
makes no complaint about it! So everywhere in
Nature! She is true and not a lie; and yet so great,
and just, and motherly in her truth. She requires of

a thing only that it *be* genuine of heart; she will protect it if so; will not, if not so. There is a soul of truth in all the things she ever gave harbor to. Alas, is not this the history of all highest Truth that comes or ever came into the world? The *body* of them all is imperfection, an element of light *in* darkness: to us they have to come embodied in mere Logic, in some merely *scientific* Theorem of the Universe; which *cannot* be complete; which cannot but be found, one day, *in*complete, erroneous, and so die and disappear. The body of all Truth dies; and yet in all, I say, there is a soul which never dies; which in new and ever-nobler embodiment lives immortal as man himself! It is the way with Nature. The genuine essence of Truth never dies. That it be genuine, a voice from the great Deep of Nature, there is the point at Nature's judgment-seat. What *we* call pure or impure, is not with her the final question. Not how much chaff is in you; but whether you have any wheat. Pure? I might say to many a man: Yes, you are pure; pure enough; but you are chaff, — insincere hypothesis, hearsay, formality; you never were in contact with the great heart of the Universe at all; you are properly neither pure nor impure; you *are* nothing, Nature has no business with you.

Mahomet's Creed we called a kind of Christianity; and really, if we look at the wild rapt earnestness with which it was believed and laid to heart, I should say a better kind than that of those miserable Syrian Sects, with their vain janglings about *Homoiousion* and *Homoousion* the head full of worthless noise, the heart empty and dead! The truth of it is embedded in portentous error and falsehood; but the truth of it makes it be believed, not the falsehood: it succeeded by its truth. A bastard kind of Christianity, but a living kind; with a heart-life in it; not dead, chopping

barren logic merely!   Out of all that rubbish of Arab
idolatries, argumentative theologies, traditions, subtleties, rumors and hypotheses of Greeks and Jews, with
their idle wiredrawings, this wild man of the Desert,
with his wild sincere heart, earnest as death and life,
with his great flashing natural eyesight, had seen into
the kernel of the matter.   Idolatry is nothing: these
Wooden Idols of yours, "ye rub them with oil and
wax, and the flies stick on them," — these are wood, I
tell you!   They can do nothing for you; they are an
impotent blasphemous pretence; a horror and abomination, if ye knew them.   God alone is; God alone
has power; He made us, He can kill us and keep us
alive: "*Allah akbar*, God is great."   Understand that
His will is the best for you; that howsoever sore to
flesh-and-blood, you will find it the wisest, best: you
are bound to take it so; in this world and in the next,
you have no other thing that you can do!

And now if the wild idolatrous men did believe this,
and with their fiery hearts lay hold of it to do it, in
what form soever it came to them, I say it was well
worthy of being believed.   In one form or the other,
I say it is still the one thing worthy of being believed
by all men.   Man does hereby become the high-priest
of this Temple of a World.   He is in harmony with
the Decrees of the Author of this World; co-operating
with them, not vainly withstanding them: I know, to
this day, no better definition of Duty than that same.
All that is *right* includes itself in this of co-operating
with the real Tendency of the World: you succeed by
this (the World's Tendency will succeed), you are
good, and in the right course there.   *Homoiousion,
Homoousion*, vain logical jangle, then or before or at
any time, may jangle itself out, and go whither and
how it likes: this is the *thing* it all struggles to mean,
if it would mean anything.   If it do not succeed in

meaning this, it means nothing. Not that Abstractions, logical Propositions, be correctly worded or incorrectly ; but that living concrete Sons of Adam do lay this to heart: that is the important point. Islam devoured all these vain jangling Sects ; and I think had right to do so. It was a Reality, direct from the great Heart of Nature once more. Arab idolatries, Syrian formulas, whatsoever was not equally real, had to go up in flame, — mere dead *fuel*, in various senses, for this which was *fire*.

It was during these wild warfarings and strugglings, especially after the Flight to Mecca, that Mahomet dictated at intervals his Sacred Book, which they name *Koran*, or *Reading*, "Thing to be read." This is the Work he and his disciples made so much of, asking all the world, Is not that a miracle? The Mahometans regard their Koran with a reverence which few Christians pay even to their Bible. It is admitted everywhere as the standard of all law and all practice ; the thing to be gone-upon in speculation and life : the message sent direct out of Heaven, which this Earth has to conform to, and walk by; the thing to be read. Their Judges decide by it; all Moslem are bound to study it, seek in it for the light of their life. They have mosques where it is all read daily; thirty relays of priests take it up in succession, get through the whole each day. There, for twelve-hundred years, has the voice of this Book, at all moments, kept sounding through the ears and the hearts of so many men. We hear of Mahometan Doctors that had read it seventy-thousand times!

Very curious: if one sought for "discrepancies of national taste," here surely were the most eminent instance of that! We also can read the Koran; our Translation of it, by Sale, is known to be a very fair one. I must say, it is as toilsome reading as I ever undertook. A wearisome confused jumble, crude, incondite; endless iterations, long-windedness, entanglement; most crude, incondite;—insupportable stupidity, in short! Nothing but a sense of duty could carry any European through the Koran. We read in it, as we might in the State-Paper Office, unreadable masses of lumber, that perhaps we may get some glimpses of a remarkable man. It is true we have it under disadvantages: the Arabs see more method in it than we. Mahomet's followers found the Koran lying all in fractions, as it had been written-down at first promulgation; much of it, they say, on shoulder-blades of mutton, flung pell-mell into a chest: and they published it, without any discoverable order as to time or otherwise;—merely trying, as would seem, and this not very strictly, to put the longest chapters first. The real beginning of it, in that way, lies almost at the end: for the earliest portions were the shortest. Read in its historical sequence it perhaps would not be so bad. Much of it, too, they say, is rhythmic; a kind of wild chanting song, in the original. This may be a great point; much perhaps has been lost in the Translation here. Yet with every allowance, one feels it difficult to see how any mortal ever could consider this Koran as a Book written in Heaven, too good for the Earth; as a well-written book, or indeed as a *book* at all; and not a bewildered rhapsody; *written*, so far as writing goes, as badly as almost any book ever was! So much for national discrepancies, and the standard of taste.

Yet I should say, it was not unintelligible how the Arabs might so love it. When once you get this confused coil of a Koran fairly off your hands, and have it behind you at a distance, the essential type of it begins to disclose itself; and in this there is a merit

quite other than the literary one. If a book come
from the heart, it will contrive to reach other hearts;
all art and authorcraft are of small amount to that.
One would say the primary character of the Koran is
this of its *genuineness*, of its being a *bona-fide* book.
Prideaux, I know, and others have represented it as a
mere bundle of juggleries; chapter after chapter got-up
to excuse and varnish the author's successive sins,
forward his ambitions and quackeries: but really it is
time to dismiss all that. I do not assert Mahomet's
continual sincerity: who is continually sincere? But
I confess I can make nothing of the critic, in these
times, who would accuse him of deceit *prepense;* of
conscious deceit generally, or perhaps at all; — still
more, of living in a mere element of conscious deceit,
and writing this Koran as a forger and juggler would
have done! Every candid eye, I think, will read the
Koran far otherwise than so. It is the confused fer-
ment of a great rude human soul; rude, untutored,
that cannot even read; but fervent, earnest, struggling
vehemently to utter itself in words. With a kind of
breathless intensity he strives to utter himself; the
thoughts crowd on him pellmell: for very multitude of
things to say, he can get nothing said. The meaning
that is in him shapes itself into no form of composi-
tion, is stated in no sequence, method, or coherence; —
they are not *shaped* at all, these thoughts of his;
flung-out unshaped, as they struggle and tumble there,
in their chaotic inarticulate state. We said "stupid:"
yet natural stupidity is by no means the character of
Mahomet's Book; it is natural uncultivation rather.
The man has not studied speaking; in the haste and
pressure of continual fighting, has not time to mature
himself into fit speech. The panting breathless haste
and vehemence of a man struggling in the thick of
battle for life and salvation; this is the mood he is in!

A headlong haste; for very magnitude of meaning, he cannot get himself articulated into words. The successive utterances of a soul in that mood, colored by the various vicissitudes of three-and-twenty years; now well uttered, now worse: this is the Koran.

For we are to consider Mahomet, through these three-and-twenty years, as the centre of a world wholly in conflict. Battles with the Koreish and Heathen, quarrels among his own people, backslidings of his own wild heart; all this kept him in a perpetual whirl, his soul knowing rest no more. In wakeful nights, as one may fancy, the wild soul of the man, tossing amid these vortices, would hail any light of a decision for them as a veritable light from Heaven; *any* making-up of his mind, so blessed, indispensable for him there, would seem the inspiration of a Gabriel. Forger and juggler? No, no! This great fiery heart, seething, simmering like a great furnace of thoughts, was not a juggler's. His life was a Fact to him; this God's Universe an awful Fact and Reality. He has faults enough. The man was an uncultured semi-barbarous Son of Nature, much of the Bedouin still clinging to him: we must take him for that. But for a wretched Simulacrum, a hungry Impostor without eyes or heart, practising for a mess of pottage such blasphemous swindlery, forgery of celestial documents, continual high-treason against his Maker and Self, we will not and cannot take him.

Sincerity, in all senses, seems to me the merit of the Koran; what had rendered it precious to the wild Arab men. It is, after all, the first and last merit in a book; gives rise to merits of all kinds, — nay, at bottom, it alone can give rise to merit of any kind. Curiously, through these incondite masses of tradition, vituperation, complaint, ejaculation in the Koran, a vein of true direct insight, of what we might almost

6

call poetry, is found straggling. The body of the
Book is made-up of mere tradition, and as it were
vehement enthusiastic extempore preaching. He returns forever to the old stories of the Prophets as they
went current in the Arab memory : how Prophet after
Prophet, the Prophet Abraham, the Prophet Hud, the
Prophet Moses, Christian and other real and fabulous
Prophets, had come to this Tribe and to that, warn-
ing men of their sin ; and been received by them even
as he Mahomet was, — which is a great solace to him.
These things he repeats ten, perhaps twenty times ;
again and ever again, with wearisome iteration ; has
never done repeating them.   A brave Samuel Johnson,
in his forlorn garret, might con-over the Biographies
of Authors in that way !   This is the great staple of
the Koran.   But curiously, through all this, comes
ever and anon some glance as of the real thinker and
seer.   He has actually an eye for the world, this
Mahomet : with a certain directness and rugged vigor,
he brings home still, to our heart, the thing his own
heart has been opened to.   I make but little of his
praises of Allah, which many praise ; they are borrowed I suppose mainly from the Hebrew, at least
they are far surpassed there.   But the eye that flashes
direct into the heart of things, and *sees* the truth of
them ; this is to me a highly interesting object.   Great
Nature's own gift ; which she bestows on all ; but
which only one in the thousand does not cast sorrow-
fully away : it is what I call sincerity of vision ; the
test of a sincere heart.

Mahomet can work no miracles ; he often answers
impatiently : I can work no miracles.   I ? " I am a Public
Preacher ; " appointed to preach this doctrine to all
creatures.   Yet the world, as we can see, had really
from of old been all one great miracle to him.   Look
over the world, says he ; is it not wonderful, the work

of Allah; wholly "a sign to you," if your eyes were open! This Earth, God made it for you; "appointed paths in it;" you can live in it, go to and fro on it. The clouds in the dry country of Arabia, to Mahomet they are very wonderful: Great clouds, he says, born in the deep bosom of the Upper Immensity, where do they come from! They hang there, the great black monsters; pour-down their rain-deluges "to revive a dead earth," and grass springs, and "tall leafy palm-trees with their date-clusters hanging round. Is not that a sign?" Your cattle too, — Allah made them; serviceable dumb creatures; they change the grass into milk; you have your clothing from them, very strange creatures; they come ranking home at evening-time, "and," adds he, "and are a credit to you!" Ships also, — he talks often about ships: Huge moving mountains, they spread-out their cloth wings, go bounding through the water there, Heaven's wind driving them; anon they lie motionless, God has withdrawn the wind, they lie dead, and cannot stir! Miracles? cries he: What miracle would you have? Are not you yourselves there? God made *you,* "shaped you out of a little clay." Ye were small once; a few years ago ye were not at all. Ye have beauty, strength, thoughts, "ye have compassion on one another." Old age comes-on you, and gray hairs; your strength fades into feebleness; ye sink down, and again are not. "Ye have compassion on one another:" this struck me much: Allah might have made you having no compassion on one another, — how had it been then! This is a great direct thought, a glance at first-hand into the very fact of things. Rude vestiges of poetic genius, of whatsoever is best and truest, are visible in this man. A strong untutored intellect; eyesight, heart: a strong wild man, — might have shaped himself into Poet, King, Priest, any kind of Hero.

To his eyes it is forever clear that this world wholly is miraculous. He sees what, as we said once before, all great thinkers, the rude Scandinavians themselves, in one way or other, have contrived to see: That this so solid-looking material world is, at bottom, in very deed, Nothing; is a visual and tactual Manifestation of God's power and presence, — a shadow hung-out by Him on the bosom of the void Infinite; nothing more. The mountains, he says, these great rock-mountains, they shall dissipate themselves "like clouds;" melt into the Blue as clouds do, and not be! He figures the Earth, in the Arab fashion, Sale tells us, as an immense Plain or flat Plate of ground, the mountains are set on that to *steady* it. At the Last Day they shall disappear "like clouds;" the whole Earth shall go spinning, whirl itself off into wreck, and as dust and vapor vanish in the Inane. Allah withdraws his hand from it, and it ceases to be. The universal empire of Allah, presence everywhere of an unspeakable Power, a Splendor, and a Terror not to be named, as the true force, essence and reality, in all things whatsoever, was continually clear to this man. What a modern talks-of by the name, Forces of Nature, Laws of Nature; and does not figure as a divine thing; not even as one thing at all, but as a set of things, undivine enough, — saieable, curious, good for propelling steamships! With our Sciences and Cyclopædias, we are apt to forget the *divineness*, in those laboratories of ours. We ought not to forget it! That once well forgotten, I know not what else were worth remembering. Most sciences, I think, were then a very dead thing; withered, contentious, empty; — a thistle in late autumn. The best science, without this, is but as the dead *timber;* it is not the growing tree and forest, — which gives ever-new timber, among other things! Man cannot *know* either, unless he can *worship* in some way. His knowledge is a pedantry, and dead thistle, otherwise.

Much has been said and written about the sensuality of Mahomet's Religion; more than was just. The indulgences, criminal to us, which he permitted, were not of his appointment; he found them practised, unquestioned from immemorial time in Arabia; what he did was to curtail them, restrict them, not on one but on many sides. His Religion is not an easy one: with rigorous fasts, lavations, strict complex formulas, prayers five times a day, and abstinence from wine, it did not "succeed by being an easy religion." As if indeed any religion, or cause holding of religion, could succeed by that! It is a calumny on men to say that they are roused to heroic action by ease, hope of pleasure, recompense, — sugar-plums of any kind, in this world or the next! In the meanest mortal there lies something nobler. The poor swearing soldier, hired to be shot, has his "honor of a soldier," different from drill-regulations and the shilling a day. It is not to taste sweet things, but to do noble and true things, and vindicate himself under God's Heaven as a god-made Man, that the poorest son of Adam dimly longs. Show him the way of doing that, the dullest daydrudge kindles into a hero. They wrong man greatly who say he is to be seduced by ease. Difficulty, abnegation, martyrdom, death are the *allurements* that act on the heart of man. Kindle the inner genial life of him, you have a flame that burns-up all lower considerations. Not happiness, but something higher: one sees this even in the frivolous classes, with their "point of honor" and the like. Not by flattering our appetites; no, by awakening the Heroic that slumbers in every heart, can any Religion gain followers.

Mahomet himself, after all that can be said about him, was not a sensual man. We shall err widely if we consider this man as a common voluptuary, intent mainly on base enjoyments, — nay on enjoyments of any kind. His household was of the frugallest; his common diet barley-bread and water: sometimes for months there was not a fire once lighted on his hearth. They record with just pride that he would mend his own shoes, patch his own cloak. A poor, hard-toiling, ill-provided man; careless of what vulgar men toil for. Not a bad man, I should say; something better in him than *hunger* of any sort, — or these wild Arab men, fighting and jostling three-and-twenty years at his hand, in close contact with him always, would not have reverenced him so! They were wild men, bursting ever and anon into quarrel, into all kinds of fierce sincerity; without right worth and manhood, no man could have commanded them. They called him Prophet, you say? Why, he stood there face to face with them; bare, not enshrined in any mystery; visibly clouting his own cloak, cobbling his own shoes; fighting, counselling, ordering in the midst of them: they must have seen what kind of a man he *was*, let him be *called* what you like! No emperor with his tiaras was obeyed as this man in a cloak of his own clouting. During three-and-twenty years of rough actual trial. I find something of a veritable Hero necessary for that, of itself.

His last words are a prayer; broken ejaculations of a heart struggling-up, in trembling hope, towards its Maker. We cannot say that his religion made him *worse;* it made him better; good, not bad. Generous things are recorded of him: when he lost his Daughter, the thing he answers is, in his own dialect, everyway sincere, and yet equivalent to that of Christians, " The Lord giveth, and the Lord taketh away; blessed be the name of the Lord." He answered in like manner of Seid, his emancipated well-beloved Slave, the second of the believers. Seid had fallen in the War of Tabûc, the first of Mahomet's fightings with the Greeks. Mahomet said, It was well; Seid had done his Master's work, Seid had now gone to his Master: it was all well with Seid. Yet Seid's daughter found him weeping over the body; — the old gray-haired man melting in tears! "What do I see?" said she. "You see a friend weeping over his friend." He went out for the last time into the mosque, two days before his death; asked, If he had injured any man? Let his own back bear the stripes. If he owed any man? A voice answered, "Yes, me three drachms," borrowed on such an occasion. Mahomet ordered them to be paid: "Better be in shame now," said he, "than at the Day of Judgment." You remember Kadijah, and the "No, by Allah!" Traits of that kind show us the genuine man, the brother of us all, brought visible through twelve centuries, — the veritable Son of our common Mother.

Withal I like Mahomet for his total freedom from cant. He is a rough self-helping son of the wilderness; does not pretend to be what he is not. There is no ostentatious pride in him; but neither does he go much upon humility: he is there as he can be, in cloak and shoes of his own clouting; speaks plainly to all manner of Persian Kings, Greek Emperors, what it is they are bound to do; knows well enough, about himself, "the respect due unto thee." In a life-and-death war with Bedouins, cruel things could not fail; but neither are acts of mercy, of noble natural pity and generosity wanting. Mahomet makes no apology for the one, no boast of the other. They were each the free dictate of his heart; each called-for, there and then. Not a mealy-mouthed man! A candid ferocity, if the case call for it, is in him; he does not mince matters! The War of Tabûc is a thing he often speaks of: his men refused, many of them, to march on that occasion; pleaded the heat of the weather, the harvest, and so forth; he can never forget that. Your harvest? It lasts for a day. What will become of your harvest through all eternity? Hot weather? Yes, it was hot; "but Hell will be hotter!" Sometimes a rough sarcasm turns-up: He says to the unbelievers, Ye shall have the just measure of your deeds at that Great Day. They will be weighed-out to you; ye shall not have short weight! — Everywhere he fixes the matter in his eye; he *sees* it: his heart, now and then, is as if struck dumb by the greatness of it. "Assuredly," he says: that word, in the Koran, is written-down sometimes as a sentence by itself: " Assuredly."

No *Dilettantism* in this Mahomet; it is a business of Reprobation and Salvation with him, of Time and Eternity: he is in deadly earnest about it! Dilettantism, hypothesis, speculation, a kind of amateur-search for Truth, toying and coquetting with Truth: this is the sorest sin. The root of all other imaginable sins. It consists in the heart and soul of the man never having been *open* to Truth; — "living in a vain show." Such a man not only utters and produces falsehoods, but *is* himself a falsehood. The rational moral principle, spark of the Divinity, is sunk deep in him, in quiet paralysis of life-death. The very falsehoods of Mahomet are truer than the truths of such a man. He is the insincere man: smooth-polished, respectable in some times and places; inoffensive, says nothing harsh to anybody; most *cleanly*, — just as carbonic acid is, which is death and poison.

We will not praise Mahomet's moral precepts as always of the superfinest sort; yet it can be said that there is always a tendency to good in them; that they are the true dictates of a heart aiming towards what is just and true. The sublime forgiveness of Christianity, turning of the other cheek when the one has been smitten, is not here : you *are* to revenge yourself, but it is to be in measure, not overmuch, or beyond justice. On the other hand, Islam, like any great Faith, and insight into the essence of man, is a perfect equalizer of men : the soul of one believer outweighs all earthly kingships ; all men, according to Islam too, are equal. Mahomet insists not on the propriety of giving alms, but on the necessity of it : he marks-down by law how much you are to give, and it is at your peril if you neglect. The tenth part of a man's annual income, whatever that may be, is the *property* of the poor, of those that are afflicted and need help. Good all this : the natural voice of humanity, of pity and equity dwelling in the heart of this wild Son of Nature speaks *so*.

Mahomet's Paradise is sensual, his Hell sensual : true ; in the one and the other there is enough that shocks all spiritual feeling in us. But we are to recollect that the Arabs already had it so, that Mahomet, in whatever he changed of it, softened and diminished all this. The worst sensualities, too, are the work of doctors, followers of his, not his work. In the Koran there is really very little said about the joys of Paradise ; they are intimated rather than insisted on. Nor is it forgotten that the highest joys even there shall be spiritual : the pure Presence of the Highest, this shall infinitely transcend all other joys. He says, " Your salutation shall be, Peace." *Salam*, Have Peace ! — the thing that all rational souls long for, and seek, vainly here below, as the one blessing. " Ye shall sit on seats, facing one another : all grudges shall be taken away out of your hearts." All grudges ! Ye shall love one another freely ; for each of you, in the eyes of his brothers, there will be Heaven enough !

In reference to this of the sensual Paradise and

Mahomet's sensuality, the sorest chapter of all for us, there were many things to be said; which it is not convenient to enter upon here. Two remarks only I shall make, and therewith leave it to your candor. The first is furnished me by Goethe; it is a casual hint of his which seems well worth taking note of. In one of his Delineations, in " Meister's Travels " it is, the hero comes-upon a Society of men with very strange ways, one of which was this: " We require," says the Master, "that each of our people shall restrict himself in one direction," shall go right against his desire in one matter, and *make* himself do the thing he does not wish, " should we allow him the greater latitude on all other sides." There seems to me a great justness in this. Enjoying things which are pleasant; that is not the evil: it is the reducing of our moral self to slavery by them that is. Let a man assert withal that he is king over his habitudes; that he could and would shake them off, on cause shown : this is an excellent law. The Month Ramadhan for the Moslem, much in Mahomet's Religion, much in his own Life, bears in that direction; if not by forethought, or clear purpose of moral improvement on his part, then by a certain healthy manful instinct, which is as good.

But there is another thing to be said about the Mahometan Heaven and Hell. This namely, that, however gross and material they may be, they are an emblem of an everlasting truth, not always so well remembered elsewhere. That gross sensual Paradise of his; that horrible flaming Hell; the great enormous Day of Judgment he perpetually insists on: what is all this but a rude shadow, in the rude Bedouin imagination, of that grand spiritual Fact, and Beginning of Facts, which it is ill for us too if we do not all know and feel: the Infinite Nature of Duty? That man's actions here are of *infinite* moment to him, and never die or end at all; that man, with his little life, reaches upwards high as Heaven, downwards low as Hell, and in his threescore years of Time holds an Eternity fearfully and wonderfully hidden: All this had burnt itself, as in flame-characters, into the wild Arab soul. As in flame and lightning, it stands written there; awful, unspeakable, ever present to him. With bursting earnestness, with a fierce savage sincerity, halt, articulating, not able to articulate, he strives to speak it, bodies it forth in that Heaven and that Hell. Bodied forth in what way you will, it is the first of all truths. It is venerable under all embodiments. What is the chief end of man here below? Mahomet has answered this question, in a way that might put some of *us* to shame! He does not, like a Bentham, a Paley, take Right and Wrong, and calculate the profit and loss, ultimate pleasure of the one and of the other; and summing all up by addition and subtraction into a net result, ask you, Whether on the whole the Right does not preponderate considerably? No; it is not *better* to do the one than the other; the one is to the other as life is to death, — as Heaven is to Hell. The one must in nowise be done, the other in nowise left undone. You shall not measure them; they are incommensurable: the one is death eternal to a man, the other is life eternal. Benthamee Utility, virtue by Profit and Loss; reducing this God's-world to a dead brute Steam-engine, the infinite celestial Soul of Man to a kind of Hay-balance for weighing hay and thistles on, pleasures and pains on: — If you ask me which gives, Mahomet or they, the beggarlier and falser view of Man and his Destinies in this Universe, I will answer, It is not Mahomet! —

On the whole, we will repeat that this Religion of Mahomet's is a kind of Christianity; has a genuine element of what is spiritually highest looking through it, not to be hidden by all its imperfections. The Scandinavian God *Wish*, the God of all rude men, — this has been enlarged into a Heaven by Mahomet; but a Heaven symbolical of sacred Duty, and to be earned by faith and welldoing, by valiant action, and a divine patience which is still more valiant. It is Scandinavian Paganism, and a truly celestial element superadded to that. Call it not false; look not at the falsehood of it, look at the truth of it. For these twelve centuries, it has been the religion and life-guidance of the fifth part of the whole kindred of Mankind. Above all things, it has been a religion heartily *believed.* These Arabs believe their religion, and try to live by it! No Christians, since the early ages, or only perhaps the English Puritans in modern times, have ever stood by their Faith as the Moslem do by theirs, — believing it wholly, fronting Time with it, and Eternity with it. This night the watchman on the streets of Cairo when he cries, "Who goes?" will hear from the passenger, along with his answer, "There is no God but God." *Allah akbar, Islam,* sounds through the souls, and whole daily existence, of these dusky millions. Zealous missionaries preach it abroad among Malays, black Papuans, brutal Idolaters; — displacing what is worse, nothing that is better or good.

To the Arab Nation it was as a birth from darkness into light; Arabia first became alive by means of it. A poor shepherd people, roaming unnoticed in its deserts since the creation of the world: a Hero-Prophet was sent down to them with a word they could believe: see, the unnoticed becomes world-notable, the small has grown world-great; within one century afterwards, Arabia is at Grenada on this hand, at Delhi on that; — glancing in valor and splendor

and the light of genius, Arabia shines through long
ages over a great section of the world.   Belief is great,
life-giving.   The history of a Nation becomes fruitful,
soul-elevating, great, so soon as it believes.   These
Arabs, the man Mahomet, and that one century, — is
it not as if a spark had fallen, one spark, on a world
of what seemed black unnoticeable sand ; but lo, the
sand proves explosive powder, blazes heaven-high
from Delhi to Grenada !   I said, the Great Man was
always as lightning out of Heaven ; the rest of men
waited for him like fuel, and then they too would
flame.

LECTURE III.

The Hero as Poet.—Dante; Shakspeare.

THE Hero as Divinity, the Hero as Prophet, are productions of old ages; not to be repeated in the new. They presuppose a certain rudeness of conception, which the progress of mere scientific knowledge puts an end to. There needs to be, as it were, a world vacant, or almost vacant of scientific forms, if men in their loving wonder are to fancy their fellow-man either a god or one speaking with the voice of a god. Divinity and Prophet are past. We are now to see our Hero in the less ambitious, but also less questionable, character of Poet; a character which does not pass. The Poet is a heroic figure belonging to all ages; whom all ages possess, when once he is produced, whom the newest age as the oldest may produce;—and will produce, always when Nature pleases. Let Nature send a Hero-soul; in no age is it other than possible that he may be shaped into a Poet.

Hero, Prophet, Poet,—many different names, in different times and places, do we give to Great Men; according to varieties we note in them, according to the sphere in which they have displayed themselves! We might give many more names, on this same principle. I will remark again, however, as a fact not unimportant to be understood, that the different *sphere* constitutes the grand origin of such distinction; that the Hero can be Poet, Prophet, King, Priest or what you will, according to the kind of world he finds himself born into. I confess, I have no notion of a truly great man that could not be *all* sorts of men. The Poet who could merely sit on a chair, and compose stanzas, would never make a stanza worth much. He could not sing the Heroic warrior, unless he himself were at least a Heroic warrior too. I fancy there is in him the Politician, the Thinker, Legislator, Philosopher; — in one or the other degree, he could have been, he is all these. So too I cannot understand how a Mirabeau, with that great glowing heart, with the fire that was in it, with the bursting tears that were in it, could not have written verses, tragedies, poems, and touched all hearts in that way, had his course of life and education led him thitherward. The grand fundamental character is that of Great Man; that the man be great. Napoleon has words in him which are like Austerlitz Battles. Louis Fourteenth's Marshals are a kind of poetical men withal; the things Turenne says are full of sagacity and geniality, like sayings of Samuel Johnson. The great heart, the clear deep-seeing eye: there it lies; no man whatever, in what province soever, can prosper at all without these. Petrarch and Boccaccio did diplomatic messages, it seems, quite well: one can easily believe it; they had done things a little harder than these! Burns, a gifted song-writer, might have made a still better Mirabeau. Shakspeare, — one knows not what *he* could not have made, in the supreme degree.

True, there are aptitudes of Nature too. Nature does not make all great men, more than all other men, in the self-same mould. Varieties of aptitude doubtless; but infinitely more of circumstance; and far oftenest it is the *latter* only that are looked to. But it is as with common men in the learning of trades. You take any man, as yet a vague capability of a man, who could be any kind of craftsman; and make him into a smith, a carpenter, a mason: he is then and thenceforth that and nothing else. And if, as Addison complains, you sometimes see a street-porter staggering under his load on spindle-shanks, and near at hand a tailor with the frame of a Samson handling a bit of cloth and small Whitechapel needle, — it cannot be considered that aptitude of Nature alone has been consulted here either! — The Great Man also, to what shall he be bound apprentice? Given your Hero, is he to become Conqueror, King, Philosopher, Poet? It is an inexplicably complex controversial-calculation between the world and him! He will read the world and its laws; the world with its laws will be there to be read. What the world, on *this* matter, shall permit and bid is, as we said, the most important fact about the world. —

Poet and Prophet differ greatly in our loose modern notions of them. In some old languages, again, the titles are synonymous; *Vates* means both Prophet and Poet: and indeed at all times, Prophet and Poet, well understood, have much kindred of meaning. Fundamentally indeed they are still the same; in this most important respect especially, That they have penetrated both of them into the sacred mystery of the Universe; what Goethe calls "the open secret." "Which is the great secret?" asks one. "The *open* secret," — open to all, seen by almost none! That divine mystery, which lies everywhere in all Beings, " the Divine Idea of the World, that which lies at the bottom of Appearance," as Fichte styles it; of which all Appearance, from the starry sky to the grass of the field, but especially the Appearance of Man and his work, is but the *vesture*, the embodiment that renders it visible. This divine mystery *is* in all times and in all places; veritably is. In most times and places it is greatly overlooked; and the Universe, definable always in one or the other dialect, as the realized Thought of God, is considered a trivial, inert, commonplace matter, — as if, says the Satirist, it were a dead thing, which some upholsterer had put together ! It could do no good, at present, to *speak* much about this; but it is a pity for every one of us if we do not know it, live ever in the knowledge of it. Really a most mournful pity ; — a failure to live at all, if we live otherwise !

But now, I say, whoever may forget this divine mystery, the *Vates*, whether Prophet or Poet, has penetrated into it; is a man sent hither to make it more impressively known to us. That always is his message; he is to reveal that to us, — that sacred mystery which he more than others lives ever present with. While others forget it, he knows it ; — I might say, he has been driven to know it; without consent asked of *him*, he finds himself living in it, bound to live in it. Once more, here is no Hearsay, but a direct Insight and Belief; this man too could not help being a sincere man ! Whosoever may live in the shows of things, it is for him a necessity of nature to live in the very fact of things. A man once more, in earnest with the Universe, though all others were but toying with it. He is a *Vates*, first of all, in virtue of being sincere. So far Poet and Prophet, participators in the "open secret," are one.

With respect to their distinction again: The *Vates* Prophet, we might say, has seized that sacred mystery rather on the moral side, as Good and Evil, Duty and Prohibition ; the *Vates* Poet on what the Germans call the æsthetic side, as Beautiful, and the like. The one we may call a revealer of what we are to do, the other of what we are to love. But indeed these two provinces run into one another, and cannot be disjoined. The Prophet too has his eye on what we are to love: how else shall he know what it is we are to do ? The

7

highest Voice ever heard on this earth said withal,
" Consider the lilies of the field ; they toil not, neither
do they spin : yet Solomon in all his glory was not
arrayed like one of these." A glance, that, into the
deepest deep of Beauty. "The lilies of the field," —
dressed finer than earthly princes, springing-up there
in the humble furrow-field ; a beautiful *eye* looking-out
on you, from the great inner Sea of Beauty ! How
could the rude Earth make these, if her Essence,
rugged as she looks and is, were not inwardly Beauty ?
In this point of view, too, a saying of Goethe's, which
has staggered several, may have meaning : " The
Beautiful," he intimates, " is higher than the Good ;
the Beautiful includes in it the Good." The *true*
Beautiful ; which however, I have said somewhere,
" differs from the *false* as Heaven does from Vauxhall !" So much for the distinction and identity of
Poet and Prophet. —

In ancient and also in modern periods we find a few
Poets who are accounted perfect ; whom it were a
kind of treason to find fault with. This is noteworthy ;
this is right : yet in strictness it is only an illusion.
At bottom, clearly enough, there is no perfect Poet !
A vein of Poetry exists in the hearts of all men ; no
man is made altogether of Poetry. We are all poets
when we *read* a poem well. The "imagination that
shudders at the Hell of Dante," is not that the same
faculty, weaker in degree, as Dante's own ? No one
but Shakspeare can embody, out of *Saxo Grammaticus*, the story of *Hamlet* as Shakspeare did : but
every one models some kind of story out of it ; every
one embodies it better or worse. We need not spend
time in defining. Where there is no specific difference, as between round and square, all definition must
be more or less arbitrary. A man that has *so* much
more of the poetic element developed in him as to

have become noticeable, will be called Poet by his neighbors. World-Poets too, those whom we are to take for perfect Poets, are settled by critics in the same way. One who rises *so* far above the general level of Poets will, to such and such critics, seem a Universal Poet; as he ought to do. And yet it is, and must be, an arbitrary distinction. All Poets, all men, have some touches of the Universal; no man is wholly made of that. Most Poets are very soon forgotten: but not the noblest Shakspeare or Homer of them can be remembered *forever;* — a day comes when he too is not!

Nevertheless, you will say, there must be a difference between true Poetry and true Speech not poetical: what is the difference? On this point many things have been written, especially by late German Critics, some of which are not very intelligible at first. They say, for example, that the Poet has an *infinitude* in him; communicates an *Unendlichkeit*, a certain character of "infinitude," to whatsoever he delineates. This, though not very precise, yet on so vague a matter is worth remembering: if well meditated, some meaning will gradually be found in it. For my own part, I find considerable meaning in the old vulgar distinction of Poetry being *metrical*, having music in it, being a Song. Truly, if pressed to give a definition, one might say this as soon as anything else: If your delineation be authentically *musical*, musical not in word only, but in heart and substance, in all the thoughts and utterances of it, in the whole conception of it, then it will be poetical; if not, not. Musical: how much lies in that! A *musical* thought is one spoken by a mind that has penetrated into the inmost heart of the thing; detected the inmost mystery of it, namely the *melody* that lies hidden in it; the inward harmony of coherence which is its soul, whereby it exists, and has a right to be, here in this world. All inmost things, we may say, are melodious; naturally utter themselves in Song. The meaning of Song goes deep. Who is there that, in logical words, can express the effect music has on us? A kind of inarticulate unfathomable speech, which leads us to the edge of the Infinite, and lets us for moments gaze into that!

Nay all speech, even the commonest speech, has something of song in it: not a parish in the world but has its parish-accent; — the rhythm or *tune* to which the people there *sing* what they have to say! Accent is a kind of chanting; all men have accent of their own, — though they only *notice* that of others. Observe too how all passionate language does of itself become musical, — with a finer music than the mere accent; the speech of a man even in zealous anger becomes a chant, a song. All deep things are Song. It seems somehow the very central essence of us, Song ; as if all the rest were but wrappages and hulls. The primal element of us; of us, and of all things. The Greeks fabled of Sphere-Harmonies: it was the feeling they had of the inner structure of Nature; that the soul of all her voices and utterances was perfect music. Poetry, therefore, we will call *musical Thought*. The Poet is he who *thinks* in that manner. At bottom, it turns still on power of intellect; it is a man's sincerity and depth of vision that makes him a Poet. See deep enough, and you see musically; the heart of Nature *being* everywhere music, if you can only reach it.

The *Vates* Poet, with his melodious Apocalypse of Nature, seems to hold a poor rank among us, in comparison with the *Vates* Prophet; his function, and our esteem of him for his function, alike slight. The Hero taken as Divinity; the Hero taken as Prophet; then next the Hero taken only as Poet: does it not look as if our estimate of the Great Man, epoch after epoch, were continually diminishing? We take him first for a god, then for one god-inspired; and now in the next stage of it, his most miraculous word gains from us only the recognition that he is a Poet, beautiful verse-maker, man of genius, or suchlike! It looks so; but I persuade myself that intrinsically it is not so. If we consider well, it will perhaps appear that in man still there is the *same* altogether peculiar admiration for the Heroic Gift, by what name soever called, that there at any time was.

I should say, if we do not now reckon a Great Man literally divine, it is that our notions of God, of the supreme unattainable Fountain of Splendor, Wisdom and Heroism, are ever rising *higher;* not altogether that our reverence for these qualities, as manifested in our like, is getting lower. This is worth taking thought of. Sceptical Dilettantism, the curse of these ages, a curse which will not last forever, does indeed in this the highest province of human things, as in all provinces, make sad work; and our reverence for great men, all crippled, blinded, paralytic as it is, comes out in poor plight, hardly recognizable. Men worship the shows of great men; the most disbelieve that there is any reality of great men to worship. The dreariest, fatallest faith; believing which, one would literally despair of human things. Nevertheless look, for example, at Napoleon! A Corsican lieutenant of artillery; that is the show of *him:* yet is he not obeyed, *worshipped* after his sort, as all the Tiaraed and Diademed of the world put together could not be? High Duchesses, and hostlers of inns, gather round the Scottish rustic, Burns;—a strange feeling dwelling in each that they never heard a man like this; that, on the whole, this is the man! In the secret heart of these people it still dimly reveals itself, though there is no accredited way of uttering it at present, that this rustic, with his black brows and flashing sun-eyes, and strange words moving laughter and tears, is of a dignity far beyond all others, incommensurable with all others. Do not we feel it so? But now, were Dilettantism, Scepticism, Triviality, and all that sorrowful brood, cast-out of us, — as, by God's blessing, they shall one day be; were faith in the shows of things entirely swept-out, replaced by clear faith in the *things*, so that a man acted on the impulse of that only, and counted the other non-extant; what a new livelier feeling towards this Burns were it!

Nay here in these ages, such as they are, have we not two mere Poets, if not deified, yet we may say beatified? Shakspeare and Dante are Saints of Poetry; really, if we will think of it, *canonized*, so that it is impiety to meddle with them. The unguided instinct of the world, working across all these perverse impediments, has arrived at such result. Dante and Shakspeare are a peculiar Two. They dwell apart, in a kind of royal solitude; none equal, none second to them : in the general feeling of the world, a certain transcendentalism, a glory as of complete perfection, invests these two. They *are* canonized, though no Pope or Cardinals took hand in doing it! Such, in spite of every perverting influence, in the most unheroic times, is still our indestructible reverence for heroism. We will look a little at these Two, the Poet Dante and the Poet Shakspeare : what little it is permitted us to say here of the Hero as Poet will most fitly arrange itself in that fashion.

Many volumes have been written by way of commentary on Dante and his Book; yet, on the whole, with no great result. His Biography is, as it were, irrecoverably lost for us. An unimportant, wandering, sorrow-stricken man, not much note was taken of him while he lived; and the most of that has vanished, in the long space that now intervenes. It is five centuries since he ceased writing and living here. After all commentaries, the Book itself is mainly what we know of him. The Book;—and one might add that Portrait commonly attributed to Giotto, which, looking on it, you cannot help inclining to think genuine, whoever did it. To me it is a most touching face; perhaps of all faces that I know, the most so. Lonely there, painted as on vacancy, with the simple laurel wound round it; the deathless sorrow and pain, the known victory which is also deathless;—significant of the whole history of Dante! I think it is the mournfulest face that ever was painted from reality; an altogether tragic heart-affecting face. There is in it, as foundation of it, the softness, tenderness, gentle affection as of a child; but all this is as if congealed into sharp contradiction, into abnegation, isolation, proud hopeless pain. A soft ethereal soul looking-out so stern, implacable, grim-trenchant, as from imprisonment of thick-ribbed ice! Withal it is a silent pain too, a silent scornful one: the lip is curled in a kind of godlike disdain of the thing that is eating-out his heart,—as if it were withal a mean insignificant thing, as if he whom it had power to torture and strangle were greater than it. The face of one wholly in protest, and life-long unsurrendering battle, against the world. Affection all converted into indignation: an implacable indignation; slow, equable, silent, like that of a god! The eye too, it looks-out as in a kind of *surprise*, a kind of inquiry, Why the world was of such a sort? This is Dante: so he looks, this "voice of ten silent centuries," and sings us "his mystic unfathomable song."

The little that we know of Dante's Life corresponds

well enough with this Portrait and this Book. He was
born at Florence, in the upper class of society, in the
year 1265. His education was the best then going;
much school-divinity, Aristotelean logic, some Latin
classics, — no inconsiderable insight into certain provinces of things : and Dante, with his earnest intelligent
nature, we need not doubt, learned better than most
all that was learnable. He has a clear cultivated
understanding, and of great subtlety; this best fruit
of education he had contrived to realize from these
scholastics. He knows accurately and well what lies
close to him; but, in such a time, without printed
books or free intercourse, he could not know well what
was distant : the small clear light, most luminous for
what is near, breaks itself into singular *chiaroscuro*
striking on what is far off. This was Dante's learning
from the schools. In life, he had gone through the
usual destinies; been twice out campaigning as a
soldier for the Florentine State, been on embassy;
had in his thirty-fifth year, by natural gradation of
talent and service, become one of the Chief Magistrates of Florence. He had met in boyhood a certain
Beatrice Portinari, a beautiful little girl of his own
age and rank, and grown-up thenceforth in partial
sight of her, in some distant intercourse with her. All
readers know his graceful affecting account of this;
and then of their being parted; of her being wedded
to another, and of her death soon after. She makes
a great figure in Dante's Poem; seems to have made
a great figure in his life. Of all beings it might seem
as if she, held apart from him, far apart at last in the
dim Eternity, were the only one he had ever with his
whole strength of affection loved. She died : Dante himself was wedded; but it seems not happily, far from
happily. I fancy, the rigorous earnest man, with his keen
excitabilities, was not altogether easy to make happy.

We will not complain of Dante's miseries: had all
gone right with him as he wished it, he might have
been Prior, Podestà, or whatsoever they call it, of
Florence, well accepted among neighbors, — and the
world had wanted one of the most notable words ever
spoken or sung. Florence would have had another
prosperous Lord Mayor; and the ten dumb centuries
continued voiceless, and the ten other listening centuries (for there will be ten of them and more) had no
" Divina Commedia " to hear! We will complain of
nothing. A nobler destiny was appointed for this
Dante; and he, struggling like a man led towards
death and crucifixion, could not help fulfilling it.
Give *him* the choice of his happiness! He knew not,
more than we do, what was really happy, what was
really miserable.

In Dante's Priorship, the Guelf-Ghibelline, Bianchi-
Neri, or some other confused disturbances rose to
such a height, that Dante, whose party had seemed
the stronger, was with his friends cast unexpectedly
forth into banishment; doomed thenceforth to a life
of woe and wandering. His property was all confis-
cated and more; he had the fiercest feeling that it
was entirely unjust, nefarious in the sight of God and
man. He tried what was in him to get reinstated;
tried even by warlike surprisal, with arms in his
hand: but it would not do; bad only had become
worse. There is a record, I believe, still extant in
the Florence Archives, dooming this Dante, wheresoever caught, to be burnt alive. Burnt alive; so it
stands, they say: a very curious civic document.
Another curious document, some considerable number
of years later, is a Letter of Dante's to the Florentine
Magistrates, written in answer to a milder proposal of
theirs, that he should return on condition of apologiz-
ing and paying a fine. He answers, with fixed stern

pride: "If I cannot return without calling myself guilty, I will never return, *nunquam revertar.*"

For Dante there was now no home in this world. He wandered from patron to patron, from place to place: proving, in his own bitter words, "How hard is the path, *Come è duro calle.*" The wretched are not cheerful company. Dante, poor and banished, with his proud earnest nature, with his moody humors, was not a man to conciliate men. Petrarch reports of him that being at Can della Scala's court, and blamed one day for his gloom and taciturnity, he answered in no courtier-like way. Della Scala stood among his courtiers, with mimes and buffoons (*nebulones ac histriones*) making him heartily merry; when turning to Dante, he said: "Is it not strange, now, that this poor fool should make himself so entertaining; while you, a wise man, sit there day after day, and have nothing to amuse us with at all?" Dante answered bitterly: "No, not strange; your Highness is to recollect the Proverb, *Like to Like;*" — given the amuser, the amusee must also be given! Such a man, with his proud silent ways, with his sarcasms and sorrows, was not made to succeed at court. By degrees, it came to be evident to him that he had no longer any resting-place, or hope of benefit, in this earth. The earthly world had cast him forth, to wander, wander; no living heart to love him now; for his sore miseries there was no solace here.

The deeper naturally would the Eternal World impress itself on him; that awful reality over which, after all, this Time-world, with its Florences and banishments, only flutters as an unreal shadow. Florence thou shalt never see: but Hell and Purgatory and Heaven thou shalt surely see! What is Florence, Can della Scala, and the World and Life altogether? ETERNITY: thither, of a truth, not elsewhither, art thou and all things bound! The great soul of Dante, homeless on earth, made its home more and more in that awful other world. Naturally his thoughts brooded on that, as on the one fact important for him. Bodied or bodiless, it is the one fact important for all men : — but to Dante, in that age, it was bodied in fixed certainty of scientific shape ; he no more doubted of that *Malebolge* Pool, that it all lay there with its gloomy circles, with its *alti guai,* and that he himself should see it, than we doubt that we should see Constantinople if we went thither. Dante's heart, long filled with this, brooding over it in speechless thought and awe, bursts forth at length into "mystic unfathomable song ;" and this his "Divine Comedy," the most remarkable of all modern Books, is the result.

It must have been a great solacement to Dante, and was, as we can see, a proud thought for him at times, That he, here in exile, could do this work ; that no Florence, nor no man or men, could hinder him from doing it, or even much help him in doing it. He knew too, partly, that it was great ; the greatest a man could do. "If thou follow thy star, *Se tu segui tua stella,*" — so could the Hero, in his forsakenness, in his extreme need, still say to himself : "Follow thou thy star, thou shalt not fail of a glorious haven !" The labor of writing, we find, and indeed could know otherwise, was great and painful for him ; he says, This Book, "which has made me lean for many years." Ah yes, it was won, all of it, with pain and sore toil, — not in sport, but in grim earnest. His Book, as indeed most good Books are, has been written, in many senses, with his heart's blood. It is his whole history, this Book. He died after finishing it ; not yet very old, at the age of fifty-six ; — broken-hearted rather, as is said. He lies buried in his death-city

Ravenna: *Hic claudor Dantes patriis extorris ab oris.* The Florentines begged back his body, in a century after; the Ravenna people would not give it. "Here am I Dante laid, shut-out from my native shores."

I said, Dante's Poem was a Song: it is Tieck who calls it "a mystic unfathomable Song;" and such is literally the character of it. Coleridge remarks very pertinently somewhere, that wherever you find a sentence musically worded, of true rhythm and melody in the words, there is something deep and good in the meaning too. For body and soul, word and idea, go strangely together here as everywhere. Song: we said before, it was the Heroic of Speech! All *old* Poems, Homer's and the rest, are authentically Songs. I would say, in strictness, that all right Poems are: that whatsoever is not *sung* is properly no Poem, but a piece of Prose cramped into jingling lines, — to the great injury of the grammar, to the great grief of the reader, for most part! What we want to get at is the *thought* the man had, if he had any: why should he twist it into jingle, if he *could* speak it out plainly? It is only when the heart of him is rapt into true passion of melody, and the very tones of him, according to Coleridge's remark, become musical by the greatness, depth and music of his thoughts, that we can give him right to rhyme and sing; that we call him a Poet, and listen to him as the Heroic of Speakers, — whose speech *is* Song. Pretenders to this are many; and to an earnest reader, I doubt, it is for most part a very melancholy, not to say an insupportable business, that of reading rhyme! Rhyme that had no inward necessity to be rhymed; — it ought to have told us plainly, without any jingle, what it was aiming at. I would advise all men who *can* speak their thought, not to sing it; to understand that, in a serious time, among serious men, there is no vocation in them for singing it. Precisely as we love the true song, and are charmed by it as by something divine, so shall we hate the false song, and account it a mere wooden noise, a thing hollow, superfluous, altogether an insincere and offensive thing.

I give Dante my highest praise when I say of his " Divine Comedy " that it is, in all senses, genuinely a Song. In the very sound of it there is a *canto fermo;* it proceeds as by a chant. The language, his simple *terza rima,* doubtless helped him in this. One reads along naturally with a sort of *lilt.* But I add, that it could not be otherwise; for the essence and material of the work are themselves rhythmic. Its depth, and rapt passion and sincerity, makes it musical; — go *deep* enough, there is music everywhere. A true inward symmetry, what one calls an architectural harmony, reigns in it, proportionates it all: architectural; which also partakes of the character of music. The three kingdoms, *Inferno, Purgatorio, Paradiso,* lookout on one another like compartments of a great edifice; a great supernatural world-cathedral, piled-up .there, stern, solemn, awful; Dante's World of Souls ! It is, at bottom, the *sincerest* of all Poems ; sincerity, here too, we find to be the measure of worth. It came deep out of the author's heart of hearts ; and it goes deep, and through long generations, into ours. The people of Verona, when they saw him on the streets, used to say, "*Eccovi l' uom ch' è stato all' Inferno,* See, there is the man that was in Hell!" Ah yes, he had been in Hell; — in Hell enough, in long severe sorrow and struggle ; as the like of him is pretty sure to have been. Commedias that come-out *divine* are not accomplished otherwise. Thought, true labor of any kind, highest virtue itself, is it not the daughter of Pain? Born as out of the black whirlwind; — true *effort*, in fact, as of a captive struggling to free him-self: that is Thought. In all ways we are "to be-come perfect through *suffering.*" But, as I say, no work known to me is so elaborated as this of Dante's. It has all been as if molten, in the hottest furnace of his soul. It had made him "lean" for many years. Not the general whole only; every compartment of it is worked-out, with intense earnestness, into truth, into clear visuality. Each answers to the other; each fits in its place, like a marble stone accurately hewn and polished. It is the soul of Dante, and in this the soul of the middle ages, rendered forever rhythmically visible there. No light task; a right in-tense one; but a task which is *done.*

Perhaps one would say, *intensity*, with the much that depends on it, is the prevailing character of Dante's genius. Dante does not come before us as a large catholic mind; rather as a narrow, and even sectarian mind: it is partly the fruit of his age and position, but partly too of his own nature. His great-ness has, in all senses, concentrated itself into fiery emphasis and depth. He is world-great not because he is world-wide, but because he is world-deep. Through all objects he pierces as it were down into the heart of Being. I know nothing so intense as Dante. Consider, for example, to begin with the outermost development of his intensity, consider how he paints. He has a great power of vision; seizes the very type of a thing; presents that and nothing more. You remember that first view he gets of the Hall of Dite: *red* pinnacle, redhot cone of iron glow-ing through the dim immensity of gloom; — so vivid, so distinct, visible at once and forever! It is as an emblem of the whole genius of Dante. There is a brevity, an abrupt precision in him: Tacitus is not briefer, more condensed; and then in Dante it seems a natural condensation, spontaneous to the man. One smiting word; and then there is silence, nothing more said. His silence is more eloquent than words. It is strange with what a sharp decisive grace he snatches the true likeness of a matter: cuts into the matter as with a pen of fire. Plutus, the blustering giant, collapses at Virgil's rebuke; it is "as the sails sink, the mast being suddenly broken." Or that poor Brunetto Latini, with the *cotto aspetto*, "face *baked*," parched brown and lean; and the "fiery snow" that falls on them there, a "fiery snow without wind," slow, deliberate, never-ending! Or the lids of those Tombs: square sarcophaguses, in that silent dim-burning Hall, each with its Soul in torment; the lids laid open there; they are to be shut at the Day of Judgment, through Eternity. And how Farinata rises; and how Cavalcante falls — at hearing of his Son, and the past tense "*fue!*" The very movements in Dante have something brief; swift, decisive, almost military. It is of the inmost essence of his genius this sort of painting. The fiery, swift Italian nature of the man, so silent, passionate, with its quick abrupt movements, its silent "pale rages," speaks itself in these things.

For though this of painting is one of the outermost developments of a man, it comes like all else from the essential faculty of him; it is physiognomical of the whole man. Find a man whose words paint you a likeness, you have found a man worth something; mark his manner of doing it, as very characteristic of him. In the first place, he could not have discerned the object at all, or seen the vital type of it, unless he had, what we may call *sympathized* with it, — had sympathy in him to bestow on objects. He must have been *sincere* about it too; sincere and sympathetic: a man without worth cannot give you the likeness of any object; he dwells in vague outwardness, fallacy and trivial hearsay, about all objects. And indeed may we not say that intellect altogether expresses itself in this power of discerning what an object is? Whatsoever of faculty a man's mind may have will come out here. Is it even of business, a matter to be done? The gifted man is he who *sees* the essential point, and leaves all the rest aside as surplusage: it is his faculty too, the man of business's faculty, that he discern the true *likeness*, not the false superficial one, of the thing he has got to work in. And how much of *morality* is in the kind of insight we get of anything; " the eye seeing in all things what it brought with it the faculty of seeing"! To the mean eye all things are trivial, as certainly as to be jaundiced they are yellow. Raphael, the Painters tell us, is the best of all Portrait-painters withal. No most gifted eye can exhaust the significance of any object. In the commonest human face there lies more than Raphael will take-away with him.

Dante's painting is not graphic only, brief, true, and of a vividness as of fire in dark night; taken on the wider scale, it is everyway noble, and the outcome of a great soul. Francesca and her Lover, what quali-ties in that! A thing woven as out of rainbows, on a ground of eternal black. A small flute-voice of infinite wail speaks there, into our very heart of hearts. A touch of womanhood in it too: *della bella persona, che mi fu tolta;* and how, even in the Pit of woe, it is a solace that *he* will never part from her! Saddest tragedy in these *alti guai.* And the racking winds, in that *aer bruno,* whirl them away again, to wail forever! Strange to think: Dante was the friend of this poor Francesca's father; Francesca herself may have sat upon the Poet's knee, as a bright innocent little child. Infinite pity, yet also infinite rigor of law: it is so

Nature is made ; it is so Dante discerned that she was made. What a paltry notion is that of his "Divine Comedy's" being a poor splenetic impotent terrestrial libel; putting those into Hell whom he could not be avenged-upon on earth! I suppose if ever pity, tender as a mother's, was in the heart of any man, it was in Dante's. But a man who does not know rigor cannot pity either. His very pity will be cowardly, egoistic, — sentimentality, or little better. I know not in the world an affection equal to that of Dante. It is a tenderness, a trembling, longing, pity-ing love: like the wail of Æolean harps, soft, soft; like a child's young heart; — and then that stern, sore-saddened heart! These longings of his towards his Beatrice; their meeting together in the "Paradiso;" his gazing in her pure transfigured eyes, her that had been purified by death so long, separated from him so far: — one likens it to the song of angels ; it is among the purest utterances of affection, perhaps the very purest, that ever came out of a human soul.

For the *intense* Dante is intense in all things ; he has got into the essence of all. His intellectual in-sight as painter, on occasion too as reasoner, is but the result of all other sorts of intensity. Morally great, above all, we must call him ; it is the beginning of all. His scorn, his grief are as transcendent as his love ; — as indeed, what are they but the *inverse* or *converse* of his love? "*A Dio spiacenti ed a' nemici sui*, Hateful to God and to the enemies of God:" lofty scorn, unappeasable silent reprobation and aversion; "*Non ragionam di lor*, We will not speak of *them*, look only and pass." Or think of this; "They have not the *hope* to die, *Non han speranza di morte.*" One day, it had risen sternly benign on the scathed heart of Dante, that he, wretched, never-rest-ing, worn as he was, would full surely *die;* "that

8

Destiny itself could not doom him not to die." Such words are in this man. For rigor, earnestness and depth, he is not to be paralleled in the modern world; to seek his parallel we must go into the Hebrew Bible, and live with the antique Prophets there.

I do not agree with much modern criticism, in greatly preferring the " Inferno " to the other two parts of the " Divine Commedia." Such preference belongs, I imagine, to our general Byronism of taste, and is like to be a transient feeling. The " Purgatorio " and " Paradiso," especially the former, one would almost say, is even more excellent than it. It is a noble thing that " Purgatorio," " Mountain of Purification ; " an emblem of the noblest conception of that age. If Sin is so fatal, and Hell is and must be so rigorous, awful, yet in Repentance too is man purified ; Repentance is the grand Christian act. It is beautiful how Dante works it out. The *tremolar dell' onde*, that " trembling " of the ocean-waves, under the first pure gleam of morning, dawning afar on the wandering Two, is as the type of an altered mood. Hope has now dawned ; never-dying Hope, if in company still with heavy sorrow. The obscure sojourn of dæmons and reprobate is underfoot ; a soft breathing of penitence mounts higher and higher, to the Throne of Mercy itself. " Pray for me," the denizens of that Mount of Pain all say to him. " Tell my Giovanna to pray for me," my daughter Giovanna ; " I think her mother loves me no more ! " They toil painfully up by that winding steep, " bent-down like corbels of a building," some of them, — crushed-together so " for the sin of pride ; " yet nevertheless in years, in ages and æons, they shall have reached the top, which is Heaven's gate, and by Mercy shall have been admitted in. The joy too of all, when one has prevailed ; the whole Mountain shakes with joy, and a psalm of praise rises, when one soul has perfected repentance and got its sin and misery left behind ! I call all this a noble embodiment of a true noble thought.

But indeed the Three compartments mutually support one another, are indispensable to one another. The " Paradiso," a kind of inarticulate music to me, is the redeeming side of the " Inferno;" the "Inferno " without it were untrue. All three make-up the true Unseen World, as figured in the Christianity of the Middle Ages; a thing forever memorable, forever true in the essence of it, to all men. It was perhaps delineated in no human soul with such depth of veracity as in this of Dante's; a man *sent* to sing it, to keep it long memorable. Very notable with what brief simplicity he passes out of the every-day reality, into the Invisible one ; and in the second or third stanza, we find ourselves in the World of Spirits; and dwell there, as among things palpable, indubitable ! To Dante they *were* so; the real world, as it is called, and its facts, was but the threshold to an infinitely higher Fact of a World. At bottom, the one was as *preter*natural as the other. Has not each man a soul ? He will not only be a spirit, but is one. To the earnest Dante it is all one visible Fact; he believes it, sees it; is the Poet of it in virtue of that. Sincerity, I say again, is the saving merit, now as always.

Dante's Hell, Purgatory, Paradise, are a symbol withal, an emblematic representation of his Belief about this Universe : — some Critic in a future age, like those Scandinavian ones the other day, who has ceased altogether to think as Dante did, may find this too all an " Allegory," perhaps an idle Allegory ! It is a sublime embodiment, or sublimest, of the soul of Christianity. It expresses, as in huge worldwide architectural emblems, how the Christian Dante felt

Good and Evil to be the two polar elements of this Creation, on which it all turns; that these two differ not by *preferability* of one to the other, but by incompatibility absolute and infinite; that the one is excellent and high as light and Heaven, the other hideous, black as Gehenna and the Pit of Hell! Everlasting Justice, yet with Penitence, with everlasting Pity,— all Christianism, as Dante and the Middle Ages had it, is emblemed here. Emblemed: and yet, as I urged the other day, with what entire truth of purpose; how unconscious of any embleming! Hell, Purgatory, Paradise: these things were not fashioned as emblems; was there, in our Modern European Mind, any thought at all of their being emblems! Were they not indubitable awful facts; the whole heart of man taking them for practically true, all Nature everywhere confirming them? So is it always in these things. Men do not believe an Allegory. The future Critic, whatever his new thought may be, who considers this of Dante to have been all got-up as an Allegory, will commit one sore mistake! Paganism we recognized as a veracious expression of the earnest awe-struck feeling of man towards the Universe; veracious, true once, and still not without worth for us. But mark here the difference of Paganism and Christianism; one great difference. Paganism emblemed chiefly the Operations of Nature; the destinies, efforts, combinations, vicissitudes of things and men in this world; Christianism emblemed the Law of Human Duty, the Moral Law of Man. One was for the sensuous nature: a rude helpless utterance of the *first* Thought of men, — the chief recognized virtue, Courage, Superiority to Fear. The other was not for the sensuous nature, but for the moral. What a progress is here, if in that one respect only! —

And so in this Dante, as we said, had ten silent centuries, in a very strange way, found a voice. The " Divina Commedia " is of Dante's writing; yet in truth *it* belongs to ten Christian centuries, only the finishing of it is Dante's. So always. The craftsman there, the smith with that metal of his, with these tools, with these cunning methods, — how little of all he does is properly *his* work! All past inventive men work there with him; — as indeed with all of us, in all things. Dante is the spokesman of the Middle Ages; the Thought they lived by stands here, in everlasting music. These sublime ideas of his, terrible and beautiful, are the fruit of the Christian Meditation of all the good men who had gone before him. Precious they; but also is not he precious? Much, had not he spoken, would have been dumb; not dead, yet living voiceless.

On the whole, is it not an utterance, this mystic Song, at once of one of the greatest human souls, and of the highest thing that Europe had hitherto realized for itself? Christianism, as Dante sings it, is another than Paganism in the rude Norse mind; another than " Bastard Christianism " half-articulately spoken in the Arab Desert seven-hundred years before! The noblest *idea* made *real* hitherto among men, is sung, and emblemed-forth abidingly, by one of the noblest men. In the one sense and in the other, are we not right glad to possess it? As I calculate, it may last yet for long thousands of years. For the thing that is uttered from the inmost parts of a man's soul, differs altogether from what is uttered by the outer part. The outer is of the day, under the empire of mode; the outer passes away, in swift endless changes; the inmost is the same yesterday, today and forever. True souls, in all generations of the world, who look on this Dante, will find a brotherhood in him; the deep sincerity of his thoughts, his woes and hopes, will speak likewise to their sincerity; they will feel that this Dante too was a brother. Napoleon in Saint-Helena is charmed with the genial veracity of old Homer. The oldest Hebrew Prophet, under a vesture the most diverse from ours, does yet, because he speaks from the heart of man, speak to all men's hearts. It is the one sole secret of continuing long memorable. Dante, for depth of sincerity, is like an antique Prophet too; his words, like theirs, come from his very heart. One need not wonder if it were predicted that his Poem might be the most enduring thing our Europe has yet made; for nothing so endures as a truly spoken word. All cathedrals, pontificalities, brass and stone, and outer arrangement never so lasting, are brief in comparison to an unfathomable heart-song like this: one feels as if it might survive, still of importance to men, when these had all sunk into new irrecognizable combinations, and had ceased individually to be. Europe has made much; great cities, great empires, encyclopædias, creeds, bodies of opinion and practice: but it has made little of the class of Dante's Thought. Homer yet *is*, veritably present face to face with every open soul of us; and Greece, where is *it?* Desolate for thousands of years; away, vanished; a bewildered heap of stones and rubbish, the life and existence of it all gone. Like a dream; like the dust of King Agamemnon! Greece was; Greece, except in the *words* it spoke, is not.

The uses of this Dante? We will not say much about his "uses." A human soul who has once got into that primal element of *Song*, and sung-forth fitly somewhat therefrom, has worked in the *depths* of our existence; feeding through long times the life-*roots* of all excellent human things whatsoever, — in a way that "utilities" will not succeed well in calculating! We will not estimate the Sun by the quantity of gaslight it saves us; Dante shall be invaluable, or of no value. One remark I may make: the contrast in this respect between the Hero-Poet and the Hero-Prophet. In a hundred years, Mahomet, as we saw, had his Arabians at Grenada and at Delhi; Dante's Italians seem to be yet very much where they were. Shall we say, then, Dante's effect on the world was small in comparison? Not so: his arena is far more restricted; but also it is far nobler, clearer; — perhaps not less but more important. Mahomet speaks to great masses of men, in the coarse dialect adapted to such; a dialect filled with inconsistencies, crudities, follies: on the great masses alone can he act, and there with good and with evil strangely blended. Dante speaks to the noble, the pure and great, in all times and places. Neither does he grow obsolete, as the other does. Dante burns as a pure star, fixed there in the firmament, at which the great and the high of all ages kindle themselves: he is the possession of all the chosen of the world for uncounted time. Dante, one calculates, may long survive Mahomet. In this way the balance may be made straight again.

But, at any rate, it is not by what is called their effect on the world by what *we* can judge of their effect there, that a man and his work are measured. Effect? Influence? Utility? Let a man *do* his work; the fruit of it is the care of Another than he. It will grow its own fruit; and whether embodied in Caliph Thrones and Arabian Conquests, so that it "fills all Morning and Evening Newspapers," and all Histories, which are a kind of distilled Newspapers; or not embodied so at all; — what matters that? That is not the real fruit of it! The Arabian Caliph, in so far only as he did something, was something. If the great Cause of Man, and Man's work in God's Earth, got no furtherance from the Arabian Caliph, then no matter how many cimeters he drew, how many gold piasters pocketed, and what uproar and blaring he made in this world, — *he* was but a loud-sounding inanity and futility; at bottom, he *was* not at all. Let us honor the great empire of *Silence*, once more! The boundless treasury which we do *not* jingle in our pockets, or count up and present before men! It is perhaps, of all things, the usefullest for each of us to do, in these loud times. —

As Dante, the Italian man, was sent into our world to embody musically the Religion of the Middle Ages, the Religion of our Modern Europe, its Inner Life; so Shakspeare, we may say, embodies for us the Outer Life of our Europe as developed then, its chivalries, courtesies, humors, ambitions, what practical way of thinking, acting, looking at the world, men then had. As in Homer we may still construe Old Greece; so in Shakspeare and Dante, after thousands of years, what our modern Europe was, in Faith and in Practice, will still be legible. Dante has given us the Faith or soul; Shakspeare, in a not less noble way, has given us the Practice or body. This latter also we were to have; a man was sent for it, the man Shakspeare. Just when that chivalry way of life had reached its last finish, and was on the point of breaking down into slow or swift dissolution, as we now see it everywhere, this other sovereign Poet, with his seeing eye, with his perennial singing voice, was sent to take note of it, to give long-enduring record of it. Two fit men: Dante, deep, fierce as the central fire of the world; Shakspeare, wide, placid, far-seeing, as the Sun, the upper light of the world. Italy produced the one world-voice; we English had the honor of producing the other.

Curious enough how, as it were by mere accident, this man came to us. I think always, so great, quiet, complete and self-sufficing is this Shakspeare, had the Warwickshire Squire not prosecuted him for deer-stealing, we had perhaps never heard of him as a Poet! The woods and skies, the rustic Life of Man in Stratford there, had been enough for this man! But indeed that strange outbudding of our whole English Existence, which we call the Elizabethan Era, did not it too come as of its own accord? The "Tree Igdrasil" buds and withers by its own laws,—too deep for our scanning. Yet it does bud and wither, and every bough and leaf of it is there, by fixed eternal laws; not a Sir Thomas Lucy but comes at the hour fit for him. Curious, I say, and not sufficiently considered: how everything does co-operate with all; not a leaf rotting on the highway but is indissoluble portion of solar and stellar systems; no thought, word or act of man but has sprung withal out of all men, and works sooner or later, recognizably or irrecognizably, on all men! It is all a Tree: circulation of sap and influences, mutual communication of every minutest leaf with the lowest talon of a root, with every other greatest and minutest portion of the whole. The Tree Igdrasil, that has its roots down in the Kingdoms of Hela and Death, and whose boughs overspread the highest Heaven! —

In some sense it may be said that this glorious Elizabethan Era with its Shakspeare, as the outcome and flowerage of all which had preceded it, is itself attributable to the Catholicism of the Middle Ages. The Christian Faith, which was the theme of Dante's Song, had produced this Practical Life which Shakspeare was to sing. For Religion then, as it now and always is, was the soul of Practice; the primary vital fact in men's life. And remark here, as rather curious, that Middle-Age Catholicism was abolished, so far as Acts of Parliament could abolish it, before Shakspeare, the noblest product of it, made his appearance. He did make his appearance nevertheless. Nature at her own time, with Catholicism or what else might be necessary, sent him forth; taking small thought of Acts of Parliament. King-Henrys, Queen-Elizabeths go their way; and Nature too goes hers. Acts of Parliament, on the whole, are small, notwithstanding the noise they make. What Act of Parliament, debate at St. Stephen's, on the hustings or elsewhere, was it that brought this Shakspeare into being? No dining at Freemasons' Tavern, opening subscription-lists, selling of shares, and infinite other jangling and true or false endeavoring! This Elizabethan Era, and all its nobleness and blessedness, came without proclamation, preparation of ours. Priceless Shakspeare was the free gift of Nature; given altogether silently; — received altogether silently, as if it had been a thing of little account. And yet, very literally, it is a priceless thing. One should look at that side of matters too.

Of this Shakspeare of ours, perhaps the opinion one sometimes hears a little idolatrously expressed is, in fact, the right one; I think the best judgment not of this country only, but of Europe at large, is slowly pointing to the conclusion, That Shakspeare is the chief of all Poets hitherto: the greatest intellect who, in our recorded world, has left record of himself in the way of Literature. On the whole, I know not such a power of vision, such a faculty of thought, if we take all the characters of it, in any other man. Such a calmness of depth; placid joyous strength;

all things imaged in that great soul of his so true and clear, as in a tranquil unfathomable sea ! It has been said, that in the constructing of Shakspeare's Dramas there is, apart from all other "faculties" as they are called, an understanding manifested, equal to that in Bacon's "Novum Organum." That is true ; and it is not a truth that strikes every one. It would become more apparent if we tried, any of us for himself, how, out of Shakspeare's dramatic materials, *we* could fashion such a result ! The built house seems all so fit, — everyway as it should be, as if it came there by its own law and the nature of things, — we forget the rude disorderly quarry it was shaped from. The very perfection of the house, as if Nature herself had made it, hides the builder's merit. Perfect, more perfect than any other man, we may call Shakspeare in this : he discerns, knows as by instinct, what condition he works under, what his materials are, what his own force and its relation to them is. It is not a transitory glance of insight that will suffice ; it is deliberate illumination of the whole matter ; it is a calmly *seeing* eye ; a great intellect, in short. How a man, of some wide thing that he has witnessed, will construct a narrative, what kind of picture and delineation he will give of it, — is the best measure you could get of what intellect is in the man. Which circumstance is vital and shall stand prominent ; which unessential, fit to be suppressed ; where is the true *beginning*, the true sequence and ending ? To find out this, you task the whole force of insight that is in the man. He must *understand* the thing ; according to the depth of his understanding, will the fitness of his answer be. You will try him so. Does like join itself to like ; does the spirit of method stir in that confusion, so that its embroilment becomes order ? Can the man say, *Fiat lux*, Let there be light ; and out of chaos make a world? Precisely as there is *light* in himself, will he accomplish this.

Or indeed we may say again, it is in what I called Portrait-painting, delineating of men and things, especially of men, that Shakspeare is great. All the greatness of the man comes out decisively here. It is unexampled, I think, that calm creative perspicacity of Shakspeare. The thing he looks at reveals not this or that face of it, but its inmost heart, and generic secret: it dissolves itself as in light before him, so that he discerns the perfect structure of it. Creative, we said: poetic creation, what is this too but *seeing* the thing sufficiently? The *word* that will describe the thing, follows of itself from such clear intense sight of the thing. And is not Shakspeare's *morality*, his valor, candor, tolerance, truthfulness; his whole victorious strength and greatness, which can triumph over such obstructions, visible there too? Great as the world! No *twisted*, poor convex-concave mirror, reflecting all objects with its own convexities and concavities; a perfectly *level* mirror; — that is to say withal, if we will understand it, a man justly related to all things and men, a good man. It is truly a lordly spectacle how this great soul takes-in all kinds of men and objects, a Falstaff, an Othello, a Juliet, a Coriolanus; sets them all forth to us in their round completeness; loving, just, the equal brother of all. "Novum Organum," and all the intellect you will find in Bacon, is of a quite secondary order; earthy, material, poor in comparison with this. Among modern men, one finds, in strictness, almost nothing of the same rank. Goethe alone, since the days of Shakspeare, reminds me of it. Of him too you say that he *saw* the object; you may say what he himself says of Shakspeare: " His characters are like watches with dial-plates of transparent crystal; they show you the hour like others, and the inward mechanism also is all visible."

The seeing eye! It is this that discloses the inner harmony of things; what Nature meant, what musical idea Nature has wrapped-up in these often rough embodiments. Something she did mean. To the seeing eye that something were discernible. Are they base, miserable things? You can laugh over them, you can weep over them; you can in some way or other genially relate yourself to them, — you can, at lowest, hold your peace about them, turn away your own and others' face from them, till the hour come for practically exterminating and extinguishing them! At bottom, it is the Poet's first gift, as it is all men's, that he have intellect enough. He will be a Poet if he have: a Poet in word; or failing that, perhaps still better, a Poet in act. Whether he write at all; and if so, whether in prose or in verse, will depend on accidents: who knows on what extremely trivial accidents, — perhaps on his having had a singing-master, on his being taught to sing in his boyhood! But the faculty which enables him to discern the inner heart of things, and the harmony that dwells there (for whatsoever exists has a harmony in the heart of it, or it would not hold together and exist), is not the result of habits or accidents, but the gift of Nature herself; the primary outfit for a Heroic Man in what sort soever. To the Poet, as to every other, we say first of all, *See.* If you cannot do that, it is of no use to keep stringing rhymes together, jingling sensibilities against each other, and *name* yourself a Poet; there is no hope for you. If you can, there is, in prose or verse, in action or speculation, all manner of hope. The crabbed old Schoolmaster used to ask, when they brought him a new pupil, "But are ye sure he's *not a dunce?*" Why, really one might ask the same thing, in regard to every man proposed for whatsoever function; and consider it as the one inquiry needful : Are ye sure he's not a dunce? There is, in this world, no other entirely fatal person.

For, in fact, I say the degree of vision that dwells in a man is a correct measure of the man. If called to define Shakspeare's faculty, I should say superiority of Intellect, and think I had included all under that. What indeed are faculties? We talk of faculties as if they were distinct, things separable; as if a man had intellect, imagination, fancy, etc., as he has hands, feet and arms. That is a capital error. Then again, we hear of a man's "intellectual nature," and of his "moral nature," as if these again were divisible, and existed apart. Necessities of language do perhaps prescribe such forms of utterance; we must speak, I am aware, in that way, if we are to speak at all. But words ought not to harden into things for us. It seems to me, our apprehension of this matter is, for most part, radically falsified thereby. We ought to know withal, and to keep forever in mind, that these divisions are at bottom but *names;* that man's spiritual nature, the vital Force which dwells in him, is essentially one and indivisible; that what we call imagination, fancy, understanding, and so forth, are but different figures of the same Power of Insight, all indissolubly connected with each other, physiognomically related; that if we knew one of them, we might know all of them. Morality itself, what we call the moral quality of a man, what is this but another *side* of the one vital Force whereby he is and works? All that a man does is physiognomical of him. You may see how a man would fight, by the way in which he sings; his courage, or want of courage, is visible in the word he utters, in the opinion he has formed, no less than in the stroke he strikes. He is *one;*

and preaches the same Self abroad in all these ways.

Without hands a man might have feet, and could still walk: but, consider it, — without morality, intellect were impossible for him; a thoroughly immoral *man* could not know anything at all! To know a thing, what we can call knowing, a man must first *love* the thing, sympathize with it: that is, be *virtuously* related to it. If he have not the justice to put down his own selfishness at every turn, the courage to stand by the dangerous-true at every turn, how shall he know? His virtues, all of them, will lie recorded in his knowledge. Nature, with her truth, remains to the bad, to the selfish and the pusillanimous forever a sealed book: what such can know of Nature is mean, superficial, small; for the uses of the day merely. But does not the very Fox know something of Nature? Exactly so: it knows where the geese lodge! The human Reynard, very frequent everywhere in the world, what more does he know but this and the like of this? Nay, it should be considered too, that if the Fox had not a certain vulpine *morality*, he could not even know where the geese were, or get at the geese! If he spent his time in splenetic atrabiliar reflections on his own misery, his ill usage by Nature, Fortune and other Foxes, and so forth; and had not courage, promptitude, practicality, and other suitable vulpine gifts and graces, he would catch no geese. We may say of the Fox too, that his morality and insight are of the same dimensions; different faces of the same internal unity of vulpine life! — These things are worth stating; for the contrary of them acts with manifold very baleful perversion, in this time: what limitations, modifications they require, your own candor will supply.

If I say, therefore, that Shakspeare is the greatest

of Intellects, I have said all concerning him. But there is more in Shakspeare's intellect than we have yet seen. It is what I call an unconscious intellect; there is more virtue in it than he himself is aware of. Novalis beautifully remarks of him, that those Dramas of his are Products of Nature too, deep as Nature herself. I find a great truth in this saying. Shakspeare's Art is not Artifice; the noblest worth of it is not there by plan or precontrivance. It grows-up from the deeps of Nature, through this noble sincere soul, who is a voice of Nature. The latest generations of men will find new meanings in Shakspeare, new elucidations of their own human being; "new harmonies with the infinite structure of the Universe; concurrences with later ideas, affinities with the higher powers and senses of man." This well deserves meditating. It is Nature's highest reward to a true simple great soul, that he get thus to be *a part of herself.* Such a man's works, whatsoever he with utmost conscious exertion and forethought shall accomplish, grow up withal *un*consciously, from the unknown deeps in him; — as the oak-tree grows from the Earth's bosom, as the mountains and waters shape themselves; with a symmetry grounded on Nature's own laws, conformable to all Truth whatsoever. How much in Shakspeare lies hid; his sorrows, his silent struggles known to himself; much that was not known at all, not speakable at all: like *roots*, like sap and forces working underground! Speech is great; but Silence is greater.

Withal the joyful tranquillity of this man is notable. I will not blame Dante for his misery: it is as battle without victory; but true battle, — the first, indispensable thing. Yet I call Shakspeare greater than Dante, in that he fought truly, and did conquer. Doubt it not, he had his own sorrows: those " Sonnets " of his will even testify expressly in what deep waters he had waded, and swum struggling for his life ; — as what man like him ever failed to have to do ? It seems to me a heedless notion, our common one, that he sat like a bird on the bough ; and sang forth, free and offhand, never knowing the troubles of other men. Not so ; with no man is it so. How could a man travel forward from rustic deer-poaching to such tragedy-writing, and not fall-in with sorrows by the way ? Or, still better, how could a man delineate a Hamlet, a Coriolanus, a Macbeth, so many suffering heroic hearts, if his own heroic heart had never suffered ? — And now, in contrast with all this, observe his mirthfulness, his genuine overflowing love of laughter! You would say, in no point does he *exaggerate* but only in laughter. Fiery objurgations, words that pierce and burn, are to be found in Shakspeare ; yet he is always in measure here ; never what Johnson would remark as a specially "good hater." But his laughter seems to pour from him in floods ; he heaps all manner of ridiculous nicknames on the butt he is bantering, tumbles and tosses him in all sorts of horse-play ; you would say, with his whole heart laughs. And then, if not always the finest, it is always a genial laughter. Not at mere weakness, at misery or poverty ; never. No man who *can* laugh, what we call laughing, will laugh at these things. It is some poor character only *desiring* to laugh, and have the credit of wit, that does so. Laughter means sympathy ; good laughter is not "the crackling of thorns under the pot." Even at stupidity and pretension this Shakspeare does not laugh otherwise than genially. Dogberry and Verges tickle our very hearts ; and we dismiss them covered with explosions of laughter : but we like the poor fellows only the better for laughing ; and hope they will get on well

9

there, and continue Presidents of the City-watch. Such laughter, like sunshine on the deep sea, is very beautiful to me.

We have no room to speak of Shakspeare's individual works; though perhaps there is much still waiting to be said on that head. Had we, for instance, all his plays reviewed as "Hamlet," in "Wilhelm Meister," is! A thing which might, one day, be done. August Wilhelm Schlegel has a remark on his Historical Plays, "Henry Fifth" and the others, which is worth remembering. He calls them a kind of National Epic. Marlborough, you recollect, said, he knew no English History but what he had learned from Shakspeare. There are really, if we look to it, few as memorable Histories. The great salient points are admirably seized; all rounds itself off, into a kind of rhythmic coherence; it is, as Schlegel says, *epic;* — as indeed all delineation by a great thinker will be. There are right beautiful things in those Pieces, which indeed together form one beautiful thing. That battle of Agincourt strikes me as one of the most perfect things, in its sort, we anywhere have of Shakspeare's. The description of the two hosts: the worn-out, jaded English; the dread hour, big with destiny, when the battle shall begin; and then that deathless valor: "Ye good yeomen, whose limbs were made in England!" There is a noble Patriotism in it, — far other than the "indifference" you sometimes hear ascribed to Shakspeare. A true English heart breathes, calm and strong, through the whole business; not boisterous, protrusive; all the better for that. There is a sound in it like the ring of steel. This man too had a right stroke in him, had it come to that! But I will say, of Shakspeare's works generally, that we have no full impress of him there; even as full as we have of many men. His works are so many windows, through which we see a glimpse of the world that was in him. All his works seem, comparatively speaking, cursory, imperfect, written under cramping circumstances; giving only here and there a note of the full utterance of the man. Passages there are that come upon you like splendor out of Heaven; bursts of radiance, illuminating the very heart of the thing: you say, " That is *true*, spoken once and for-ever; wheresoever and whensoever there is an open human soul, that will be recognized as true ! " Such bursts, however, make us feel that the surrounding matter is not radiant; that it is, in part, temporary, conventional. Alas, Shakspeare had to write for the Globe Playhouse : his great soul had to crush itself, as it could, into that and no other mould. It was with him, then, as it is with us all. No man works save under conditions. The sculptor cannot set his own free Thought before us ; but his Thought as he could translate it into the stone that was given, with the tools that were given. *Disjecta membra* are all that we find of any Poet, or of any man.

Whoever looks intelligently at this Shakspeare may recognize that he too was a *Prophet*, in his way ; of an insight analogous to the Prophetic, though he took it up in another strain. Nature seemed to this man also divine; *un*speakable, deep as Tophet, high as Heaven: "We are such stuff as Dreams are made of ! " That scroll in Westminster Abbey, which few read with understanding, is of the depth of any seer. But the man sang; did not preach, except musically. We called Dante the melodious Priest of Middle-Age Catholicism. May we not call Shakspeare the still more melodious Priest of a *true* Catholicism, the " Universal Church " of the Future and of all times?

No narrow superstition, harsh asceticism, intolerance, fanatical fierceness or perversion: a Revelation, so far as it goes, that such a thousandfold hidden beauty and divineness dwells in all Nature; which let all men worship as they can! We may say without offence, that there rises a kind of universal Psalm out of this Shakspeare too; not unfit to make itself heard among the still more sacred Psalms. Not in disharmony with these, if we understood them, but in harmony! I cannot call this Shakspeare a "Sceptic," as some do; his indifference to the creeds and theological quarrels of his time misleading them. No: neither unpatriotic, though he says little about his Patriotism; nor sceptic, though he says little about his Faith. Such "indifference" was the fruit of his greatness withal: his whole heart was in his own grand sphere of worship (we may call it such); these other controversies, vitally important to other men, were not vital to him.

But call it worship, call it what you will, is it not a right glorious thing, and set of things, this that Shakspeare has brought us? For myself, I feel that there is actually a kind of sacredness in the fact of such a man being sent into this Earth. Is he not an eye to us all; a blessed heaven-sent Bringer of Light?— And, at bottom, was it not perhaps far better that this Shakspeare, everyway an unconscious man, was *conscious* of no Heavenly message? He did not feel, like Mahomet, because he saw into those internal Splendors, that he specially was the "Prophet of God": and was he not greater than Mahomet in that? Greater; and also, if we compute strictly, as we did in Dante's case, more successful. It was intrinsically an error that notion of Mahomet's, of his supreme Prophethood; and has come down to us inextricably involved in error to this day; dragging along with it such a coil of fables, impurities, intolerances, as makes

it a questionable step for me here and now to say, as
I have done, that Mahomet was a true Speaker at all,
and not rather an ambitious charlatan, perversity and
simulacrum ; no Speaker, but a Babbler ! Even in Arabia, as I compute, Mahomet will have exhausted himself and become obsolete, while this Shakspeare, this
Dante may still be young ; — while this Shakspeare
may still pretend to be a Priest of Mankind, of Arabia
as of other places, for unlimited periods to come !

Compared with any speaker or singer one knows,
even with Æschylus or Homer, why should he not, for
veracity and universality, last like them ? He is *sincere*
as they ; reaches deep down like them, to the universal and perennial. But as for Mahomet, I think it
had been better for him *not* to be so conscious ! Alas,
poor Mahomet ; all that he was *conscious* of was a
mere error ; a futility and triviality, — as indeed such
ever is. The truly great in him too was the unconscious : that he was a wild Arab lion of the desert,
and did speak-out with that great thunder-voice of his,
not by words which he *thought* to be great, but by
actions, by feelings, by a history which *were* great !
His Koran has become a stupid piece of prolix ab-
surdity ; we do not believe, like him, that God wrote
that ! The Great Man here too, as always, is a Force
of Nature : whatsoever is truly great in him springs-up
from the *in*articulate deeps.

Well : this is our poor Warwickshire Peasant, who
rose to be Manager of a Playhouse, so that he could
live without begging ; whom the Earl of Southampton
cast some kind glances on ; whom Sir Thomas Lucy,
many thanks to him, was for sending to the Tread-
mill ! We did not account him a god, like Odin,
while he dwelt with us ; on which point there were
much to be said. But I will say rather, or repeat : In

spite of the sad state Hero-worship now lies in, consider what this Shakspeare has actually become among
us. Which Englishman we ever made, in this land of
ours, which million of Englishmen, would we not give-
up rather than the Stratford Peasant? There is no
regiment of highest Dignitaries that we would sell him
for. He is the grandest thing we have yet done. For
our honor among foreign nations, as an ornament to
our English Household, what item is there that we
would not surrender rather than him? Consider now,
if they asked us, Will you give-up your Indian Empire
or your Shakspeare, you English; never have had any
Indian Empire, or never have had any Shakspeare?
Really it were a grave question. Official persons
would answer doubtless in official language; but we,
for our part too, should not we be forced to answer:
Indian Empire or no Indian Empire; we cannot do
without Shakspeare! Indian Empire will go, at any
rate, some day; but this Shakspeare does not go,
he lasts forever with us; we cannot give-up our
Shakspeare!

Nay, apart from spiritualities; and considering him
merely as a real, marketable, tangibly-useful possession.
England, before long, this Island of ours, will hold but
a small fraction of the English: in America, in New
Holland, east and west to the very Antipodes, there
will be a Saxondom covering great spaces of the
Globe, and now, what is it that can keep all these
together into virtually one Nation, so that they do not
fall-out and fight, but live at peace, in brotherlike
intercourse, helping one another? This is justly regarded as the greatest practical problem, the thing all
manner of sovereignties and governments are here to
accomplish: What is it that will accomplish this?
Acts of Parliament, administrative prime-ministers
cannot. America is parted from us, so far as Parlia-

ment could part it. Call it not fantastic, for there is much reality in it: Here, I say, is an English King, whom no time or chance, Parliament or combination of Parliaments, can dethrone! This King Shakspeare, does not he shine, in crowned sovereignty, over us all, as the noblest, gentlest, yet strongest of rallying-signs; *in*destructible; really more valuable in that point of view than any other means or appliance whatsoever? We can fancy him as radiant aloft over all the Nations of Englishmen, a thousand years hence. From Paramatta, from New York, wheresoever, under what sort of Parish-Constable soever, English men and women are, they will say to one another: "Yes, this Shakspeare is ours; we produced him, we speak and think by him; we are of one blood and kind with him." The most common-sense politician, too, if he pleases, may think of that.

Yes, truly, it is a great thing for a Nation that it get an articulate voice; that it produce a man who will speak-forth melodiously what the heart of it means! Italy, for example, poor Italy lies dismembered, scattered asunder, not appearing in any protocol or treaty as a unity at all; yet the noble Italy is actually *one:* Italy produced its Dante; Italy can speak! The Czar of all the Russias, he is strong, with so many bayonets, Cossacks and cannons; and does a great feat in keeping such a tract of Earth politically together; but he cannot yet speak. Something great in him, but it is a dumb greatness. He has had no voice of genius, to be heard of all men and times. He must learn to speak. He is a great dumb monster hitherto. His cannons and Cossacks will all have rusted into nonentity, while that Dante's voice is still audible. The Nation that has a Dante is bound together as no dumb Russia can be. We must here end what we had to say of the *Hero-Poet.*

LECTURE IV.

THE HERO AS PRIEST. — LUTHER: REFORMATION; KNOX: PURITANISM.

OUR present discourse is to be of the Great Man as Priest. We have repeatedly endeavored to explain that all sorts of Heroes are intrinsically of the same material; that given a great soul, open to the Divine Significance of Life, then there is given a man fit to speak of this, to sing of this, to fight and work for this, in a great, victorious, enduring manner; there is given a Hero, — the outward shape of whom will depend on the time and the environment he finds himself in. The Priest too, as I understand it, is a kind of Prophet; in him too there is required to be a light of inspiration, as we must name it. He presides over the worship of the people; is the Uniter of them with the Unseen Holy. He is the spiritual Captain of the people; as the Prophet is their spiritual King with many captains: he guides them heavenward, by wise guidance through this Earth and its work. The ideal of him is, that he too be what we can call a voice from the unseen Heaven; interpreting, even as the Prophet did, and in a more familiar manner unfolding the same to men. The unseen Heaven, — the "open secret of the Universe," — which so few have an eye for! He is the Prophet shorn of his more awful splendor; burning with mild equable radiance, as the enlightener of daily life. This, I say, is the ideal of a Priest. So in old times; so in these, and in all times. One knows very well that, in reducing ideals to practice, great latitude of tolerance is needful; very great. But a priest who is not this at all, who does not any longer aim or try to be this, is a character — of whom we had rather not speak in this place.

Luther and Knox were by express vocation Priests, and did faithfully perform that function in its common sense. Yet it will suit us better here to consider them chiefly in their historical character, rather as Reformers than Priests. There have been other Priests perhaps equally notable, in calmer times, for doing faithfully the office of a Leader of Worship; bringing down, by faithful heroism in that kind, a light from Heaven into the daily life of their people; leading them forward, as under God's guidance, in the way wherein they were to go. But when this same *way* was a rough one, of battle, confusion and danger, the spiritual Captain, who led through that, becomes, especially to us who live under the fruit of his leading, more notable than any other. He is the warfaring and battling Priest; who led his people, not to quiet faithful labor as in smooth times, but to faithful valorous conflict, in times all violent, dismembered: a more perilous service, and a more memorable one, be it higher or not. These two men we will account our best Priests, inasmuch as they were our best Reformers. Nay I may ask, Is not every true Reformer, by the nature of him, a *Priest* first of all? He appeals to Heaven's invisible justice against Earth's visible force; knows that it, the invisible, is strong and alone strong. He is a believer in the divine truth of things; a *seer*, seeing through the shows of things; a worshipper, in one way or the other, of the divine truth of things; a Priest, that is. If he be not first a Priest, he will never be good for much as a Reformer.

Thus then, as we have seen Great Men, in various situations, building-up Religions, heroic Forms of human Existence in this world, Theories of Life worthy to be sung by a Dante, Practices of Life by a Shakspeare, — we are now to see the reverse process; which also is necessary, which also may be carried-on in the Heroic manner. Curious how this should be necessary: yet necessary it is. The mild shining of the Poet's light has to give place to the fierce lightning of the Reformer: unfortunately the Reformer too is a personage that cannot fail in History! The Poet indeed, with his mildness, what is he but the product and ultimate adjustment of Reform, or Prophecy, with its fierceness? No wild Saint Dominics and Thebaïd Eremites, there had been no melodious Dante; rough Practical Endeavor, Scandinavian and other, from Odin to Walter Raleigh, from Ulfila to Cranmer, enabled Shakspeare to speak. Nay the finished Poet, I remark sometimes, is a symptom that his epoch itself has reached perfection and is finished; that before long there will be a new epoch, new Reformers needed.

Doubtless it were finer, could we go along always in the way of *music;* be tamed and taught by our Poets, as the rude creatures were by their Orpheus of old. Or failing this rhythmic *musical* way, how good were it could we get so much as into the *equable* way; I mean, if *peaceable* Priests, reforming from day to day, would always suffice us! But it is not so; even this latter has not yet been realized. Alas, the battling Reformer too is, from time to time, a needful and inevitable phenomenon. Obstructions are never wanting: the very things that were once indispensable furtherances become obstructions; and need to be shaken-off, and left behind us, — a business often of enormous difficulty. It is notable enough, surely, how a Theorem or spiritual Representation, so we may call it, which once took-in the whole Universe, and was completely satisfactory in all parts of it to the highly-discursive acute intellect of Dante, one of the greatest in the world, — had in the course of another century become dubitable to common intellects; become deniable; and is now, to every one of us, flatly incredible, obsolete as Odin's Theorem! To Dante, human Existence, and God's ways with men, were all well represented by those *Malebolges, Purgatorios;* to Luther not well. How was this? Why could not Dante's Catholicism continue; but Luther's Protestantism must needs follow? Alas, nothing will *continue.*

I do not make much of " Progress of the Species," as handled in these times of ours; nor do I think you would care to hear much about it. The talk on that subject is too often of the most extravagant, confused sort. Yet I may say, the fact itself seems certain enough; nay we can trace-out the inevitable necessity of it in the nature of things. Every man, as I have stated somewhere, is not only a learner but a doer: he learns with the mind given him what has been; but with the same mind he discovers farther, he invents and devises somewhat of his own. Absolutely without originality there is no man. No man whatever believes, or can believe, exactly what his grandfather believed: he enlarges somewhat, by fresh discovery, his view of the Universe, and consequently his Theorem of the Universe, — which is an *infinite* Universe, and can never be embraced wholly or finally by any view or Theorem, in any conceivable enlargement: he enlarges somewhat, I say; finds somewhat that was credible to his grandfather incredible to him, false to him, inconsistent with some new thing he has discovered or observed. It is the history of every man; and in the history of Mankind we see it summed-up into great historical amounts, — revolutions, new epochs. Dante's Mountain of Purgatory does *not* stand "in the ocean of the other Hemisphere," when Columbus has once sailed thither! Men find no such thing extant in the other Hemisphere. It is not there. It must cease to be believed to be there. So with all beliefs whatsoever in this world, — all Systems of Belief, and Systems of Practice that spring from these.

If we add now the melancholy fact, that when Belief waxes uncertain, Practice too becomes unsound, and errors, injustices and miseries everywhere more and more prevail, we shall see material enough for revolution. At all turns, a man who will *do* faithfully, needs to believe firmly. If he have to ask at every turn the world's suffrage; if he cannot dispense with the world's suffrage, and make his own suffrage serve, he is a poor eye-servant; the work committed to him will be *mis*done. Every such man is a daily contributor to the inevitable downfall. Whatsoever work he does, dishonestly, with an eye to the outward look of it, is a new offence, parent of new misery to somebody or other. Offences accumulate till they become insupportable; and are then violently burst through, cleared off as by explosion. Dante's sublime Catholicism, incredible now in theory, and defaced still worse by faithless, doubting and dishonest practice, has to be torn asunder by a Luther; Shakspeare's noble Feudalism, as beautiful as it once looked and was, has to end in a French Revolution. The accumulation of offences is, as we say, too literally *exploded*, blasted asunder volcanically; and there are long troublous periods, before matters come to a settlement again.

Surely it were mournful enough to look only at this face of the matter, and find in all human opinions and arrangements merely the fact that they were uncertain,

temporary, subject to the law of death! At bottom,
it is not so : all death, here too we find, is but of the
body, not of the essence or soul; all destruction, by
violent revolution or howsoever it be, is but new creation on a wider scale. Odinism was *Valor;* Christianism was *Humility,* a nobler kind of Valor. No
thought that ever dwelt honestly as true in the heart
of man but *was* an honest insight into God's truth on
man's part, and *has* an essential truth in it which
endures through all changes, an everlasting possession
for us all. And, on the other hand, what a melancholy notion is that, which has to represent all men,
in all countries and times except our own, as having
spent their life in blind condemnable error, mere lost
Pagans, Scandinavians, Mahometans, only that we
might have the true ultimate knowledge! All generations of men were lost and wrong, only that this
present little section of a generation might be saved
and right. They all marched forward there, all generations since the beginning of the world, like the
Russian soldiers into the ditch of Schweidnitz Fort,
only to fill-up the ditch with their dead bodies, that
we might march-over and take the place! It is an
incredible hypothesis.

Such incredible hypothesis we have seen maintained
with fierce emphasis; and this or the other poor individual man, with his sect of individual men, march-
ing as over the dead bodies of all men, towards sure
victory: but when he too, with his hypothesis and
ultimate infallible credo, sank into the ditch, and
became a dead body, what was to be said? Withal,
it is an important fact in the nature of man, that he
tends to reckon his own insight as final, and goes
upon it as such. He will always do it, I suppose, in
one or the other way; but it must be in some wider,
wiser way than this. Are not all true men that live,

or that ever lived, soldiers of the same army, enlisted, under Heaven's captaincy, to do battle against the same enemy, the empire of Darkness and Wrong? Why should we misknow one another, fight not against the enemy but against ourselves, from mere difference of uniform? All uniforms shall be good, so they hold in them true valiant men. All fashions of arms, the Arab turban and swift cimeter, Thor's strong hammer smiting down *Jötuns*, shall be welcome. Luther's battle-voice, Dante's march-melody, all genuine things are with us, not against us. We are all under one Captain, soldiers of the same host. Let us now look a little at this Luther's fighting; what kind of battle it was, and how he comported himself in it. Luther too was of our spiritual Heroes; a Prophet to his country and time.

As introductory to the whole, a remark about Idol-atry will perhaps be in place here. One of Mahomet's characteristics, which indeed belongs to all Prophets, is unlimited implacable zeal against Idolatry. It is the grand theme of Prophets: Idolatry, the worshipping of dead Idols as the Divinity, is a thing they cannot away-with, but have to denounce continually, and brand with inexpiable reprobation; it is the chief of all the sins they see done under the sun. This is worth noting. We will not enter here into the theological question about Idolatry. Idol is *Eidolon*, a thing seen, a symbol. It is not God, but a Symbol of God; and perhaps one may question whether any the most be-nighted mortal ever took it for more than a Symbol. I fancy, he did not think that the poor image his own hands had made *was* God; but that God was em-blemed by it, that God was in it some way or other. And now in this sense, one may ask, Is not all wor-ship whatsoever a worship by Symbols, by *eidola*, or things seen? Whether *seen*, rendered visible as an image or picture to the bodily eye; or visible only to the inward eye, to the imagination, to the intellect: this makes a superficial, but no substantial difference. It is still a Thing Seen, significant of Godhead; an Idol. The most rigorous Puritan has his Confession of Faith, and intellectual Representation of Divine things, and worships thereby; thereby is worship first made possible for him. All creeds, liturgies, religious forms, conceptions that fitly invest religious feelings, are in this sense *eidola*, things seen. All worship whatsoever must proceed by Symbols, by Idols: — we may say, all Idolatry is comparative, and the worst Idolatry is only *more* idolatrous.

Where, then, lies the evil of it? Some fatal evil must lie in it, or earnest prophetic men would not on all hands so reprobate it. Why is Idolatry so hateful to Prophets? It seems to me as if, in the worship of those poor wooden symbols, the thing that had chiefly provoked the Prophet, and filled his inmost soul with indignation and aversion, was not exactly what suggested itself to his own thought, and came out of him in words to others, as the thing. The rudest heathen that worshipped Canopus, or the Caabah Black-Stone, he, as we saw, was superior to the horse that worshipped nothing at all! Nay there was a kind of lasting merit in that poor act of his; analogous to what is still meritorious in Poets: recognition of a certain endless *divine* beauty and significance in stars and all natural objects whatsoever. Why should the Prophet so mercilessly condemn him? The poorest mortal worshipping his Fetish, while his heart is full of it, may be an object of pity, of contempt and avoidance, if you will; but cannot surely be an object of hatred. Let his heart *be* honestly full of it, the whole space of his dark narrow mind illuminated thereby;

in one word, let him entirely *believe* in his Fetish, — it will then be, I should say, if not well with him, yet as well as it can readily be made to be, and you will leave him alone, unmolested there.

But here enters the fatal circumstance of Idolatry, that, in the era of the Prophets, no man's mind *is* any longer honestly filled with his Idol or Symbol. Before the Prophet can arise who, seeing through it, knows it to be mere wood, many men must have begun dimly to doubt that it was little more. Condemnable Idolatry is *insincere* Idolatry. Doubt has eaten-out the heart of it: a human soul is seen clinging spasmodically to an Ark of the Covenant, which it half-feels now to have become a Phantasm. This is one of the balefulest sights. Souls are no longer *filled* with their Fetish; but only pretend to be filled, and would fain make themselves feel that they are filled. " You do not believe," said Coleridge; " you only believe that you believe." It is the final scene in all kinds of Worship and Symbolism; the sure symptom that death is now nigh. It is equivalent to what we call Formulism, and Worship of Formulas, in these days of ours. No more immoral act can be done by a human creature; for it is the beginning of all immorality, or rather it is the impossibility henceforth of any morality whatsoever: the innermost moral soul is paralyzed thereby, cast into fatal magnetic sleep! Men are no longer *sincere* men. I do not wonder that the earnest man denounces this, brands it, prosecutes it with inextinguishable aversion. He and it, all good and it, are at death-feud. Blamable Idolatry is *Cant*, and even what one may call Sincere-Cant. Sincere-Cant: that is worth thinking of! Every sort of Worship ends with this phasis.

I find Luther to have been a Breaker of Idols, no less than any other Prophet. The wooden gods of the Koreish, made of timber and bees-wax, were not more hateful to Mahomet than Tetzel's Pardons of Sin, made of sheepskin and ink, were to Luther. It is the property of every Hero, in every time, in every place and situation, that he come back to reality; that he stand upon things, and not shows of things. According as he loves, and venerates, articulately or with deep speechless thought, the awful realities of things, so will the hollow shows of things, however regular, decorous, accredited by Koreishes or Conclaves, be intolerable and detestable to him. Protestantism too is the work of a Prophet: the prophet-work of that sixteenth century. The first stroke of honest demolition to an ancient thing grown false and idolatrous; preparatory afar off to a new thing, which shall be true and authentically divine! —

At first view it might seem as if Protestantism were entirely destructive to this that we call Hero-worship, and represent as the basis of all possible good, religious or social, for mankind. One often hears it said that Protestantism introduced a new era, radically different from any the world had ever seen before: the era of "private judgment," as they call it. By this revolt against the Pope, every man became his own Pope; and learnt, among other things, that he must never trust any Pope, or spiritual Hero-captain, any more! Whereby, is not spiritual union, all hierarchy and subordination among men, henceforth an impossibility? So we hear it said. Now I need not deny that Protestantism was a revolt against spiritual sovereignties, Popes and much else. Nay I will grant that English Puritanism, revolt against earthly sovereignties, was the second act of it; that the enormous French Revolution itself was the third act, whereby all sovereignties earthly and spiritual were, as might seem, abolished or made sure of abolition. Protestantism is the grand root from which our whole subsequent European History branches out. For the spiritual will always body itself forth in the temporal history of men; the spiritual is the beginning of the temporal. And now, sure enough, the cry is everywhere for Liberty and Equality, Independence and so forth; instead of *Kings*, Ballot-boxes and Electoral suffrages: it seems made out that any Hero-sovereign, or loyal obedience of men to a man, in things temporal or things spiritual, has passed away forever from the world. I should despair of the world altogether, if so. One of my deepest convictions is, that it is not so. Without sovereigns, true sovereigns, temporal and spiritual, I see nothing possible but an anarchy; the hatefulest of things. But I find Protestantism, whatever anarchic democracy it have produced, to be the beginning of new genuine sovereignty and order. I find it to be a revolt against *false* sovereigns; the painful but indispensable first preparative for *true* sovereigns getting place among us! This is worth explaining a little.

Let us remark, therefore, in the first place, that this of " private judgment " is, at bottom, not a new thing in the world, but only new at that epoch of the world. There is nothing generically new or peculiar in the Reformation; it was a return to Truth and Reality in opposition to Falsehood and Semblance, as all kinds of Improvement and genuine Teaching are and have been. Liberty of private judgment, if we will consider it, must at all times have existed in the world. Dante had not put-out his eyes, or tied shackles on himself; he was at home in that Catholicism of his, a free-seeing soul in it, — if many a poor Hogstraten, Tetzel and Dr. Eck had now become slaves in it. Liberty of judgment? No iron chain, or outward force of any kind, could ever compel the soul of a man to believe or to disbelieve : it is his own indefeasible light, that judgment of his ; he will reign, and believe there, by the grace of God alone ! The sorriest sophistical Bellarmine, preaching sightless faith and passive obedience, must first, by some kind of *conviction*, have abdicated his right to be convinced. His "private judgment" indicated that, as the advisablest step *he* could take. The right of private judgment will subsist, in full force, wherever true men subsist. A true man *believes* with his whole judgment, with all the illumination and discernment that is in him, and has always so believed. A false man, only struggling to "believe that he believes," will naturally manage it in some other way. Protestantism said to this latter, Woe! and to the former, Well done! At bottom, it was no new saying ; it was a return to all old sayings that ever had been said. Be genuine, be sincere : that was, once more, the meaning of it. Mahomet believed with his whole mind ; Odin with his whole mind, — he, and all *true* Followers of Odinism. They, by their private judgment, had "judged" — *so*.

And now I venture to assert, that the exercise of private judgment, faithfully gone about, does by no means necessarily end in selfish independence, isolation ; but rather ends necessarily, in the opposite of that. It is not honest inquiry that makes anarchy ; but it is error, insincerity, half-belief and untruth that make it. A man protesting against error is on the way towards uniting himself with all men that believe in truth. There is no communion possible among men who believe only in hearsays. The heart of each is lying dead ; has no power of sympathy even with *things*, — or he would believe *them* and not hearsays. No sympathy even with things ; how much less with his fellow-men ! He cannot unite with men ; he is an anarchic man. Only in a world of sincere men is unity possible;—and there, in the longrun, it is as good as *certain.*

For observe one thing, a thing too often left out of view, or rather altogether lost sight of, in this controversy: That it is not necessary a man should himself have *discovered* the truth he is to believe in, and never so *sincerely* to believe in. A Great Man, we said, was always sincere, as the first condition of him. But a man need not be great in order to be sincere; that is not the necessity of Nature and all Time, but only of certain corrupt unfortunate epochs of Time. A man can believe, and make his own, in the most genuine way, what he has received from another;—and with boundless gratitude to that other! The merit of *originality* is not novelty; it is sincerity. The believing man is the original man; whatsoever he believes, he believes it for himself, not for another. Every son of Adam can become a sincere man, an original man, in this sense; no mortal is doomed to be an insincere man. Whole ages, what we call ages of Faith, are original; all men in them, or the most of men in them, sincere. These are the great and fruitful ages: every worker, in all spheres, is a worker not on semblance but on substance; every work issues in a result: the general sum of such work is great; for all of it, as genuine, tends towards one goal; all of it is *additive,* none of it subtractive. There is true union, true kingship, loyalty, all true and blessed things, so far as the poor Earth can produce blessedness for men.

Hero-worship? Ah me, that a man be self-subsistent, original, true, or what we call it, is surely the farthest in the world from indisposing him to reverence and believe other men's truth! It only disposes, necessitates and invincibly compels him to *dis*believe other men's dead formulas, hearsays and untruths. A

man embraces truth with his eyes open, and because
his eyes are open: does he need to shut them before
he can love his Teacher of truth? He alone can love,
with a right gratitude and genuine loyalty of soul, the
Hero-Teacher who has delivered him out of darkness
into light. Is not such a one a true Hero and Serpent-
queller; worthy of all reverence! The black monster,
Falsehood, our one enemy in this world, lies prostrate
by his valor; it was he that conquered the world for
us! See, accordingly, was not Luther himself reverenced as a true Poet, or Spiritual Father, *being*
verily such? Napoleon, from amid boundless revolt of
Sansculottism, became a King. Hero-worship never
dies, nor can die. Loyalty and Sovereignty are everlasting in the world: — and there is this in them, that
they are grounded not on garnitures and semblances,
but on realities and sincerities. Not by shutting your
eyes, your "private judgment;" no, but by opening
them, and by having something to see! Luther's
message was deposition and abolition to all false Popes
and Potentates, but life and strength, though afar off
to new genuine ones.

All this of Liberty and Equality, Electoral suffrages,
Independence and so forth, we will take, therefore, to
be a temporary phenomenon, by no means a final one.
Though likely to last a long time, with sad enough
embroilments for us all, we must welcome it, as the
penalty of sins that are past, the pledge of inestimable
benefits that are coming. In all ways, it behooved
men to quit simulacra and return to fact; cost what it
might, that did behoove to be done. With spurious
Popes, and Believers having no private judgment, —
quacks pretending to command over dupes, — what
can you do? Misery and mischief only. You cannot
make an association out of insincere men; you cannot build an edifice except by plummet and level, — at

right-angles to one another! In all this wild revolutionary work, from Protestantism downwards, I see the blessedest result preparing itself: not abolition of Hero-worship, but rather what I would call a whole World of Heroes. If Hero mean *sincere man*, why may not every one of us be a Hero? A world all sincere, a believing world: the like has been; the like will again be, — cannot help being. That were the right sort of Worshippers for Heroes: never could the truly Better be so reverenced as where all were True and Good! But we must hasten to Luther and his Life.

Luther's birthplace was Eisleben in Saxony; he came into the world there on the 10th of November 1483. It was an accident that gave this honor to Eisleben. His parents, poor mine-laborers in a village of that region, named Mohra, had gone to the Eisleben Winter-Fair: in the tumult of this scene the Frau Luther was taken with travail, found refuge in some poor house there, and the boy she bore was named MARTIN LUTHER. Strange enough to reflect upon it. This poor Frau Luther, she had gone with her husband to make her small merchandisings; perhaps to sell the lock of yarn she had been spinning, to buy the small winter-necessaries for her narrow hut or household; in the whole world, that day, there was not a more entirely unimportant-looking pair of people than this Miner and his Wife. And yet what were all Emperors, Popes and Potentates, in comparison? There was born here, once more, a Mighty Man; whose light was to flame as the beacon over long centuries and epochs of the world; the whole world and its history was waiting for this man. It is strange, it is great. It leads us back to another Birth-hour, in a still meaner environment, Eighteen Hundred years ago, — of which it is fit that we *say* nothing, that we think only in silence ; for what words are there ! The Age of Miracles past? The Age of Miracles is for-ever here ! —

I find it altogether suitable to Luther's function in this Earth, and doubtless wisely ordered to that end by the Providence presiding over him and us and all things, that he was born poor, and brought-up poor, one of the poorest of men. He had to beg, as the school-children in those times did ; singing for alms and bread, from door to door. Hardship, rigorous Necessity was the poor boy's companion ; no man nor no thing would put-on a false face to flatter Martin Luther. Among things, not among the shows of things, had he to grow. A boy of rude figure, yet with weak health, with his large greedy soul, full of all faculty and sensibility, he suffered greatly. But it was his task to get acquainted with *realities*, and keep acquainted with them, at whatever cost : his task was to bring the whole world back to reality, for it had dwelt too long with semblance ! A youth nursed-up in wintry whirlwinds, in desolate darkness and diffi-culty, that he may step-forth at last from his stormy Scandinavia, strong as a true man, as a god : a Christian Odin, — a right Thor once more, with his thunder-hammer, to smite asunder ugly enough *Jötuns* and Giant-monsters : —

Perhaps the turning incident of his life, we may fancy, was that death of his friend Alexis, by light-ning, at the gate of Erfurt. Luther had struggled-up through boyhood, better and worse ; displaying, in spite of all hindrances, the largest intellect, eager to learn : his father judging doubtless that he might pro-mote himself in the world, set him upon the study of Law. This was the path to rise ; Luther, with little will in it either way, had consented : he was now nine-

teen years of age. Alexis and he had been to see the
old Luther people at Mansfeldt; were got back again
near Erfurt, when a thunderstorm came on; the bolt
struck Alexis, he fell dead at Luther's feet. What is
this Life of ours? — gone in a moment, burnt-up like
a scroll, into the blank Eternity! What are all earthly
preferments, Chancellorships, Kingships? They lie
shrunk together — there! The Earth has opened on
them; in a moment they are not, and Eternity is.
Luther, struck to the heart, determined to devote himself to God and God's service alone. In spite of all
dissuasions from his father and others, he became a
Monk in the Augustine Convent at Erfurt.

This was probably the first light-point in the history
of Luther his purer will now first decisively uttering
itself; but, for the present, it was still as one light-
point in an element all of darkness. He says he was
a pious monk, *ich bin ein frommer Mönch gewesen;*
faithfully, painfully struggling to work-out the truth of
this high act of his; but it was to little purpose. His
misery had not lessened; had rather, as it were, in-
creased into infinitude. The drudgeries he had to do,
as novice in his Convent, all sorts of slave-work, were
not his grievance: the deep earnest soul of the man
had fallen into all manner of black scruples, dubita-
tions; he believed himself likely to die soon, and far
worse than die. One hears with a new interest for
poor Luther that, at this time, he lived in terror of the
unspeakable misery; fancied that he was doomed to
eternal reprobation. Was it not the humble sincere
nature of the man? What was he, that he should be
raised to Heaven! He that had known only misery,
and mean slavery: the news was too blessed to be
credible. It could not become clear to him how, by
fasts, vigils, formalities and mass-work, a man's soul
could be saved. He fell into the blackest wretched-

ness; had to wander staggering as on the verge of bottomless Despair.

It must have been a most blessed discovery, that of an old Latin Bible which he found in the Erfurt Library about this time. He had never seen the Book before. It taught him another lesson than that of fasts and vigils. A brother monk too, of pious experience, was helpful. Luther learned now that a man was saved not by singing masses, but by the infinite grace of God: a more credible hypothesis. He gradually got himself founded, as on the rock. No wonder he should venerate the Bible, which had brought this blessed help to him. He prized it as the Word of the Highest must be prized by such a man. He determined to hold by that; as through life and to death he firmly did.

This, then, is his deliverance from darkness, his final triumph over darkness, what we call his conversion; for himself the most important of all epochs. That he should now grow daily in peace and clearness; that, unfolding now the great talents and virtues implanted in him, he should rise to importance in his Convent, in his country, and be found more and more useful in all honest business of life, is a natural result. He was sent on missions by his Augustine Order, as a man of talent and fidelity fit to do their business well: the Elector of Saxony, Friedrich, named the Wise, a truly wise and just prince, had cast his eye on him as a valuable person; made him Professor in his new University of Wittenberg, Preacher too at Wittenberg; in both which capacities, as in all duties he did, this Luther, in the peaceable sphere of common life, was gaining more and more esteem with all good men.

It was in his twenty-seventh year that he first saw Rome; being sent thither, as I said, on mission from his Convent. Pope Julius the Second, and what was going-on at Rome, must have filled the mind of Luther with amazement. He had come as to the Sacred City, throne of God's Highpriest on Earth; and he found it — what we know! Many thoughts it must have given the man; many which we have no record of, which perhaps he did not himself know how to utter. This Rome, this scene of false priests, clothed not in the beauty of holiness, but in far other vesture, is *false:* but what is it to Luther? A mean man he, how shall he reform a world? That was far from his thoughts. A humble, solitary man, why should he at all meddle with the world? It was the task of quite higher men than he. His business was to guide his own footsteps wisely through the world. Let him do his own obscure duty in it well; the rest, horrible and dismal as it looks, is in God's hand, not in his.

It is curious to reflect what might have been the issue, had Roman Popery happened to pass this Luther by; to go on in its great wasteful orbit, and not come athwart his little path, and force him to assault it! Conceivable enough that, in this case, he might have held his peace about the abuses of Rome; left Providence, and God on high, to deal with them! A modest quiet man; not prompt he to attack irreverently persons in authority. His clear task, as I say, was to do his own duty; to walk wisely in this world of confused wickedness, and save his own soul alive. But the Roman Highpriesthood did come athwart him: afar off at Wittenberg he, Luther, could not get lived in honesty for it; he remonstrated, resisted, came to extremity; was struck-at, struck again, and so it came to wager of battle between them! This is worth attending to in Luther's history. Perhaps no man of so humble, peaceable a disposition ever filled the world with contention. We cannot but see that he would have loved privacy, quiet diligence in the shade; that it was against his will he ever became a notoriety. Notoriety: what would that do for him? The goal of his march through this world was the Infinite Heaven; an indubitable goal for him: in a few years, he should either have attained that, or lost it forever! We will say nothing at all, I think, of that sorrowfulest of theories, of its being some mean shop-keeper grudge, of the Augustine Monk against the Dominican, that first kindled the wrath of Luther, and produced the Protestant Reformation. We will say to the People who maintain it, if indeed any such exist now: Get first into the sphere of thought by which it is so much as possible to judge of Luther, or of any man like Luther, otherwise than distractedly; we may then begin arguing with you.

The Monk Tetzel, sent out carelessly in the way of trade, by Leo Tenth, — who merely wanted to raise a little money, and for the rest seems to have been a Pagan rather than a Christian, so far as he was any-thing, — arrived at Wittenberg, and drove his scanda-lous trade there. Luther's flock bought indulgences; in the confessional of his Church people pleaded to him that they had already got their sins pardoned. Luther, if he would not be found wanting at his own post, a false sluggard and coward at the very centre of the little space of ground that was his own and no other man's, had to step-forth against Indulgences, and declare aloud that *they* were a futility and sor-rowful mockery, that no man's sins could be pardoned by *them*. It was the beginning of the whole Reforma-tion. We know how it went; forward from this first public challenge of Tetzel, on the last day of October 1517, through remonstrance and argument; — spread-ing ever wider, rising ever higher; till it became unquenchable, and enveloped all the world. Luther's heart's-desire was to have this grief and other griefs amended ; his thought was still far other than that of introducing separation in the Church, or revolting against the Pope, Father of Christendom.   The elegant Pagan Pope cared little about this Monk and his doctrines ; wished, however, to have done with the noise of him : in a space of some three years, having tried various softer methods, he thought good to end it by *fire.*   He dooms the Monk's writings to be burnt by the hangman, and his body to be sent bound to Rome, — probably for a similar purpose.   It was the way they had ended with Huss, with Jerome, the century before.   A short argument, fire.   Poor Huss : he came to that Constance Council, with all imaginable promises and safe-conducts ; an earnest, not rebellious kind of man : they laid him instantly in a stone dungeon "three-feet wide, six-feet high, seven-feet long ; " *burnt* the true voice of him out of this world ; choked it in smoke and fire.   That was *not* well done !

I, for one, pardon Luther for now altogether revolting against the Pope.   The elegant Pagan, by this fire-decree of his, had kindled into noble just wrath the bravest heart then living in this world.   The bravest, if also one of the humblest, peaceablest ; it was now kindled.   These words of mine, words of truth and soberness, aiming faithfully, as human inability would allow, to promote God's truth on Earth, and save men's souls, you, God's vicegerent on earth, answer them by the hangman and fire ?   You will burn me and them, for answer to the God's-message they strove to bring you ? *You* are not God's vicegerent ; you are another's than his, I think !   I take your Bull as an emparchmented Lie, and burn *it.*   You will do what you see good next : this is what I do.   It was on the 10th of December 1520, three years after the beginning of the business, that Luther, "with a great concourse of people," took this indignant step of burning the Pope's fire-decree " at the Elster-Gate of Wittenberg." Wittenberg looked on "with shoutings;" the whole world was looking on. The Pope should not have provoked that "shout"! It was the shout of the awakening of nations. The quiet German heart, modest, patient of much, had at length got more than it could bear. Formulism, Pagan Popeism, and other Falsehood and corrupt Semblance had ruled long enough: and here once more was a man found who durst tell all men that God's-world stood not on semblances but on realities; that Life was a truth, and not a lie!

At bottom, as was said above, we are to consider Luther as a Prophet Idol-breaker; a bringer-back of men to reality. It is the function of great men and teachers. Mahomet said, These idols of yours are wood; you put wax and oil on them, the flies stick on them: they are not God, I tell you, they are black wood! Luther said to the Pope, This thing of yours that you call a Pardon of Sins, it is a bit of rag-paper with ink. It *is* nothing else; it, and so much like it, is nothing else. God alone can pardon sins. Popeship, spiritual Fatherhood of God's Church, is that a vain semblance, of cloth and parchment? It is an awful fact. God's Church is not a semblance, Heaven and Hell are not semblances. I stand on this, since you drive me to it. Standing on this, I a poor German Monk am stronger than you all. I stand solitary, friendless, but on God's Truth; you with your tiaras, triple-hats, with your treasuries and armories, thunders spiritual and temporal, stand on the Devil's Lie, and are not so strong! —

The Diet of Worms, Luther's appearance there on the 17th of April 1521, may be considered as the greatest scene in Modern European History; the point, indeed, from which the whole subsequent history of civilization takes its rise. After multiplied negotiations, disputations, it had come to this. The young Emperor Charles Fifth, with all the Princes of Germany, Papal nuncios, dignitaries spiritual and temporal, are assembled there: Luther is to appear and answer for himself, whether he will recant or not. The world's pomp and power sits there on this hand: on that, stands-up for God's Truth, one man, the poor miner Hans Luther's Son. Friends had reminded him of Huss, advised him not to go; he would not be advised. A large company of friends rode-out to meet him, with still more earnest warnings; he answered, " Were there as many Devils in Worms as there are roof-tiles, I would on." The people, on the morrow, as he went to the Hall of the Diet, crowded the windows and housetops, some of them calling out to him, in solemn words, not to recant: " Whosoever denieth me before men!" they cried to him, — as in a kind of solemn petition and adjuration. Was it not in reality our petition too, the petition of the whole world, lying in dark bondage of soul, paralyzed under a black spectral Nightmare and tripple-hatted Chimera, calling itself Father in God, and what not: " Free us; it rests with thee; desert us not!"

Luther did not desert us. His speech of two hours, distinguished itself by its respectful, wise and honest tone; submissive to whatsoever could lawfully claim submission, not submissive to any more than that. His writings, he said, were partly his own, partly derived from the word of God. As to what was his own, human infirmity entered into it; unguarded anger, blindness, many things doubtless which it were a blessing for him could he abolish altogether. But as to what stood on sound truth and the Word of God, he could not recant it. How could he? " Confute me," he concluded, "by proofs of Scripture, or else by plain just arguments: I cannot recant otherwise. For it is neither safe nor prudent to do aught against conscience. Here stand I; I can do no other: God assist me!" It is, as we say, the greatest moment in the Modern History of Men. English Puritanism, England and its Parliaments, Americas, and vast work these two centuries; French Revolution, Europe and its work everywhere at present: the germ of it all lay there: had Luther in that moment done other, it had all been otherwise! The European World was asking him: Am I to sink ever lower into falsehood, stagnant putrescence, loathsome accursed death; or, with whatever paroxysm, to cast the falsehoods out of me, and be cured and live? —

Great wars, contentions and disunion followed out of this Reformation; which last down to our day, and are yet far from ended. Great talk and crimination has been made about these. They are lamentable, undeniable; but after all, what has Luther or his cause to do with them? It seems strange reasoning to charge the Reformation with all this. When Hercules turned the purifying river into King Augeas's stables, I have no doubt the confusion that resulted was considerable all around: but I think it was not Hercules's blame; it was some other's blame! The Reformation might bring what results it liked when it came, but the Reformation simply could not help coming. To all Popes and Popes' advocates, expostulating, lamenting and accusing, the answer of the world is: Once for all, your Popehood has become untrue. No matter how good it was, how good you say it is, we cannot believe it; the light of our whole mind, given us to walk-by from Heaven above, finds it henceforth a thing unbelievable. We will not believe it, we

will not try to believe it, — we dare not! The thing
is *untrue;* we were traitors against the Giver of all
Truth, if we durst pretend to think it true. Away
with it; let whatsoever likes come in the place of it:
with *it* we can have no farther trade! Luther and
his Protestantism is not responsible for wars; the
false Simulacra that forced him to protest, they are
responsible. Luther did what every man that God
has made has not only the right, but lies under the
sacred duty, to do: answered a falsehood when it
questioned him, Dost thou believe me? No! At
what cost soever, without counting of costs, this thing
behooved to be done. Union, organization spiritual
and material, a far nobler than any Popedom or
Feudalism in their truest days, I never doubt, is coming for the world; sure to come. But on Fact alone,
not on Semblance and Simulacrum, will it be able
either to come, or to stand when come. With union
grounded on falsehood, and ordering us to speak and
act lies, we will not have anything to do. Peace? A
brutal lethargy is peaceable, the noisome grave is
peaceable. We hope for a living peace, not a dead
one!

And yet, in prizing justly the indispensable bless-
ings of the New, let us not be unjust to the Old. The
Old *was* true, if it no longer is. In Dante's days it
needed no sophistry, self-blinding or other dishonesty,
to get itself reckoned true. It was good then; nay
there is in the soul of it a deathless good. The cry
of "No Popery" is foolish enough in these days.
The speculation that Popery is on the increase, building new chapels and so forth, may pass for one of the
idlest ever started. Very curious: to count-up a few
Popish chapels, listen to a few Protestant logic-
choppings, — to much dull-droning drowsy inanity
that still calls itself Protestant, and say: See, Pro-

THE HERO AS PRIEST.

testantism is *dead;* Popeism is more alive than it, will be alive after it! Drowsy inanities, not a few, that call themselves Protestant are dead; but *Protestantism* has not died yet, that I hear of! Protestantism, if we will look, has in these days produced its Goethe, its Napoleon; German Literature and the French Revolution; rather considerable signs of life! Nay, at bottom, what else is alive *but* Protestantism? The life of most else that one meets is a galvanic one merely, — not a pleasant, not a lasting sort of life!

Popery can build new chapels; welcome to do so, to all lengths. Popery cannot come back, any more than Paganism can, — *which* also still lingers in some countries. But, indeed, it is with these things, as with the ebbing of the sea: you look at the waves oscillating hither, thither on the beach; for *minutes* you cannot tell how it is going; look in half an hour where it is, — look in half a century where your Popehood is! Alas, would there were no greater danger to our Europe than the poor old Pope's revival! Thor may as soon try to revive. And withal this oscillation has a meaning. The poor old Popehood will not die away entirely, as Thor has done, for some time yet; nor ought it. We may say, the Old never dies till this happen, Till all the soul of good that was in it have got itself transfused into the practical New. While a good work remains capable of being done by the Romish form; or, what is inclusive of all, while a *pious life* remains capable of being led by it, just so long, if we consider, will this or the other human soul adopt it, go about as a living witness of it. So long it will obtrude itself on the eye of us who reject it, till we in our practice too have appropriated whatsoever of truth was in it. Then, but also not till then, it will have no charm more for any man. It lasts here for a purpose. Let it last as long as it can. —

11

Of Luther I will add now, in reference to all these wars and bloodshed, the noticeable fact that none of them began so long as he continued living. The controversy did not get to fighting so long as he was there. To me it is proof of his greatness in all senses, this fact. How seldom do we find a man that has stirred-up some vast commotion, who does not himself perish, swept-away in it! Such is the usual course of Revolutionists. Luther continued, in a good degree, sovereign of this greatest revolution; all Protestants, of what rank or function soever, looking much to him for guidance: and he held it peaceable, continued firm at the centre of it. A man to do this must have a kingly faculty: he must have the gift to discern at all turns where the true heart of the matter lies, and to plant himself courageously on that, as a strong true man, that other true men may rally round him there. He will not continue leader of men otherwise. Luther's clear deep force of judgment, his force of all sorts, of *silence*, of tolerance and moderation, among others, are very notable in these circumstances.

Tolerance, I say; a very genuine kind of tolerance: he distinguishes what is essential, and what is not; the unessential may go very much as it will. A complaint comes to him that such and such a Reformed Preacher "will not preach without a cassock." Well, answers Luther, what harm will a cassock do the man? "Let him have a cassock to preach in; let him have three cassocks if he find benefit in them!" His conduct in the matter of Karlstadt's wild image-breaking; of the Anabaptists; of the Peasants' War, show a noble strength, very different from spasmodic violence. With sure prompt insight he discriminates what is what: a strong just man, he speaks-forth what is the wise course, and all men follow him in that. Luther's Written Works give similar testimony of him. The dialect of these speculations is now grown obsolete for us; but one still reads them with a singular attraction. And indeed the mere grammatical diction is still legible enough; Luther's merit in literary history is of the greatest; his dialect became the language of all writing. They are not well written, these Four-and-twenty Quartos of his; written hastily, with quite other than literary objects. But in no Books have I found a more robust, genuine, I will say noble faculty of a man than in these. A rugged honesty, homeliness, simplicity; a rugged sterling sense and strength. He flashes-out illumination from him; his smiting idiomatic phrases seem to cleave into the very secret of the matter. Good humor too, nay tender affection, nobleness, and depth: this man could have been a Poet too! He had to *work* an Epic Poem, not write one. I call him a great Thinker; as indeed his greatness of heart already betokens that.

Richter says of Luther's words, "his words are half-battles." They may be called so. The essential quality of him was, that he could fight and conquer; that he was a right piece of human Valor. No more valiant man, no mortal heart to be called *braver*, that one has record of, ever lived in that Teutonic Kindred, whose character is valor. His defiance of the " Devils " in Worms was not a mere boast, as the like might be if now spoken. It was a faith of Luther's that there were Devils, spiritual denizens of the Pit, continually besetting men. Many times, in his writings, this turns-up; and a most small sneer has been grounded on it by some. In the room of the Wartburg where he sat translating the Bible, they still show you a black spot on the wall; the strange memorial of one of these conflicts. Luther sat translating one of the Psalms; he was worn-down with long labor, with sickness, abstinence from food: there rose before him some hideous indefinable Image, which he took for the Evil One, to forbid his work: Luther started-up, with fiend defiance; flung his inkstand at the spectre, and it disappeared! The spot still remains there; a curious monument of several things. Any apothecary's apprentice can now tell us what we are to think of this apparition, in a scientific sense: but the man's heart that dare rise defiant, face to face, against Hell itself, can give no higher proof of fearlessness. The thing he will quail before exists not on this Earth or under it. Fearless enough! "The Devil is aware," writes he on one occasion, "that this does not proceed out of fear in me. I have seen and defied innumerable Devils. Duke George," of Leipzig, a great enemy of his, "Duke George is not equal to one Devil," — far short of a Devil! "If I had business at Leipzig, I would ride into Leipzig, though it rained Duke-Georges for nine days running." What a reservoir of Dukes to ride into! —

At the same time, they err greatly who imagine that this man's courage was ferocity, mere coarse disobedient obstinacy and savagery, as many do. Far from that. There may be an absence of fear which arises from the absence of thought or affection, from the presence of hatred and stupid fury. We do not value the courage of the tiger highly! With Luther it was far otherwise; no accusation could be more unjust than this of mere ferocious violence brought against him. A most gentle heart withal, full of pity and love, as indeed the truly valiant heart ever is. The tiger before a *stronger* foe — flies: the tiger is not what we call valiant, only fierce and cruel. I know few things more touching than those soft breathings of affection, soft as a child's or a mother's, in this great wild heart of Luther. So honest, unadulterated with any cant;

homely, rude in their utterances; pure as water welling from the rock. What, in fact, was all that down-pressed mood of despair and reprobation, which we saw in his youth, but the outcome of pre-eminent thoughtful gentleness, affections too keen and fine? It is the course such men as the poor Poet Cowper fall into. Luther to a slight observer might have seemed a timid, weak man; modesty, affectionate shrinking tenderness the chief distinction of him. It is a noble valor which is roused in a heart like this, once stirred-up into defiance, all kindled into a heavenly blaze.

In Luther's "Table-Talk," a posthumous Book of anecdotes and sayings collected by his friends, the most interesting now of all the Books proceeding from him, we have many beautiful unconscious displays of the man, and what sort of nature he had. His behavior at the deathbed of his little Daughter, so still, so great and loving, is among the most affecting things. He is resigned that his little Magdalene should die, yet longs inexpressibly that she might live; — follows, in awestruck thought, the flight of her little soul through those unknown realms. Awe-struck; most heartfelt, we can see; and sincere, — for after all dogmatic creeds and articles, he feels what nothing it is that we know, or can know: His little Magdalene shall be with God, as God wills; for Luther too that is all; *Islam* is all.

Once, he looks-out from his solitary Patmos, the Castle of Coburg, in the middle of the night: The great vault of Immensity, long flights of clouds sailing through it, — dumb, gaunt, huge : — who supports all that? "None ever saw the pillars of it; yet it is supported." God supports it. We must know that God is great, that God is good; and trust, where we cannot see. Returning home from Leipzig once, he is struck by the beauty of the harvest-fields: How it stands, that golden yellow corn, on its fair taper stem, its golden head bent, all rich and waving there, — the meek Earth, at God's kind bidding, has produced it once again; the bread of man!   In the garden at Wittenberg one evening at sunset, a little bird has perched for the night: That little bird, says Luther, above it are the stars and deep Heaven of worlds; yet it has folded its little wings; gone trustfully to rest there as in its home: the Maker of it has given it too a home!   Neither are mirthful turns wanting: there is a great free human heart in this man.   The common speech of him has a rugged nobleness, idiomatic, expressive, genuine; gleams here and there with beautiful poetic tints.   One feels him to be a great brother man.   His love of Music, indeed, is not this, as it were, the summary of all these affections in him? Many a wild unutterability he spoke-forth from him in the tones of his flute.   The Devils fled from his flute, he says.   Death-defiance on the one hand, and such love of music on the other; I could call these the two opposite poles of a great soul; between these two all great things had room.

Luther's face is to me expressive of him; in Kranach's best portraits I find the true Luther.   A rude plebeian face; with its huge crag-like brows and bones, the emblem of rugged energy; at first, almost a repulsive face.   Yet in the eyes especially there is a wild silent sorrow; an unnamable melancholy, the element of all gentle and fine affections; giving to the rest the true stamp of nobleness.   Laughter was in this Luther, as we said; but tears also were there. Tears also were appointed him; tears and hard toil. The basis of his life was Sadness, Earnestness.   In his latter days, after all triumphs and victories, he expresses himself heartily weary of living; he considers that God alone can and will regulate the course things are taking, and that perhaps the Day of Judgment is not far. As for him, he longs for one thing: that God would release him from his labor, and let him depart and be at rest. They understand little of the man who cite this in *dis*credit of him! I will call this Luther a true Great Man; great in intellect, in courage, affection and integrity; one of our most lovable and precious men. Great, not as a hewn obelisk; but as an Alpine mountain, — so simple, honest, spontaneous, not setting-up to be great at all; there for quite another purpose than being great! Ah yes, unsubduable granite, piercing far and wide into the Heavens; yet in the clefts of it fountains, green beautiful valleys with flowers! A right Spiritual Hero and Prophet; once more, a true Son of Nature and Fact, for whom these centuries, and many that are to come yet, will be thankful to Heaven.

The most interesting phasis which the Reformation anywhere assumes, especially for us English, is that of Puritanism. In Luther's own country Protestantism soon dwindled into a rather barren affair: not a religion or faith, but rather now a theological jangling of argument, the proper seat of it not the heart; the essence of it sceptical contention: which indeed has jangled more and more, down to Voltaireism itself,— through Gustavus-Adolphus contentions onward to French-Revolution ones! But in our Island there arose a Puritanism, which even got itself established as a Presbyterianism and National Church among the Scotch; which came forth as a real business of the heart; and has produced in the world very notable fruit. In some senses, one may say it is the only phasis of Protestantism that ever got to the rank of being a Faith, a true heart-communication with Heaven, and of exhibiting itself in History as such. We must spare a few words for Knox; himself a brave and remarkable man; but still more important as Chief Priest and Founder, which one may consider him to be, of the Faith that became Scotland's, New England's, Oliver Cromwell's. History will have something to say about this, for some time to come!

We may censure Puritanism as we please; and no one of us, I suppose, but would find it a very rough defective thing. But we, and all men, may understand that it was a genuine thing; for Nature has adopted it, and it has grown, and grows. I say sometimes, that all goes by wager-of-battle in this world; that *strength*, well understood, is the measure of all worth. Give a thing time; if it can succeed, it is a right thing. Look now at American Saxondom; and at that little Fact of the sailing of the Mayflower, two-hundred years ago, from Delft Haven in Holland! Were we of open sense as the Greeks were, we had found a Poem here; one of Nature's own Poems, such as she writes in broad facts over great continents. For it was properly the beginning of America: there were straggling settlers in America before, some material as of a body was there; but the soul of it was first this. These poor men, driven-out of their own country, not able well to live in Holland, determine on settling in the New World. Black untamed forests are there, and wild savage creatures; but not so cruel as Starchamber hangmen. They thought the Earth would yield them food, if they tilled honestly; the everlasting heaven would stretch, there too, overhead; they should be left in peace, to prepare for Eternity by living well in this world of Time; worshipping in what they thought the true, not the idolatrous way. They clubbed their small means together; hired a ship, the little ship Mayflower, and made ready to set sail.

In Neal's " History of the Puritans " is an account of the ceremony of their departure : solemnity, we might call it rather, for it was a real act of worship. Their minister went down with them to the beach, and their brethren whom they were to leave behind; all joined in solemn prayer, That God would have pity on His poor children, and *go* with them into that waste wilderness, for He also had made that, He was there also as well as here. Hah ! These men, I think, had a work ! The weak thing, weaker than a child, becomes strong one day, if it be a true thing. Puritanism was only despicable, laughable then ; but nobody can manage to laugh at it now. Puritanism has got weapons and sinews ; it has fire-arms, war-navies ; it has cunning in its ten fingers, strength in its right arm ; it can steer ships, fell forests, remove mountains ; — it is one of the strongest things under this sun at present !

In the history of Scotland, too, I can find properly but one epoch : we may say, it contains nothing of world-interest at all but this Reformation by Knox. A poor barren country, full of continual broils, dissensions, massacrings ; a people in the last state of rudeness and destitution, little better perhaps than Ireland at this day. Hungry fierce barons, not so much as able to form any arrangement with each other *how to divide* what they fleeced from these poor drudges ; but obliged, as the Columbian Republics are at this day, to make of every alteration a revolution ; no way of changing a ministry but by hanging the old ministers on gibbets : this is a historical spectacle of no very singular significance ! " Bravery " enough, I doubt not ; fierce fighting in abundance : but not braver or fiercer than that of their old Scandinavian Sea-king ancestors ; *whose* exploits we have not found worth dwelling on ! It is a country as yet without a soul : nothing developed in it but what is rude, external, semi-animal. And now at the Reformation, the internal life is kindled, as it were, under the ribs of this outward material death. A cause, the noblest of causes kindles itself, like a beacon set on high; high as Heaven, yet attainable from Earth; — whereby the meanest man becomes not a Citizen only, but a Member of Christ's visible Church; a veritable Hero, if he prove a true man!

Well; this is what I mean by a whole "nation of heroes;" a *believing* nation. There needs not a great soul to make a hero; there needs a god-created soul which will be true to its origin; that will be a great soul! The like has been seen, we find. The like will be again seen, under wider forms than the Presbyterian: there can be no lasting good done till then. Impossible! say some. Possible? Has it not *been*, in this world, as a practised fact? Did Hero-worship fail in Knox's case? Or are we made of other clay now? Did the Westminster Confession of Faith add some new property to the soul of man? God made the soul of man. He did not doom any soul of man to live as a Hypothesis and Hearsay, in a world filled with such, and with the fatal work and fruit of such! —

But to return: This that Knox did for his Nation, I say, we may really call a resurrection as from death. It was not a smooth business; but it was welcome surely, and cheap at that price, had it been far rougher. On the whole, cheap at any price; — as life is. The people began to *live :* they needed first of all to do that, at what cost and costs soever. Scotch Literature and Thought, Scotch Industry; James Watt, David Hume, Walter Scott, Robert Burns: I find Knox and the Reformation acting in the heart's core of every one of these persons and phenomena; I find that without the Reformation they would not have been. Or what of Scotland? The Puritanism of Scotland became that of England, of New England. A tumult in the High Church of Edinburgh spread into a universal battle and struggle over all these realms; — there came out, after fifty-years struggling, what we all call the "*Glorious* Revolution," a *Habeas-Corpus* Act, Free Parliaments, and much else! Alas, is it not too true what we said, That many men in the van do always, like Russian soldiers, march into the ditch of Schweidnitz, and fill it up with their dead bodies, that the rear may pass-over them dry-shod, and gain the honor? How many earnest rugged Cromwells, Knoxes, poor Peasant Covenanters, wrestling, battling for very life, in rough miry places, have to struggle, and suffer, and fall, greatly censured, *bemired*, — before a beautiful Revolution of Eighty-eight can step-over them in official pumps and silk-stockings, with universal three-times-three!

It seems to me hard measure that this Scottish man, now after three-hundred years, should have to plead like a culprit before the world; intrinsically for having been, in such way as it was then possible to be, the bravest of all Scotchmen! Had he been a poor Half-and-half, he could have crouched into the corner, like so many others; Scotland had not been delivered; and Knox had been without blame. He is the one Scotchman to whom, of all others, his country and the world owe a debt. He has to plead that Scotland would forgive him for having been worth to it any million "unblamable" Scotchmen that need no forgiveness! He bared his breast to the battle; had to row in French galleys, wander forlorn in exile, in clouds and storms; was censured, shot-at through his windows; had a right sore fighting life: if this world were his place of recompense, he had made but a bad venture of it. I cannot apologize for Knox. To him it is very indifferent, these two-hundred-and-fifty years or more, what men say of him. But we, having got above all those details of his battle, and living now in clearness on the fruits of his victory, we, for our own sake, ought to look through the rumors and controversies enveloping the man, into the man himself.

For one thing, I will remark that this post of Prophet to his Nation was not of his seeking; Knox had lived forty years quietly obscure, before he became conspicuous. He was the son of poor parents; had got a college education; become a Priest; adopted the Reformation, and seemed well content to guide his own steps by the light of it, nowise unduly intruding it on others. He had lived as Tutor in gentlemen's families; preaching when any body of persons wished to hear his doctrine: resolute he to walk by the truth, and speak the truth when called to do it: not ambitious of more; not fancying himself capable of more. In this entirely obscure way he had reached the age of forty; was with the small body of Reformers who were standing siege in St. Andrew's Castle, — when one day in their chapel, the Preacher after finishing his exhortation to these fighters in the forlorn hope, said suddenly, That there ought to be other speakers, that all men who had a priest's heart and gift in them ought now to speak; — which gifts and heart one of their own number, John Knox the name of him, had: Had he not? said the Preacher, appealing to all the audience: what then is *his* duty? The people answered affirmatively; it was a criminal forsaking of his post, if such a man held the word that was in him silent. Poor Knox was obliged to stand-up; he attempted to reply; he could say no word; — burst into a flood of tears, and ran out. It is worth remembering, that scene. He was in grievous trouble for some days. He felt what a small faculty was his for this great work. He felt what a baptism he was called to be baptized withal. He " burst into tears."

Our primary characteristic of a Hero, that he is sincere, applies emphatically to Knox. It is not denied anywhere that this, whatever might be his other qualities or faults, is among the truest of men. With a singular instinct he holds to the truth and fact; the truth alone is there for him, the rest a mere shadow and deceptive nonentity. However feeble, forlorn the reality may seem, on that and that only *can* he take his stand. In the Galleys of the River Loire, whither Knox and the others, after their Castle of St. Andrew's was taken, had been sent as Galley-slaves, — some officer or priest, one day, presented them an Image of the Virgin Mother, requiring that they, the blasphemous heretics, should do it reverence. Mother? Mother of God? said Knox, when the turn came to him: This is no Mother of God: this is "a *pented bredd*," — a piece of wood, I tell you, with paint on it! She is fitter for swimming, I think, than for being worshipped, added Knox; and flung the thing into the river. It was not very cheap jesting there: but come of it what might, this thing to Knox was and must continue nothing other than the real truth; it was a *pented bredd:* worship it he would not.

He told his fellow-prisoners, in this darkest time, to be of courage; the Cause they had was the true one, and must and would prosper; the whole world could not put it down. Reality is of God's making; it is alone strong. How many *pented bredds*, pretending to be real, are fitter to swim than to be worshipped! — This Knox cannot live but by fact: he clings to reality as the shipwrecked sailor to the cliff. He is an instance to us how a man, by sincerity itself, becomes heroic: it is the grand gift he has. We find in Knox a good honest intellectual talent, no transcendent one; — a narrow, inconsiderable man, as compared with Luther: but in heartfelt instinctive adherence to truth, in *sincerity*, as we say, he has no superior; nay, one might ask, What equal he has? The heart of him is of the true Prophet cast. "He lies there," said the Earl of Morton at his grave, "who never feared the face of man." He resembles, more than any of the moderns, an Old-Hebrew Prophet. The same inflexibility, intolerance, rigid narrow-looking adherence to God's truth, stern rebuke in the name of God to all that forsake truth: an Old-Hebrew Prophet in the guise of an Edinburgh Minister of the Sixteenth Century. We are to take him for that; not require him to be other.

Knox's conduct to Queen Mary, the harsh visits he used to make in her own palace, to reprove her there, have been much commented upon. Such cruelty, such coarseness fills us with indignation. On reading the actual narrative of the business, what Knox said, and what Knox meant, I must say one's tragic feeling is rather disappointed. They are not so coarse, these speeches; they seem to me about as fine as the circumstances would permit! Knox was not there to do the courtier; he came on another errand. Whoever, reading these colloquies of his with the Queen, thinks they are vulgar insolences of a plebeian priest to a delicate high lady, mistakes the purport and essence of them altogether. It was unfortunately not possible to be polite with the Queen of Scotland, unless one proved untrue to the Nation and Cause of Scotland. A man who did not wish to see the land of his birth made a hunting-field for intriguing ambitious Guises, and the Cause of God trampled underfoot of Falsehoods, Formulas and the Devil's Cause, had no method of making himself agreeable! "Better

that women weep," said Morton, "than that bearded
men be forced to weep." Knox was the constitutional opposition-party in Scotland : the Nobles of the
country, called by their station to take that post, were
not found in it; Knox had to go, or no one. The
hapless Queen ; — but the still more hapless Country,
if *she* were made happy! Mary herself was not without sharpness enough, among her other qualities :
"Who are you," said she once, "that presume to
school the nobles and sovereign of this realm?"
"Madam, a subject born within the same," answered he. Reasonably answered! If the "subject"
have truth to speak, it is not the "subject's" footing
that will fail him here. —

We blame Knox for his intolerance. Well, surely
it is good that each of us be as tolerant as possible.
Yet, at bottom, after all the talk there is and has been
about it, what is tolerance? Tolerance has to tolerate
the *un*essential; and to see well what that is. Tolerance has to be noble, measured, just in its very wrath,
when it can tolerate no longer. But, on the whole,
we are not altogether here to tolerate! We are here
to resist, to control and vanquish withal. We do not
"tolerate" Falsehoods, Thieveries, Iniquities, when
they fasten on us; we say to them, Thou art false,
thou art not tolerable! We are here to extinguish
Falsehoods, and put an end to them, in some wise
way! I will not quarrel so much with the way; the
doing of the thing is our great concern. In this sense
Knox was, full surely, intolerant.

A man sent to row in French Galleys, and suchlike,
for teaching the Truth in his own land, cannot always
be in the mildest humor! I am not prepared to say
that Knox had a soft temper; nor do I know that he
had what we call an ill temper. An ill nature he
decidedly had not. Kind honest affections dwelt in

the much-enduring, hard-worn, ever-battling man. That he *could* rebuke Queens, and had such weight among those proud turbulent Nobles, proud enough whatever else they were; and could maintain to the end a kind of virtual Presidency and Sovereignty in that wild realm, he who was only a "subject born within the same:" this of itself will prove to us that he was found, close at hand, to be no mean acrid man; but at heart a healthful, strong, sagacious man. Such alone can bear rule in that kind. They blame him for pulling-down cathedrals, and so forth, as if he were a seditious rioting demagogue: precisely the reverse is seen to be the fact, in regard to cathedrals and the rest of it, if we examine! Knox wanted no pulling-down of stone edifices; he wanted leprosy and darkness to be thrown out of the lives of men. Tumult was not his element; it was the tragic feature of his life that he was forced to dwell so much in that. Every such man is the born enemy of Disorder; hates to be in it: but what then? Smooth Falsehood is not Order; it is the general sumtotal of *Dis*order. Order is *Truth*,—each thing standing on the basis that belongs to it: Order and Falsehood cannot subsist together.

Withal, unexpectedly enough, this Knox has a vein of drollery in him; which I like much, in combination with his other qualities. He has a true eye for the ridiculous. His "History," with its rough earnestness is curiously enlivened with this. When the two Prelates, entering Glasgow Cathedral, quarrel about precedence; march rapidly up, take to hustling one another, twitching one another's rochets, and at last flourishing their crosiers like quarter-staves, it is a great sight for him everyway! Not mockery, scorn, bitterness alone; though there is enough of that too. But a true, loving, illuminating laugh mounts-up over the earnest visage; not a loud laugh; you would say, a laugh in the *eyes* most of all. An honest-hearted, brotherly man; brother to the high, brother also to the low; sincere in his sympathy with both. He had his pipe of Bourdeaux too, we find, in that old Edinburgh house of his; a cheery social man, with faces that loved him! They go far wrong who think this Knox was a gloomy, spasmodic, shrieking fanatic. Not at all; he is one of the solidest of men. Practical, cautious-hopeful, patient; a most shrewd, observing, quietly discerning man. In fact, he has very much the type of character we assign to the Scotch at present : a certain sardonic taciturnity is in him; insight enough; and a stouter heart than he himself knows of. He has the power of holding his peace over many things which do not vitally concern him, —"They? what are they?" But the thing which does vitally concern him, that thing he will speak of; and in a tone the whole world shall be made to hear : all the more emphatic for his long silence.

This Prophet of the Scotch is to me no hateful man! He had a sore fight of an existence : wrestling with Popes and Principalities; in defeat, contention, life-long struggle; rowing as a galley-slave, wandering as an exile. A sore fight: but he won it. "Have you hope?" they asked him in his last moment, when he could no longer speak. He lifted his finger, "pointed upwards with his finger," and so died. Honor to him! His works have not died. The letter of his work dies, as of all men's; but the spirit of it never.

One word more as to the letter of Knox's work. The unforgivable offence in him is, that he wished to set-up Priests over the head of Kings. In other words, he strove to make the Government of Scotland a *Theocracy*. This indeed is properly the sum of his

12

offences, the essential sin; for which what pardon can there be? It is most true, he did, at bottom, consciously or unconsciously, mean a Theocracy, or Government of God. He did mean that Kings and Prime Ministers, and all manner of persons, in public or private, diplomatizing or whatever else they might be doing, should walk according to the Gospel of Christ, and understand that this was their Law, supreme over all laws. He hoped once to see such a thing realized; and the Petition, *Thy Kingdom come*, no longer an empty word. He was sore grieved when he saw the greedy worldly Barons clutch hold of the Church's property; when he expostulated that it was not secular property, that it was spiritual property, and should be turned to *true* churchly uses, education, schools, worship; — and the Regent Murray had to answer, with a shrug of the shoulders, " It is a devout imagination!" This was Knox's scheme of right and truth; this he zealously endeavored after, to realize it. If we think his scheme of truth was too narrow, was not true, we may rejoice that he could not realize it; that it remained after two centuries of effort, unrealizable, and is a " devout imagination " still. But how shall we blame *him* for struggling to realize it? Theocracy, Government of God, is precisely the thing to be struggled for! All Prophets, zealous Priests, are there for that purpose. Hildebrand wished a Theocracy; Cromwell wished it, fought for it; Mahomet attained it. Nay, is it not what all zealous men, whether called Priests, Prophets, or whatsoever else called, do essentially wish, and must wish? That right and truth, or God's Law, reign supreme among men, this is the Heavenly Ideal (well named in Knox's time, and namable in all times, a revealed " Will of God ") towards which the Reformer will insist that all be more and more approximated. All true Reformers, as I said, are by the nature of them Priests, and strive for a Theocracy.

How far such Ideals can ever be introduced into Practice, and at what point our impatience with their non-introduction ought to begin, is always a question. I think we may say safely, Let them introduce themselves as far as they can contrive to do it! If they are the true faith of men, all men ought to be more or less impatient always where they are not found introduced. There will never be wanting Regent-Murrays enough to shrug their shoulders, and say, "A devout imagination!" We will praise the Hero-priest rather, who does what is in *him* to bring them in; and wears-out, in toil, calumny, contradiction, a noble life, to make a God's Kingdom of this Earth. The Earth will not become too godlike!

LECTURE V.

THE HERO AS MAN OF LETTERS. — JOHNSON,
ROUSSEAU, BURNS.

HERO–GODS, Prophets, Poets, Priests are forms of Heroism that belong to the old ages, make their appearance in the remotest times ; some of them have ceased to be possible long since, and cannot any more show themselves in this world. The Hero as *Man of Letters*, again, of which class we are to speak today, is altogether a product of these new ages ; and so long as the wondrous art of *Writing*, or of Ready-writing which we call *Printing*, subsists, he may be expected to continue, as one of the main forms of Heroism for all future ages. He is, in various respects, a very singular phenomenon.

He is new, I say ; he has hardly lasted above a century in the world yet. Never, till about a hundred years ago, was there seen any figure of a Great Soul living apart in that anomalous manner ; endeavoring to speak-forth the inspiration that was in him by Printed Books, and find place and subsistence by what the world would please to give him for doing that. Much had been sold and bought, and left to make its own bargain in the marketplace ; but the inspired wisdom of a Heroic Soul never till then, in that naked manner. He, with his copy-wrights and copy-wrongs, in his squalid garret, in his rusty coat ; ruling (for this is what he does), from his grave, after death, whole nations and generations who would, or would not, give him bread while living, — is a rather curious spectacle! Few shapes of Heroism can be more unexpected.

Alas, the Hero from of old has had to cramp himself into strange shapes: the world knows not well at any time what to do with him, so foreign is his aspect in the world! It seemed absurd to us, that men, in their rude admiration, should take some wise great Odin for a god, and worship him as such; some wise great Mahomet for one god-inspired, and religiously follow his Law for twelve centuries: but that a wise great Johnson, a Burns, a Rousseau, should be taken for some idle nondescript, extant in the world to amuse idleness, and have a few coins and applauses thrown him, that he might live thereby; *this* perhaps, as before hinted, will one day seem a still absurder phasis of things! Meanwhile, since it is the spiritual always that determines the material, this same Man-of-Letters Hero must be regarded as our most important modern person. He, such as he may be, is the soul of all. What he teaches, the whole world will do and make. The world's manner of dealing with him is the most significant feature of the world's general position. Looking well at his life, we may get a glance, as deep as is readily possible for us, into the life of those singular centuries which have produced him, in which we ourselves live and work.

There are genuine Men of Letters, and not genuine; as in every kind there is a genuine and a spurious. If *Hero* be taken to mean genuine, then I say the Hero as Man of Letters will be found discharging a function for us which is ever honorable, ever the highest; and was once well known to be the highest. He is uttering-forth, in such way as he has, the inspired soul of him; all that a man, in any case, can do. I say *inspired;* for what we call "originality," "sincerity," "genius," the heroic quality we have no good name for, signifies that. The Hero is he who lives in the inward sphere of things, in the True, Divine and Eternal, which exists always, unseen to most, under the Temporary, Trivial: his being is in that; he declares that abroad, by act or speech as it may be, in declaring himself abroad. His life, as we said before, is a piece of the everlasting heart of Nature herself: all men's life is, — but the weak many know not the fact, and are untrue to it, in most times; the strong few are strong, heroic, perennial, because it cannot be hidden from them. The Man of Letters, like every Hero, is there to proclaim this in such sort as he can. Intrinsically it is the same function which the old generations named a man Prophet, Priest, Divinity for doing; which all manner of Heroes, by speech or by act, are sent into the world to do.

Fichte the German Philosopher delivered, some forty years ago at Erlangen, a highly remarkable Course of Lectures on this subject: "*Ueber das Wesen des Gelehrten*, On the Nature of the Literary Man." Fichte, in conformity with the Transcendental Philosophy, of which he was a distinguished teacher, declares first: That all things which we see or work with in this Earth, especially we ourselves and all persons, are as a kind of vesture or sensuous Appearance: that under all there lies, as the essence of them, what he calls the " Divine Idea of the World;" this is the Reality which "lies at the bottom of all Appearance." To the mass of men no such Divine Idea is recognizable in the world; they live merely, says Fichte, among the superficialities, practicalities and shows of the world, not dreaming that there is anything divine under them. But the Man of Letters is sent hither specially that he may discern for himself, and make manifest to us, this same Divine Idea: in every new generation it will manifest itself in a new dialect; and he is there for the purpose of doing that. Such is Fichte's phraseology; with which we need not quarrel. It is his way of naming what I here, by other words, am striving imperfectly to name; what there is at present no name for: The unspeakable Divine Significance, full of splendor, of wonder and terror, that lies in the being of every man, of every thing, — the Presence of the God who made every man and thing. Mahomet taught this in his dialect; Odin in his: it is the thing which all thinking hearts, in one dialect or another, are here to teach.

Fichte calls the Man of Letters, therefore, a Prophet, or as he prefers to phrase it, a Priest, continually unfolding the God-like to men: Men of Letters are a perpetual Priesthood, from age to age, teaching all men that a God is still present in their life; that all "Appearance," whatsoever we see in the world, is but as a vesture for the "Divine Idea of the World," for "that which lies at the bottom of Appearance." In the true Literary Man there is thus ever, acknowledged or not by the world, a sacredness: he is the light of the world; the world's Priest; — guiding it, like a sacred Pillar of Fire, in its dark pilgrimage through the waste of Time. Fichte discriminates with sharp zeal the *true* Literary Man, what we here call the *Hero* as Man of Letters, from multitudes of false unheroic. Whoever lives not wholly in this Divine Idea, or living partially in it, struggles not, as for the one good, to live wholly in it, — he is, let him live where else he like, in what pomps and prosperities he like, no Literary Man; he is, says Fichte, a "Bungler, *Stümper*." Or at best, if he belong to the prosaic provinces, he may be a "Hodman;" Fichte even calls him elsewhere a "Nonentity," and has in short no mercy for him, no wish that *he* should continue happy among us! This is Fichte's notion of the Man of Letters.   It means, in its own form, precisely what we here mean.

In this point of view, I consider that, for the last hundred years, by far the notablest of all Literary Men is Fichte's countryman, Goethe.   To that man too, in a strange way, there was given what we may call a life in the Divine Idea of the World; vision of the inward divine mystery: and strangely, out of his Books, the world rises imaged once more as godlike, the workmanship and temple of a God.   Illuminated all, not in fierce impure fire-splendor as of Mahomet, but in mild celestial radiance; — really a Prophecy in these most unprophetic times; to my mind, by far the greatest, though one of the quietest, among all the great things that have come to pass in them.   Our chosen specimen of the Hero as Literary Man would be this Goethe.   And it were a very pleasant plan for me here to discourse of his heroism: for I consider him to be a true Hero; heroic in what he said and did, and perhaps still more in what he did not say and did not do; to me a noble spectacle : a great heroic ancient man, speaking and keeping silence as an ancient Hero, in the guise of a most modern, high-bred, high-cultivated Man of Letters !   We have had no such spectacle; no man capable of affording such, for the last hundred-and-fifty years.

But at present, such is the general state of knowledge about Goethe, it were worse than useless to attempt speaking of him in this case.   Speak as I might, Goethe, to the great majority of you, would remain problematic, vague ; no impression but a false one could be realized.   Him we must leave to future times.   Johnson, Burns, Rousseau, three great figures from a prior time, from a far inferior state of circumstances, will suit us better here.   Three men of the Eighteenth Century ; the conditions of their life far

more resemble what those of ours still are in England,
than what Goethe's in Germany were. Alas, these
men did not conquer like him; they fought bravely,
and fell. They were not heroic bringers of the light,
but heroic seekers of it. They lived under galling
conditions; struggling as under mountains of impedi-
ment, and could not unfold themselves into clearness,
or victorious interpretation of that " Divine Idea." It
is rather the *Tombs* of three Literary Heroes that I
have to show you. There are the monumental heaps,
under which three spiritual giants lie buried. Very
mournful, but also great and full of interest for us.
We will linger by them for a while.

Complaint is often made, in these times, of what we
call the disorganized condition of society: how ill
many arranged forces of society fulfil their work; how
many powerful forces are seen working in a wasteful,
chaotic, altogether unarranged manner. It is too just
a complaint, as we all know. But perhaps if we look
at this of Books and the Writers of Books, we shall
find here, as it were, the summary of all other disorganization; — a sort of *heart*, from which, and to
which, all other confusion circulates in the world!
Considering what Book-writers do in the world, and
what the world does with Book-writers, I should say,
It is the most anomalous thing the world at present
has to show. We should get into a sea far beyond
sounding, did we attempt to give account of this: but
we must glance at it for the sake of our subject. The
worst element in the life of these three Literary
Heroes was, that they found their business and position such a chaos. On the beaten road there is tolerable travelling; but it is sore work, and many have to
perish, fashioning a path through the impassable!

Our pious Fathers, feeling well what importance lay
in the speaking of man to men, founded churches,

made endowments, regulations; everywhere in the civilized world there is a Pulpit, environed with all manner of complex dignified appurtenances and furtherances, that therefrom a man with the tongue may, to best advantage, address his fellow-men. They felt that this was the most important thing; that without this there was no good thing. It is a right pious work, that of theirs; beautiful to behold! But now with the art of Writing, with the art of Printing, a total change has come over that business. The Writer of a Book, is not he a Preacher preaching not to this parish or that, on this day or that, but to all men in all times and places? Surely it is of the last importance that *he* do his work right, whoever do it wrong; — that the *eye* report not falsely, for then all the other members are astray! Well; how he may do his work, whether he do it right or wrong, or do it at all, is a point which no man in the world has taken the pains to think of. To a certain shopkeeper, trying to get some money for his books, if lucky, he is of some importance; to no other man of any. Whence he came, whither he is bound, by what ways he arrived, by what he might be furthered on his course, no one asks. He is an accident in society. He wanders like a wild Ishmaelite, in a world of which he is as the spiritual light, either the guidance or the misguidance!

Certainly the Art of Writing is the most miraculous of all things man has devised. Odin's " Runes " were the first form of the work of a Hero; *Books*, written words, are still miraculous " Runes," the latest form! In Books lies the *soul* of the whole Past Time; the articulate audible voice of the Past, when the body and material substance of it has altogether vanished like a dream. Mighty fleets and armies, harbors and arsenals, vast cities, high-domed, many-engined, —

they are precious, great: but what do they become? Agamemnon, the many Agamemnons, Pericleses, and their Greece; all is gone now to some ruined fragments, dumb mournful wrecks and blocks: but the Books of Greece! There Greece to every thinker, still very literally lives; can be called-up again into life. No magic " Rune " is stranger than a Book. All that Mankind has done, thought, gained or been: it is lying as in magic preservation in the pages of Books. They are the chosen possession of men.

Do not Books still accomplish *miracles*, as *Runes* were fabled to do? They persuade men. Not the wretchedest circulating-library novel, which foolish girls thumb and con in remote villages, but will help to regulate the actual practical weddings and households of those foolish girls. So " Celia " felt, so " Clifford " acted: the foolish Theorem of Life, stamped into those young brains, comes out as a solid Practice one day. Consider whether any *Rune* in the wildest imagination of Mythologists ever did such wonders as, on the actual firm Earth, some Books have done! What built St. Paul's Cathedral? Look at the heart of the matter, it was that divine Hebrew BOOK, — the word partly of the man Moses, an outlaw tending his Midianitish herds, four-thousand years ago, in the wilderness of Sinai! It is the strangest of things, yet nothing is truer. With the art of Writing, of which Printing is a simple, an inevitable and comparatively insignificant corollary, the true reign of miracles for mankind commenced. It related, with a wondrous new contiguity and perpetual closeness, the Past and Distant with the Present in time and place; all times and all places with this our actual Here and Now. All things were altered for men; all modes of important work of men: teaching, preaching, governing, and all else.

To look at Teaching, for instance. Universities are a notable, respectable product of the modern ages. Their existence too is modified, to the very basis of it, by the existence of Books. Universities arose while there were yet no Books procurable; while a man, for a single Book, had to give an estate of land. That, in those circumstances, when a man had some knowledge to communicate, he should do it by gathering the learners round him, face to face, was a necessity for him. If you wanted to know what Abelard knew, you must go and listen to Abelard. Thousands, as many as thirty-thousand, went to hear Abelard and that metaphysical theology of his. And now for any other teacher who had also something of his own to teach, there was a great convenience opened: so many thousands eager to learn were already assembled yonder; of all places the best place for him was that. For any third teacher it was better still; and grew ever the better, the more teachers there came. It only needed now that the King took notice of this new phenomenon; combined or agglomerated the various schools into one school; gave it edifices, privileges, encouragements, and named it *Universitas*, or School of all Sciences; the University of Paris, in its essential characters, was there. The model of all subsequent Universities; which down even to these days, for six centuries now, have gone on to found themselves. Such, I conceive, was the origin of Universities.

It is clear, however, that with this simple circumstance, facility of getting Books, the whole conditions of the business from top to bottom were changed. Once invent Printing, you metamorphosed all Universities, or superseded them! The Teacher needed not now to gather men personally round him, that he might *speak* to them what he knew: print it in a

Book, and all learners far and wide, for a trifle, had it each at his own fireside, much more effectually to learn it! Doubtless there is still peculiar virtues in Speech; even writers of Books may still, in some circumstances, find it convenient to speak also, — witness our present meeting here! There is, one would say, and must ever remain while man has a tongue, a distinct province for Speech as well as for Writing and Printing. In regard to all things this must remain; to Universities among others. But the limits of the two have nowhere yet been pointed out, ascertained; much less put in practice: the University which would completely take-in that great new fact, of the existence of Printed Books, and stand on a clear footing for the Nineteenth Century as the Paris one did for the Thirteenth, has not yet come into existence. If we think of it, all that a University, or final highest School can do for us, is still but what the first School began doing, — teach us to *read*. We learn to *read*, in various languages, in various sciences; we learn the alphabet and letters of all manner of Books. But the place where we are to get knowledge, even theoretic knowledge, is the Books themselves! It depends on what we read, after all manner of Professors have done their best for us. The true University of these days is a Collection of Books.

But to the Church itself, as I hinted already, all is changed, in its preaching, in its working, by the introduction of Books. The Church is the working recognized Union of our Priests or Prophets, of those who by wise teaching guide the souls of men. While there was no Writing, even while there was no Easy-writing or *Printing*, the preaching of the voice was the natural sole method of performing this. But now with Books! He that can write a true Book, to persuade England, is not he the Bishop and Archbishop, the Primate of England and of All England? I many a time say, the writers of Newspapers, Pamphlets, Poems, Books, these *are* the real working effective Church of a modern country. Nay not only our preaching, but even our worship, is not it too accomplished by means of Printed Books? The noble sentiment which a gifted soul has clothed for us in melodious words, which brings melody into our hearts, — is not this essentially, if we will understand it, of the nature of worship? There are many, in all countries, who, in this confused time, have no other method of worship. He who, in any way, shows us better than we knew before that a lily of the fields is beautiful, does he not show it us as an effluence of the Fountain of all Beauty; as the *handwriting*, made visible there, of the great Maker of the Universe? He has sung for us, made us sing with him, a little verse of a sacred Psalm. Essentially so. How much more he who sings, who says, or in any way brings home to our heart the noble doings, feelings, darings and endurances of a brother man! He has verily touched our hearts as with a live coal *from the altar.* Perhaps there is no worship more authentic.

Literature, so far as it is Literature, is an "apocalypse of Nature," a revealing of the "open secret." It may well enough be named, in Fichte's style, a "continuous revelation" of the Godlike in the Terrestrial and Common. The Godlike does ever, in very truth, endure there; is brought out, now in this dialect, now in that, with various degrees of clearness: all true gifted Singers and Speakers are, consciously or unconsciously, doing so. The dark stormful indignation of a Byron, so wayward and perverse, may have touches of it; nay the withered mockery of a French sceptic, — his mockery of the False, a love and worship of the True. How much more the sphere-harmony of a

Shakspeare, of a Goethe; the cathedral-music of a Milton! They are something too, those humble genuine lark-notes of a Burns, — skylark, starting from the humble furrow, far overhead into the blue depths, and singing to us so genuinely there! For all true singing is of the nature of worship; as indeed all true *working* may be said to be, — whereof such *singing* is but the record, and fit melodious representation, to us. Fragments of a real " Church Liturgy " and " Body of Homilies," strangely disguised from the common eye, are to be found weltering in that huge froth-ocean of Printed Speech we loosely call Literature! Books are our Church too.

Or turning now to the Government of men. Witenagemote, old Parliament, was a great thing. The affairs of the nation were there deliberated and decided; what we were to *do* as a nation. But does not, though the name Parliament subsists, the parliamentary debate go on now, everywhere and at all times, in a far more comprehensive way, *out* of Parliament altogether? Burke said there were Three Estates in Parliament; but, in the Reporters' Gallery yonder, there sat a *Fourth Estate* more important far than they all. It is not a figure of speech, or a witty saying; it is a literal fact, — very momentous to us in these times. Literature is our Parliament too. Printing, which comes necessarily out of Writing, I say often, is equivalent to Democracy: invent Writing, Democracy is inevitable. Writing brings Printing; brings universal everyday extempore Printing, as we see at present. Whoever can speak, speaking now to the whole nation, becomes a power, a branch of government, with inalienable weight in lawmaking, in all acts of authority. It matters not what rank he has, what revenues or garnitures : the requisite thing is, that he have a tongue which others will listen to; this and nothing more is requisite. The nation is governed by all that has tongue in the nation: Democracy is virtually *there.* Add only, that whatsoever power exists will have itself, by and by, organized; working secretly under bandages, obscurations, obstructions, it will never rest till it get to work free, unencumbered, visible to all. Democracy virtually extant will insist on becoming palpably extant. —

On all sides, are we not driven to the conclusion that, of the things which man can do or make here below, by far the most momentous, wonderful and worthy are the things we call Books! Those poor bits of rag-paper with black ink on them; — from the Daily Newspaper to the sacred Hebrew BOOK, what have they not done, what are they not doing! For indeed whatever be the outward form of the thing (bits of paper, as we say, and black ink), is it not verily, at bottom, the highest act of man's faculty that produces a Book? It is the *Thought* of man; the true thaumaturgic virtue; by which man works all things whatsoever. All that he does, and brings to pass, is the vesture of a Thought. This London City, with all its houses, palaces, steamengines, cathedrals, and huge immeasurable traffic and tumult, what is it but a Thought, but millions of Thoughts made into One; a huge immeasurable Spirit of a THOUGHT, embodied in brick, in iron, smoke, dust, Palaces, Parliaments, Hackney Coaches, Katherine Docks, and the rest of it! Not a brick was made but some man had to *think* of the making of that brick. The thing we called "bits of paper with traces of black ink," is the *purest* embodiment a Thought of man can have. No wonder it is, in all ways, the activest and noblest.

All this, of the importance and supreme importance of the Man of Letters in modern Society, and how the Press is to such a degree superseding the Pulpit, the

Senate, the *Senatus Academicus* and much else, has been admitted for a good while; and recognized often enough, in late times, with a sort of sentimental triumph and wonderment. It seems to me, the Sentimental by and by will have to give place to the Practical. If Men of Letters *are* so incalculaby influential, actually performing such work for us from age to age, and even from day to day, then I think we may conclude that Men of Letters will not always wander like unrecognized unregulated Ishmaelites among us! Whatsoever thing, as I said above, has virtual unnoticed power will cast-off its wrappages, bandages, and step-forth one day with palpably articulated, universally visible power. That one man wear the clothes, and take the wages, of a function which is done by quite another: there can be no profit in this; this is not right, it is wrong. And yet, alas, the *making* of it right, — what a business, for long times to come! Sure enough, this that we call Organization of the Literary Guild is still a great way off, encumbered with all manner of complexities. If you asked me what were the best possible organization for the Men of Letters in modern society; the arrangement of furtherance and regulation, grounded the most accurately on the actual facts of their position and of the world's position, — I should beg to say that the problem far exceeded my faculty! It is not one man's faculty; it is that of many successive men turned earnestly upon it, that will bring-out even an approximate solution. What the best arrangement were, none of us could say. But if you ask, Which is the worst? I answer: This which we now have, that Chaos should sit umpire in it; this is the worst. To the best, or any good one, there is yet a long way.

One remark I must not omit, That royal or parliamentary grants of money are by no means the chief thing wanted! To give our Men of Letters stipends, endowments and all furtherance of cash, will do little towards the business. On the whole, one is weary of hearing about the omnipotence of money. I will say rather that, for a genuine man, it is no evil to be poor; that there ought to be Literary Men poor, — to show whether they are genuine or not! Mendicant Orders, bodies of good men doomed to *beg*, were instituted in the Christian Church; a most natural and even necessary development of the spirit of Christianity. It was itself founded on Poverty, on Sorrow, Contradiction, Crucifixion, every species of worldly Distress and Degradation. We may say, that he who has not known those things, and learned from them the priceless lessons they have to teach, has missed a good opportunity of schooling. To beg, and go barefoot, in coarse woollen cloak with a rope round your loins, and be despised of all the world, was no beautiful business; — nor an honorable one in any eye, till the nobleness of those who did so had made it honored of some!

Begging is not in our course at the present time: but for the rest of it, who will say that a Johnson is not perhaps the better for being poor? It is needful for him, at all rates, to know that outward profit, that success of any kind is *not* the goal he has to aim at. Pride, vanity, ill-conditioned egoism of all sorts, are bred in his heart, as in every heart; need, above all, to be cast-out of his heart, — to be, with whatever pangs, torn-out of it, cast-forth from it, as a thing worthless. Byron, born rich and noble, made-out even less than Burns, poor and plebeian. Who knows but, in that same "best possible organization" as yet far off, Poverty may still enter as an important element? What if our Men of Letters, men setting-up to be Spiritual Heroes, were still *then*, as they now are, a kind of "involuntary monastic order;" bound still to this same ugly Poverty, — till they had tried what was in it too, till they had learned to make it too do for them! Money, in truth, can do much, but it cannot do all. We must know the province of it, and confine it there; and even spurn it back, when it wishes to get farther.

Besides, were the money-furtherances, the proper season for them, the fit assigner of them, all settled, — how is the Burns to be recognized that merits these? He must pass through the ordeal, and prove himself. *This* ordeal; this wild welter of a chaos which is called Literary Life: this too is a kind of ordeal! There is clear truth in the idea that a struggle from the lower classes of society, towards the upper regions and rewards of society, must ever continue. Strong men are born there, who ought to stand elsewhere than there. The manifold, inextricably complex, universal struggle of these constitutes, and must constitute, what is called the progress of society. For Men of Letters, as for all other sorts of men. How to regulate that struggle? There is the whole question. To leave it as it is, at the mercy of blind Chance; a whirl of distracting atoms, one cancelling the other; one of the thousand arriving saved, nine-hundred-and-ninety-nine lost by the way; your royal Johnson languishing inactive in garrets, or harnessed to the yoke of Printer Cave; your Burns dying broken-hearted as a Gauger; your Rousseau driven into mad exasperation, kindling French Revolutions by his paradoxes: this, as we said, is clearly enough the *worst* regulation. The *best*, alas, is far from us!

And yet there can be no doubt but it is coming; advancing on us, as yet hidden in the bosom of centuries : this is a prophecy one can risk. For so soon as men get to discern the importance of a thing, they do infallibly set about arranging it, facilitating, forwarding it; and rest not till, in some approximate degree, they have accomplished that. I say, of all Priesthoods, Aristocracies, Governing Classes at present extant in the world, there is no class comparable for importance to that Priesthood of the Writers of Books. This is a fact which he who runs may read, — and draw inferences from. "Literature will take care of itself," answered Mr. Pitt, when applied-to for some help for Burns. "Yes," adds Mr. Southey, "it will take care of itself; *and of you too*, if you do not look to it!"

The result to individual Men of Letters is not the momentous one; they are but individuals, an infinitesimal fraction of the great body; they can struggle on, and live or else die, as they have been wont. But it deeply concerns the whole society, whether it will set its *light* on high places, to walk thereby; or trample it under foot, and scatter it in all ways of wild waste (not without conflagration), as heretofore! Light is the one thing wanted for the world. Put wisdom in the head of the world, the world will fight its battle victoriously, and be the best world man can make it. I call this anomaly of a disorganic Literary Class the heart of all other anomalies, at once product and parent; some good arrangement for that would be as the *punctum saliens* of a new vitality and just arrangement for all. Already, in some European countries, in France, in Prussia, one traces some beginnings of an arrangement for the Literary Class; indicating the gradual possibility of such. I believe that it is possible; that it will have to be possible.

By far the most interesting fact I hear about the Chinese is one on which we cannot arrive at clearness, but which excites endless curiosity even in the dim state: this namely, that they do attempt to make their Men of Letters their Governors! It would be rash to say, one understood how this was done, or with what degree of success it was done. All such things must be very *un*successful; yet a small degree of success is precious; the very attempt how precious! There does seem to be, all over China, a more or less active search everywhere to discover the men of talent that grow up in the young generation. Schools there are for every one: a foolish sort of training, yet still a sort. The youths who distinguish themselves in the lower school are promoted into favorable stations in the higher, that they may still more distinguish themselves, — forward and forward: it appears to be out of these that the Official Persons, and incipient Governors, are taken. These are they whom they *try* first, whether they can govern or not. And surely with the best hope: for they are the men that have already shown intellect. Try them: they have not governed or administered as yet; perhaps they cannot; but there is no doubt they *have* some Understanding, — without which no man can! Neither is Understanding a *tool*, as we are too apt to figure; "it is a *hand* which can handle any tool." Try these men: they are of all others the best worth trying. Surely there is no kind of government, constitution, revolution, social apparatus or arrangement, that I know of in this world, so promising to one's scientific curiosity as this. The man of intellect at the top of affairs: this is the aim of all constitutions and revolutions, if they have any aim. For the man of true intellect, as I assert and believe always, is the noble-hearted man withal, the true, just, humane and valiant man. Get *him* for governor, all is got; fail to get him, though you had Constitutions plentiful as blackberries, and a Parliament in every village, there is nothing yet got! —

These things look strange, truly; and are not such

as we commonly speculate upon. But we are fallen into strange times; these things will require to be speculated upon; to be rendered practicable, to be in some way put in practice. These, and many others. On all hands of us, there is the announcement, audible enough, that the old Empire of Routine has ended; that to say a thing has long been, is no reason for its continuing to be. The things which have been are fallen into decay, are fallen into incompetence; large masses of mankind, in every society of our Europe, are no longer capable of living at all by the things which have been. When millions of men can no longer by their utmost exertion gain food for themselves, and " the third man for thirty-six weeks each year is short of third-rate potatoes," the things which have been must decidedly prepare to alter themselves! I will **now** quit this of the organization of Men of Letters.

Alas, the evil that pressed heaviest on those Literary Heroes of ours was not the want of organization for Men of Letters, but a far deeper one; out of which, indeed, this and so many other evils for the Literary Man, and for all men, had, as from their fountain, taken rise. That our Hero as Man of Letters had to travel without highway, companionless, through an inorganic chaos, — and to leave his own life and faculty lying there, as a partial contribution towards *pushing* some highway through it: this, had not his faculty itself been so perverted and paralyzed, he might have put-up with, might have considered to be but the common lot of Heroes. His fatal misery was the *spiritual paralysis*, so we may name it, of the Age in which his life lay; whereby his life too, do what he might, was half-paralyzed! The Eighteenth was a *Sceptical* Century; in which little word there is a

whole Pandora's Box of miseries. Scepticism means
not intellectual Doubt alone, but moral Doubt; all
sorts of *in*fidelity, insincerity, spiritual paralysis. Perhaps, in few centuries that one could specify since the
world began, was a life of Heroism more difficult for
a man. That was not an age of Faith, — an age of
Heroes! The very possibility of Heroism had been,
as it were, formally abnegated in the minds of all.
Heroism was gone forever: Triviality, Formulism
and Commonplace were come forever. The "age of
miracles" had been, or perhaps had not been; but
it was not any longer. An effete world; wherein
Wonder, Greatness, Godhood could not now dwell; —
in one word, a godless world!

How mean, dwarfish are their ways of thinking, in
this time, — compared not with the Christian Shakspeares and Miltons, but with the old Pagan Skalds,
with any species of believing men! The living Tree
Igdrasil, with the melodious prophetic waving of its
world-wide boughs, deep-rooted as Hela, has died-out
into the clanking of a World-Machine. "Tree" and
"Machine:" contrast these two things. I, for my
share, declare the world to be no machine! I say
that it does *not* go by wheel-and-pinion "motives,"
self-interests, checks, balances; that there is something far other in it than the clank of spinning-jennies,
and parliamentary majorities; and, on the whole, that
it is not a machine at all! The old Norse Heathen
had a truer notion of God's-world than these poor
Machine-Sceptics: the old Heathen Norse were *sincere* men. But for these poor Sceptics there was no
sincerity, no truth. Half-truth and hearsay was called
truth. Truth, for most men, meant plausibility; to be
measured by the number of votes you could get.
They had lost any notion that sincerity was possible,
or of what sincerity was. How many Plausibilities

asking, with unaffected surprise and the air of offended virtue, What! am not I sincere? Spiritual Paralysis, I say, nothing left but a Mechanical life, was the characteristic of that century. For the common man, unless happily he stood *below* his century and belonged to another prior one, it was impossible to be a Believer, a Hero; he lay buried, unconscious, under these baleful influences. To the strongest man, only with infinite struggle and confusion was it possible to work himself half-loose; and lead as it were, in an enchanted, most tragical way, a spiritual death-in-life, and be a Half-Hero!

Scepticism is the name we give to all this; as the chief symptom, as the chief origin of all this. Concerning which so much were to be said! It would take many Discourses, not a small fraction of one Discourse, to state what one feels about that Eighteenth Century and its ways. As indeed this, and the like of this, which we now call Scepticism, is precisely the black malady and life-foe, against which all teaching and discoursing since man's life began has directed itself: the battle of Belief against Unbelief is the never-ending battle! Neither is it in the way of crimination that one would wish to speak. Scepticism, for that century, we must consider as the decay of old ways of believing, the preparation afar off for new, better and wider ways, — an inevitable thing. We will not blame men for it; we will lament their hard fate. We will understand that destruction of old *forms* is not destruction of everlasting *substances;* that Scepticism, as sorrowful and hateful as we see it, is not an end but a beginning.

The other day speaking, without prior purpose that way, of Bentham's theory of man and man's life, I chanced to call it a more beggarly one than Mahomet's. I am bound to say, now when it is once uttered, that such is my deliberate opinion. Not that one would mean offence against the man Jeremy Bentham, or those who respect and believe him. Bentham himself, and even the creed of Bentham, seems to me comparatively worthy of praise. It is a determinate *being* what all the world, in a cowardly half-and-half manner, was tending to be. Let us have the crisis; we shall either have death or the cure. I call this gross, steamengine Utilitarianism an approach towards new Faith. It was a laying-down of cant; a saying to oneself: "Well then, this world is a dead iron machine, the god of it Gravitation and selfish Hunger; let us see what, by checking and balancing, and good adjustment of tooth and pinion, can be made of it!" Benthamism has something complete, manful, in such fearless committal of itself to what it finds true; you may call it Heroic, though a Heroism with its *eyes* put out! It is the culminating point, and fearless ultimatum, of what lay in the half-and-half state, pervading man's whole existence in that Eighteenth Century. It seems to me, all deniers of Godhood, and all lip-believers of it, are bound to be Benthamites, if they have courage and honesty. Benthamism is an *eyeless* Heroism: the Human Species, like a hapless blinded Samson grinding in the Philistine Mill, clasps convulsively the pillars of its Mill; brings huge ruin down, but ultimately deliverance withal. Of Bentham I meant to say no harm.

But this I do say, and would wish all men to know and lay to heart, that he who discerns nothing but Mechanism in the Universe has in the fatalest way missed the secret of the Universe altogether. That all Godhood should vanish out of men's conception of this Universe seems to me precisely the most brutal error, — I will not disparage Heathenism by calling it a Heathen error, — that men could fall into. It is

not true ; it is false at the very heart of it.   A man
who thinks so will think *wrong* about all things in the
world ; this original sin will vitiate all other conclu-
sions he can form.   One might call it the most lamentable of Delusions, — not forgetting Witchcraft itself !
Witchcraft worshipped at least a living Devil ; but
this worships a dead iron Devil ; no God, not even a
Devil !   Whatsoever is noble, divine, inspired, drops
thereby out of life.   There remains everywhere in life
a despicable *caput-mortuum ;* the mechanical hull, all
soul fled out of it.   How can a man act heroically?
The "Doctrine of Motive" will teach him that it is,
under more or less disguise, nothing but a wretched
love of Pleasure, fear of Pain ;   that Hunger, of ap-
plause, of cash, of whatsoever victual it may be, is the
ultimate fact of man's life.   Atheism, in brief ; —
which does indeed frightfully punish itself.   The
man, I say, is become spiritually a paralytic man ; this
godlike Universe a dead mechanical steamengine, all
working by motives, checks, balances, and I know
not what ; wherein, as in the detestable belly of some
Phalaris'-Bull of his own contriving, he the poor
Phalaris sits miserably dying !

Belief I define to be the healthy act of a man's
mind.   It is a mysterious indescribable process, that
of getting to believe ; — indescribable, as all vital acts
are.   We have our mind given us, not that it may
cavil and argue, but that it may see into something,
give us clear belief and understanding about something,
whereon we are then to proceed to act.   Doubt, truly,
is not itself a crime.   Certainly we do not rush out,
clutch-up the first thing we find, and straightway
believe that !   All manner of doubt, inquiry, σκέψις as
it is named, about all manner of objects, dwells in
every reasonable mind.   It is the mystic working of the
mind, on the object it is *getting* to know and believe.

Belief comes out of all this, above ground, like the tree from its hidden *roots*. But now if, even on common things, we require that a man keep his doubts *silent*, and not babble of them till they in some measure become affirmations or denials; how much more in regard to the highest things, impossible to speak-of in words at all! That a man parade his doubt, and get to imagine that debating and logic (which means at best only the manner of *telling* us your thought, your belief or disbelief, about a thing) is the triumph and true work of what intellect he has: alas, this is as if you should *overturn* the tree, and instead of green boughs, leaves and fruits, show us ugly taloned roots turned-up into the air, — and no growth, only death and misery going-on!

For the Scepticism, as I said, is not intellectual only; it is moral also; a chronic atrophy and disease of the whole soul. A man lives by believing something; not by debating and arguing about many things. A sad case for him when all that he can manage to believe is something he can button in his pocket, and with one or the other organ eat and digest! Lower than that he will not get. We call those ages in which he gets so low the mournfulest, sickest and meanest of all ages. The world's heart is palsied, sick: how can any limb of it be whole? Genuine Acting ceases in all departments of the world's work; dextrous Similitude of Acting begins. The world's wages are pocketed, the world's work is not done. Heroes have gone-out; Quacks have come-in. Accordingly, what Century, since the end of the Roman world, which also was a time of scepticism, simulacra and universal decadence, so abounds with Quacks as that Eighteenth? Consider them, with their tumid sentimental vaporing about virtue, benevolence, — the wretched Quack-squadron, Cagliostro at

the head of them ! Few men were without quackery ;
they had got to consider it a necessary ingredient and
amalgam for truth. Chatham, our brave Chatham
himself, comes down to the House, all wrapt and ban-
daged ; he " has crawled out in great bodily suffering,"
and so on ; — *forgets*, says Walpole, that he is acting
the sick man ; in the fire of debate, snatches his arm
from the sling, and oratorically swings and brandishes
it ! Chatham himself lives the strangest mimetic life,
half-hero, half-quack, all along. For indeed the world
is full of dupes ; and you have to gain the *world's* suffrage ! How the duties of the world will be done in
that case, what quantites of error, which means failure,
which means sorrow and misery, to some and to many,
will gradually accumulate in all provinces of the world's
business, we need not compute.

It seems to me, you lay your finger here on the
heart of the world's maladies, when you call it a Sceptical World. An insincere world ; a godless untruth
of a world ! It is out of this, as I consider, that the
whole tribe of social pestilences, French Revolutions,
Chartisms, and what not, have derived their being, —
their chief necessity to be. This must alter. Till this
alter, nothing can beneficially alter. My one hope of
the world, my inexpugnable consolation in looking at
the miseries of the world, is that this is altering.
Here and there one does now find a man who knows,
as of old, that this world is a Truth, and no Plausibility and Falsity ; that he himself is alive, not dead or
paralytic ; and that the world is alive, instinct with Godhood, beautiful and awful, even as in the beginning of
days ! One man once knowing this, many men, all
men, must by and by come to know it. It lies there
clear, for whosoever will take the *spectacles* off his
eyes and honestly look, to know ! For such a man the
Unbelieving Century, with its unblessed Products, is

already past : a new century is already come. The old unblessed Products and Performances, as solid as they look, are Phantasms, preparing speedily to vanish. To this and the other noisy, very great-looking Simulacrum with the whole world huzzahing at its heels, he can say, composedly stepping aside : Thou art not *true;* thou art not extant, only semblant ; go thy way ! Yes, hollow Formulism, gross Benthamism, and other unheroic atheistic Insincerity is visibly and even rapidly declining. An unbelieving Eighteenth Century is but an exception, — such as now and then occurs. I prophesy that the world will once more become *sincere;* a believing world ; with *many* Heroes in it, a heroic world ! It will then be a victorious world; never till then.

Or indeed what of the world and its victories ? Men speak too much about the world. Each one of us here, let the world go how it will, and be victorious or not victorious, has he not a Life of his own to lead ? One Life ; a little gleam of Time between two Eternities ; no second chance to us forevermore ! It were well for *us* to live not as fools and simulacra, but as wise and realities. The world's being saved will not save us ; nor the world's being lost destroy us. We should look to ourselves : there is great merit here in the " duty of staying at home " ! And, on the whole, to say truth, I never heard of " worlds " being " saved " in any other way. That mania of saving worlds is itself a piece of the Eighteenth Century with his windy sentimentalism. Let us not follow it too far. For the saving of the *world* I will trust confidently to the Maker of the world ; and look a little to my own saving, which I am more competent to ! In brief, for the world's sake, and for our own, we will rejoice greatly that Scepticism, Insincerity, Mechanical Atheism, with all their poison-dews, are going, and as good as gone.

Now it was under such conditions, in those times of Johnson, that our Men of Letters had to live. Times in which there was properly no truth in life. Old truths had fallen nigh dumb; the new lay yet hidden, not trying to speak. That Man's Life here below was a Sincerity and Fact, and would forever continue such, no new intimation, in that dusk of the world, had yet dawned. No intimation; not even any French Revolution, — which we define to be a Truth once more, though a Truth clad in hellfire! How different was the Luther's pilgrimage, with its assured goal, from the Johnson's, girt with mere traditions, suppositions, grown now incredible, unintelligible! Mahomet's Formulas were of "wood waxed and oiled," and could be *burnt* out of one's way: poor Johnson's were far more difficult to burn. The strong man will ever find *work*, which means difficulty, pain, to the full measure of his strength. But to make-out a victory, in those circumstances of our poor Hero as Man of Letters, was perhaps more difficult than in any. Not obstruction, disorganization, Bookseller Osborne and Fourpence-halfpenny a day; not this alone; but the light of his own soul was taken from him. No landmark on the Earth; and, alas, what is that to having no loadstar in the Heaven! We need not wonder that none of those Three men rose to victory. That they fought truly is the highest praise. With a mournful sympathy we will contemplate, if not three living victorious Heroes, as I said, the Tombs of three fallen Heroes! They fell for us too; making a way for us. There are the mountains which they hurled abroad in their confused War of the Giants; under which, their strength and life spent, they now lie buried.

I have already written of these three Literary Heroes, expressly or incidentally; what I suppose is known to most of you; what need not be spoken or written a second time. They concern us here as the singular *Prophets* of that singular age; for such they virtually were; and the aspect they and their world exhibit, under this point of view, might lead us into reflections enough! I call them, all three, Genuine Men more or less; faithfully, for most part unconsciously, struggling, to be genuine, and plant themselves on the everlasting truth of things. This to a degree that eminently distinguishes them from the poor artificial mass of their contemporaries; and renders them worthy to be considered as Speakers, in some measure, of the everlasting truth, as Prophets in that age of theirs. By Nature herself a noble necessity was laid on them to be so. They were men of such magnitude that they could not live on unrealities, — clouds, froth and all inanity gave-way under them: there was no footing for them but on firm earth; no rest or regular motion for them, if they got not footing there. To a certain extent, they were Sons of Nature once more in an age of Artifice; once more, Original Men.

As for Johnson, I have always considered him to be, by nature, one of our great English souls. A strong and noble man; so much left undeveloped in him to the last: in a kindlier element what might he not have been, — Poet, Priest, sovereign Ruler! On the whole, a man must not complain of his "element," of his "time," or the like; it is thriftless work doing so. His time is bad: well then, he is there to make it better! Johnson's youth was poor, isolated, hopeless, very miserable. Indeed, it does not seem possible that, in any the favorablest outward circumstances, Johnson's life could have been other than a painful one. The world might have had more of profitable *work* out of him, or less; but his *effort* against the

world's work could never have been a light one.
Nature, in return for his nobleness, had said to him,
Live in an element of diseased sorrow. Nay, perhaps
the sorrow and the nobleness were intimately and even
inseparably connected with each other. At all events,
poor Johnson had to go about girt with continual
hypochondria, physical and spiritual pain. Like a
Hercules with the burning Nessus'-shirt on him, which
shoots-in on him dull incurable misery: the Nessus'-
shirt not to be stript-off, which is his own natural skin!
In this manner *he* had to live. Figure him there, with
his scrofulous diseases, with his great greedy heart,
and unspeakable chaos of thoughts; stalking mournful as a stranger in this Earth; eagerly devouring
what spiritual thing he could come at: school languages and other merely grammatical stuff, if there
were nothing better! The largest soul that was in all
England; and provision made for it of "fourpence-
halfpenny a day." Yet a giant invincible soul; a true
man's. One remembers always that story of the shoes
at Oxford: the rough, seamy-faced, rawboned College
Servitor stalking about, in winter-season, with his
shoes worn-out; how the charitable Gentleman Com-
moner secretly places a new pair at his door; and the
rawboned Servitor, lifting them, looking at them near,
with his dim eyes, with what thoughts, — pitches them
out of window! Wet feet, mud, frost, hunger or what
you will; but not beggary: we cannot stand beggary!
Rude stubborn self-help here; a whole world of
squalor, rudeness, confused misery and want, yet of
nobleness and manfulness withal. It is a type of the
man's life, this pitching-away of the shoes. An original man; — not a secondhand, borrowing or begging
man. Let us stand on our own basis, at any rate!
On such shoes as we ourselves can get. On frost and
mud, if you will, but honestly on that; — on the reality

and substance which Nature gives *us*, not on the semblance, on the thing she has given another than us ! —

And yet with all this rugged pride of manhood and self-help, was there ever soul more tenderly affectionate, loyally submissive to what was really higher than he ? Great souls are always loyally submissive, reverent to what is over them; only small mean souls are otherwise. I could not find a better proof of what I said the other day, That the sincere man was by nature the obedient man; that only in a World of Heroes was there loyal Obedience to the Heroic. The essence of *originality* is not that it be *new :* Johnson believed altogether in the old; he found the old opinions credible for him, fit for him; and in a right heroic manner lived under them. He is well worth study in regard to that. For we are to say that Johnson was far other than a mere man of words and formulas; he was a man of truths and facts. He stood by the old formulas; the happier was it for him that he could so stand : but in all formulas that *he* could stand by, there needed to be a most genuine substance. Very curious how, in that poor Paper-age, so barren, artificial, thick-quilted with Pedantries, Hearsays, the great Fact of this Universe glared in, forever wonderful, indubitable, unspeakable, divine-infernal, upon this man too ! How he harmonized his Formulas with it, how he managed at all under such circumstances : that is a thing worth seeing. A thing " to be looked at with reverence, with pity, with awe." That Church of St. Clement Danes, where Johnson still *worshipped* in the era of Voltaire, is to me a venerable place.

It was in virtue of his *sincerity*, of his speaking still in some sort from the heart of Nature, though in the current artificial dialect, that Johnson was a Prophet. Are not all dialects " artificial " ? Artificial things

14

are not all false; — nay every true Product of Nature will infallibly *shape* itself; we may say all artificial things are, at the starting of them, *true*. What we call "Formulas" are not in their origin bad; they are indispensably good. Formula is *method*, habitude; found wherever man is found. Formulas fashion themselves as Paths do, as beaten Highways, leading towards some sacred or high object, whither many men are bent. Consider it. One man, full of heart-felt earnest impulse, finds-out a way of doing some-what, — were it of uttering his soul's reverence for the Highest, were it but of fitly saluting his fellow-man. An inventor was needed to do that, a *poet;* he has articulated the dim-struggling thought that dwelt in his own and many hearts. This is his way of doing that; these are his footsteps, the beginning of a "Path." And now see: the second man travels nat-urally in the footsteps of his foregoer, it is the *easiest* method. In the footsteps of his foregoer; yet with improvements, with changes where such seem good; at all events with enlargements, the Path ever *widen-ing* itself as more travel it; — till at last there is a broad Highway whereon the whole world may travel and drive. While there remains a City or Shrine, or any Reality to drive to, at the farther end, the High-way shall be right welcome! When the City is gone, we will forsake the Highway. In this manner all Institutions, Practices, Regulated Things in the world have come into existence, and gone out of existence. Formulas all begin by being *full* of substance; you may call them the *skin*, the articulation into shape, into limbs and skin, of a substance that is already there: *they* had not been there otherwise. Idols, as we said, are not idolatrous till they become doubtful, empty for the worshipper's heart. Much as we talk against Formulas, I hope no one of us is ignorant withal of the high significance of *true* Formulas; that they were, and will ever be, the indispensablest furniture of our habitation in this world.

Mark, too, how little Johnson boasts of his "sincerity." He has no suspicion of his being particularly sincere, — of his being particularly anything! A hard-struggling, weary-hearted man, or "scholar" as he calls himself, trying hard to get some honest livelihood in the world, not to starve, but to live — without stealing! A noble unconsciousness is in him. He does not "engrave *Truth* on his watch-seal;" no, but he stands by truth, speaks by it, works and lives by it. Thus it ever is. Think of it once more. The man whom Nature has appointed to do great things is, first of all, furnished with that openness to Nature which renders him incapable of being *in*sincere! To his large, open, deep-feeling heart Nature is a Fact: all hearsay is hearsay; the unspeakable greatness of this Mystery of Life, let him acknowledge it or not, nay even though he seem to forget it or deny it, is ever present to *him*, — fearful and wonderful, on this hand and on that. He has a basis of sincerity; unrecognized, because never questioned or capable of question. Mirabeau, Mahomet, Cromwell, Napoleon: all the Great Men I ever heard-of have this as the primary material of them. Innumerable commonplace men are debating, are talking everywhere their commonplace doctrines, which they have learned by logic, by rote, at secondhand: to that kind of man all this is still nothing. He must have truth; truth which *he* feels to be true. How shall he stand otherwise? His whole soul, at all moments, in all ways, tells him that there is no standing. He is under the noble necessity of being true. Johnson's way of thinking about this world is not mine, any more than Mahomet's was: but I recognize the everlasting element of heart-*sincerity* in both; and see with pleasure how neither of them remains ineffectual. Neither of them is as *chaff* sown; in both of them is something which the seed-field will *grow*.

Johnson was a Prophet to his people; preached a Gospel to them, — as all like him always do. The highest Gospel he preached we may describe as a kind of Moral Prudence: "in a world where much is to be done, and little is to be known," see how you will *do* it! A thing well worth preaching. "A world where much is to be done, and little is to be known:" do not sink yourselves in boundless bottomless abysses of Doubt, of wretched god-forgetting Unbelief; — you were miserable then, powerless, mad: how could you *do* or work at all? Such Gospel Johnson preached and taught; — coupled, theoretically and practically, with this other great Gospel, "Clear your mind of Cant!" Have no trade with Cant: stand on the cold mud in the frosty weather, but let it be in your own *real* torn shoes: "that will be better for you," as Mahomet says! I call this, I call these two things *joined together*, a great Gospel, the greatest perhaps that was possible at that time.

Johnson's Writings, which once had such currency and celebrity, are now, as it were, disowned by the young generation. It is not wonderful; Johnson's opinions are fast becoming obsolete: but his style of thinking and of living, we may hope, will never become obsolete. I find in Johnson's Books the indisputablest traces of a great intellect and great heart; — ever welcome, under what obstructions and perversions soever. They are *sincere* words, those of his; he means things by them. A wondrous buckram style, — the best he could get to then; a measured grandiloquence, stepping or rather stalking along in a very solemn way, grown obsolete now; sometimes a tumid *size* of phraseology not in proportion to the contents of it : all this you will put-up with. For the phraseology, tumid or not, has always *something within it.* So many beautiful styles and books, with *nothing* in them ; — a man is a *male*factor to the world who writes such ! *They* are the avoidable kind ! Had Johnson left nothing but his *Dictionary*, one might have traced there a great intellect, a genuine man. Looking to its clearness of definition, its general solidity, honesty, insight and successful method, it may be called the best of all Dictionaries. There is in it a kind of architectural nobleness ; it stands there like a great solid square-built edifice, finished, symmetrically complete : you judge that a true Builder did it.

One word, in spite of our haste, must be granted to poor Bozzy. He passes for a mean, inflated, gluttonous creature ; and was so in many senses. Yet the fact of his reverence for Johnson will ever remain noteworthy. The foolish conceited Scotch Laird, the most conceited man of his time, approaching in such awestruck attitude the great dusty irascible Pedagogue in his mean garret there : it is a genuine reverence for Excellence ; a *worship* for Heroes, at a time when neither Heroes nor worship were surmised to exist. Heroes, it would seem, exist always, and a certain worship of them ! We will also take the liberty to deny altogether that of the witty Frenchman, that no man is a Hero to his valet-de-chambre. Or if so, it is not the Hero's blame, but the Valet's : that his soul, namely, is a mean *valet*-soul ! He expects his Hero to advance in royal stage-trappings, with measured step, trains borne behind him, trumpets sounding before him. It should stand rather, No man can be a *Grand-Monarque* to his valet-de-chambre. Strip your Louis Quatorze of his king-gear, and there *is* left nothing but a poor forked radish with a head fantastically carved;—admirable to no valet. The Valet does not know a Hero when he sees him! Alas, no: it requires a kind of *Hero* to do that;—and one of the world's wants, in *this* as in other senses, is for most part want of such.

On the whole, shall we not say, that Boswell's admiration was well bestowed; that he could have found no soul in all England so worthy of bending down before? Shall we not say, of this great mournful Johnson too, that he guided his difficult confused existence wisely; led it *well*, like a right-valiant man? That waste chaos of Authorship by trade; that waste chaos of Scepticism in religion and politics, in life-theory and life-practice; in his poverty, in his dust and dimness, with the sick body and the rusty coat: he made it do for him, like a brave man. Not wholly without a loadstar in the Eternal; he had still a loadstar, as the brave all need to have: with his eye set on that, he would change his course for nothing in these confused vortices of the lower sea of Time. "To the Spirit of Lies, bearing death and hunger, he would in no wise strike his flag." Brave old Samuel: *ultimus Romanorum!*

Of Rousseau and his Heroism I cannot say so much. He is not what I call a strong man. A morbid, excitable, spasmodic man; at best, intense rather than strong. He had not "the talent of Silence," an invaluable talent; which few Frenchmen, or indeed men of any sort in these times, excel in! The suffering man ought really "to consume his own smoke;" there is no good in emitting *smoke* till you have made it into *fire*,—which, in the metaphorical sense too, all smoke is capable of becoming! Rousseau has not depth or width, not calm force for difficulty; the first characteristic of true greatness. A fundamental mistake to call vehemence and rigidity strength! A man is not strong who takes convulsion-fits; though six men cannot hold him then. He that can walk under the heaviest weight without staggering, he is the strong man. We need forever, especially in these loud-shrieking days, to remind ourselves of that. A man who cannot *hold his peace*, till the time come for speaking and acting, is no right man.

Poor Rousseau's face is to me expressive of him. A high but narrow contracted intensity in it: bony brows; deep, strait-set eyes, in which there is something bewildered-looking, — bewildered, peering with lynx-eagerness. A face full of misery, even ignoble misery, and also of the antagonism against that; something mean, plebeian there, redeemed only by *intensity* : the face of what is called a Fanatic, — a sadly *contracted* Hero! We name him here because, with all his drawbacks, and they are many, he has the first and chief characteristic of a Hero : he is heartily *in earnest*. In earnest, if ever man was; as none of these French *Philosophes* were. Nay, one would say, of an earnestness too great for his otherwise sensitive, rather feeble nature; and which indeed in the end drove him into the strangest incoherences, almost delirations. There had come, at last, to be a kind of madness in him : his Ideas *possessed* him like demons; hurried him so about, drove him over steep places! —

The fault and misery of Rousseau was what we easily name by a single word, *Egoism ;* which is indeed the source and summary of all faults and miseries whatsoever. He had not perfected himself into victory over mere Desire; a mean Hunger, in many sorts, was still the motive principle of him. I am afraid he was a very vain man; hungry for the praises of men. You remember Genlis's experience of him. She took Jean Jacques to the Theatre; he bargaining for a strict incognito, — "*He* would not be seen there for the world!" The curtain did happen nevertheless to be drawn aside: the Pit recognized Jean Jacques, but took no great notice of him! He expressed the bitterest indignation; gloomed all evening, spake no other than surly words. The glib Countess remained entirely convinced that his anger was not at being seen, but at not being applauded when seen. How the whole nature of the man is poisoned; nothing but suspicion, self-isolation, fierce moody ways! He could not live with anybody. A man of some rank from the country, who visited him often, and used to sit with him, expressing all reverence and affection for him, comes one day; finds Jean Jacques full of the sourest unintelligible humor. "Monsieur," said Jean Jacques, with flaming eyes, "I know why you come here. You come to see what a poor life I lead; how little is in my poor pot that is boiling there. Well, look into the pot! There is half a pound of meat, one carrot and three onions; that is all: go and tell the whole world that, if you like, Monsieur!" A man of this sort was far gone. The whole world got itself supplied with anecdotes, for light laughter, for a certain theatrical interest, from these perversions and contortions of poor Jean Jacques. Alas, to him they were not laughing or theatrical; too real to him! The contortions of a dying gladiator: the crowded amphitheatre looks-on with entertainment; but the gladiator is in agonies and dying.

And yet this Rousseau, as we say, with his passionate appeals to Mothers, with his *Contrat-social*, with his celebrations of Nature, even of savage life in Nature, did once more touch upon Reality, struggle towards Reality; was doing the function of a Prophet to his Time. As *he* could, and as the Time could! Strangely through all that defacement, degradation and almost madness, there is in the inmost heart of poor Rousseau a spark of real heavenly fire. Once more, out of the element of that withered mocking Philosophism, Scepticism and Persiflage, there has arisen in this man the ineradicable feeling and knowledge that this Life of ours is *true;* not a Scepticism, Theorem, or Persiflage, but a Fact, an awful Reality. Nature had made that revelation to him; had ordered him to speak it out. He got it spoken out; if not well and clearly, then ill and dimly, — as clearly as he could. Nay what are all errors and perversities of his, even those stealings of ribbons, aimless confused miseries and vagabondisms, if we will interpret them kindly, but the blinkard dazzlement and staggerings to and fro of a man sent on an errand he is too weak for, by a path he cannot yet find? Men are led by strange ways. One should have tolerance for a man, hope of him; leave him to try yet what he will do. While life lasts, hope lasts for every man.

Of Rousseau's literary talents, greatly celebrated still among his countrymen, I do not say much. His Books, like himself, are what I call unhealthy; not the good sort of Books. There is a sensuality in Rousseau. Combined with such an intellectual gift as his, it makes pictures of a certain gorgeous attractiveness: but they are not genuinely poetical. Not white sunlight: something *operatic;* a kind of rosepink, artificial bedizenment. It is frequent, or rather it is universal, among the French since his time. Madame de Staël has something of it; St. Pierre; and down onwards to the present astonishing convulsionary "Literature of Desperation," it is everywhere abundant. That same *rosepink* is not the right hue. Look at a Shakspeare, at a Goethe, even at a Walter Scott! He who has once seen into this, has seen the difference of the True from the Sham-True, and will discriminate them ever afterwards.

We had to observe in Johnson how much good a Prophet, under all disadvantages and disorganizations, can accomplish for the world. In Rousseau we are called to look rather at the fearful amount of evil which, under such disorganization, may accompany the good. Historically it is a most pregnant spectacle, that of Rousseau. Banished into Paris garrets, in the gloomy company of his own Thoughts and Necessities there; driven from post to pillar; fretted, exasperated till the heart of him went mad, he had grown to feel deeply that the world was not his friend nor the world's law. It was expedient, if any way possible, that such a man should *not* have been set in flat hostility with the world. He could be cooped into garrets, laughed at as a maniac, left to starve like a wild-beast in his cage;—but he could not be hindered from setting the world on fire. The French Revolution found its Evangelist in Rousseau. His semi-delirious speculations on the miseries of civilized life, the preferability of the savage to the civilized, and suchlike, helped well to produce a whole delirium in France generally. True, you may well ask, What could the world, the governors of the world, do with such a man? Difficult to say what the governors of the world could do with him! What he could do with them is unhappily clear enough,—*guillotine* a great many of them! Enough now of Rousseau.

It was a curious phenomenon, in the withered, unbelieving, secondhand Eighteenth Century, that of a Hero starting up, among the artificial pasteboard figures and productions, in the guise of a Robert Burns. Like a little well in the rocky desert places,—like a sudden splendor of Heaven in the artificial Vauxhall! People knew not what to make of it. They took it for a piece of the Vauxhall fire-work;

alas, it *let* itself be so taken, though struggling half-blindly, as in bitterness of death, against that! Perhaps no man had such a false reception from his fellow-men. Once more a very wasteful life-drama was enacted under the sun.

The tragedy of Burns's life is known to all of you. Surely we may say, if discrepancy between place held and place merited constitute perverseness of lot for a man, no lot could be more perverse than Burns's. Among those secondhand acting-figures, *mimes* for most part, of the Eighteenth Century, once more a giant Original Man; one of those men who reach down to the perennial Deeps, who take rank with the Heroic among men : and he was born in a poor Ayrshire hut. The largest soul of all the British lands came among us in the shape of a hard-handed Scottish Peasant.

His Father, a poor toiling man, tried various things; did not succeed in any; was involved in continual difficulties. The Steward, Factor as the Scotch call him, used to send letters and threatenings, Burns says, "which threw us all into tears." The brave, hard-toiling, hard-suffering Father, his brave heroine of a wife; and those children, of whom Robert was one! In this Earth, so wide otherwise, no shelter for *them*. The letters "threw us all into tears": figure it. The brave Father, I say always; — a *silent* Hero and Poet; without whom the son had never been a speaking one! Burns's Schoolmaster came afterwards to London, learnt what good society was; but declares that in no meeting of men did he ever enjoy better discourse than at the hearth of this peasant. And his poor "seven acres of nursery-ground," — not that, nor the miserable patch of clay-farm, nor anything he tried to get a living by, would prosper with him; he had a sore unequal battle all his days. But he stood to it valiantly; a wise, faithful, unconquerable man;— swallowing-down how many sore sufferings daily into silence; fighting like an unseen Hero,—nobody publishing newspaper paragraphs about his nobleness; voting pieces of plate to him! However, he was not lost: nothing is lost. Robert is there; the outcome of him,—and indeed of many generations of such as him.

This Burns appeared under every disadvantage: uninstructed, poor, born only to hard manual toil; and writing, when it came to that, in a rustic special dialect, known only to a small province of the country he lived in. Had he written, even what he did write, in the general language of England, I doubt not he had already become universally recognized as being, or capable to be, one of our greatest men. That he should have tempted so many to penetrate through the rough husk of that dialect of his, is proof that there lay something far from common within it. He has gained a certain recognition, and is continuing to do so over all quarters of our wide Saxon world: wheresoever a Saxon dialect is spoken, it begins to be understood, by personal inspection of this and the other, that one of the most considerable Saxon men of the Eighteenth Century was an Ayrshire Peasant named Robert Burns. Yes, I will say, here too was a piece of the right Saxon stuff: strong as the Harz-rock, rooted in the depths of the world;—rock, yet with wells of living softness in it! A wild impetuous whirlwind of passion and faculty slumbered quiet there; such heavenly *melody* dwelling in the heart of it. A noble rough genuineness; homely, rustic, honest; true simplicity of strength; with its lightning-fire, with its soft dewy pity;—like the old Norse Thor, the Peasant-god!—

Burns's Brother Gilbert, a man of much sense and

worth, has told me that Robert, in his young days, in spite of their hardship, was usually the gayest of speech; a fellow of infinite frolic, laughter, sense and heart; far pleasanter to hear there, stript cutting peats in the bog, or suchlike, than he ever afterwards knew him. I can well believe it. This basis of mirth ("*fond gaillard,*" as old Marquis Mirabeau calls it), a primal-element of sunshine and joyfulness, coupled with his other deep and earnest qualities, is one of the most attractive characteristics of Burns. A large fund of Hope dwells in him; spite of his tragical history, he is not a mourning man. He shakes his sorrows gallantly aside; bounds forth victorious over them. It is as the lion shaking " dew-drops from his mane; " as the swift-bounding horse, that *laughs* at the shaking of the spear. But indeed, Hope, Mirth, of the sort like Burns's, are they not the outcome properly of warm generous affection, — such as is the beginning of all to every man?

You would think it strange if I called Burns the most gifted British soul we had in all that century of his: and yet I believe the day is coming when there will be little danger in saying so. His writings, all that he *did* under such obstructions, are only a poor fragment of him. Professor Stewart remarked very justly, what indeed is true of all Poets good for much, that his poetry was not any particular faculty; but the general result of a naturally vigorous original mind expressing itself in that way. Burns's gifts, expressed in conversation, are the theme of all that ever heard him. All kinds of gifts: from the gracefulest utterances of courtesy, to the highest fire of passionate speech; loud floods of mirth, soft wailings of affection, laconic emphasis, clear piercing insight; all was in him. Witty duchesses celebrate him as a man whose speech "led them off their feet." This is beautiful: but still more beautiful that which Mr. Lockhart has recorded, which I have more than once alluded to, How the waiters and hostlers at inns would get out of bed, and come crowding to hear this man speak! Waiters and hostlers: — they too were men, and here was a man! I have heard much about his speech; but one of the best things I ever heard of it was, last year, from a venerable gentleman long familiar with him. That it was speech distinguished by always *having something in it.* " He spoke rather little than much," this old man told me; " sat rather silent in those early days, as in the company of persons above him; and always when he did speak, it was to throw new light on the matter." I know not why any one should ever speak otherwise! But if we look at his general force of soul, his healthy *robustness* everyway, the rugged downrightness, penetration, generous valor and manfulness that was in him, — where shall we readily find a better-gifted man?

Among the great men of the Eighteenth Century, I sometimes feel as if Burns might be found to resemble Mirabeau more than any other. They differ widely in vesture; yet look at them intrinsically. There is the same burly thick-necked strength of body as of soul; — built, in both cases, on what the old Marquis calls a *fond gaillard.* By nature, by course of breeding, indeed by nation, Mirabeau has much more of bluster; a noisy, forward, unresting man. But the characteristic of Mirabeau too is veracity and sense, power of true *insight*, superiority of vision. The thing that he says is worth remembering. It is a flash of insight into some object or other: so do both these men speak. The same raging passions; capable too in both of manifesting themselves as the tenderest noble affections. Wit, wild laughter, energy, directness, sincerity: these were in both. The types of the two

men are not dissimilar. Burns too could have governed, debated in National Assemblies; politicized,
as few could. Alas, the courage which had to exhibit
itself in capture of smuggling schooners in the Solway
Frith; in keeping *silence* over so much, where no
good speech, but only inarticulate rage was possible:
this might have bellowed forth Ushers de Brézé and
the like; and made itself visible to all men, in man-
aging of kingdoms, in ruling of great ever-memorable
epochs! But they said to him reprovingly, his Official
Superiors said, and wrote: "You are to work, not
think." Of your *thinking*-faculty, the greatest in this
land, we have no need; you are to gauge beer there;
for that only are *you* wanted. Very notable; — and
worth mentioning, though we know what is to be said
and answered! As if Thought, Power of Thinking,
were not, at all time, in all places and situations of
the world, precisely the thing that *was* wanted. The
fatal man, is he not always the *un*thinking man, the
man who cannot think and *see;* but only grope, and
hallucinate, and *mis*see the nature of the thing he
works with? He misses it, mis*takes* it as we say;
takes it for one thing, and it *is* another thing, — and
leaves him standing like a Futility there! He is the
fatal man; unutterably fatal, put in the high places of
men. "Why complain of this?" say some: "Strength
is mournfully denied its arena; that was true from of
old." Doubtless; and the worse for the *arena*, answer I! *Complaining* profits little; stating of the
truth may profit. That a Europe, with its French
Revolution just breaking out, finds no need of a Burns
except for gauging beer, — is a thing I, for one, cannot
rejoice at!

Once more we have to say here, that the chief
quality of Burns is the *sincerity* of him. So in his
Poetry, so in his Life. The Song he sings is not of

fantasticalities ; it is of a thing felt, really there ; the prime merit of this, as of all in him, and of his Life generally, is truth. The Life of Burns is what we may call a great tragic sincerity. A sort of savage sincerity, — not cruel, far from that ; but wild, wrestling naked with the truth of things. In that sense, there is something of the savage in all great men.

Hero-worship, — Odin, Burns ? Well ; these Men of Letters too were not without a kind of Hero-worship : but what a strange condition has that got into now! The waiters and hostlers of Scotch inns, prying about the door, eager to catch any word that fell from Burns, were doing unconscious reverence to the Heroic. Johnson had his Boswell for worshipper. Rosseau had worshippers enough ; princes calling on him in his mean garret ; the great, the beautiful doing reverence to the poor moonstruck man. For himself a most portentous contradiction ; the two ends of his life not to be brought into harmony. He sits at the tables of grandees ; and has to copy music for his own living. He cannot even get his music copied. " By dint of dining out," says he, "I run the risk of dying by starvation at home." For his worshippers too a most questionable thing ! If doing Hero-worship well or badly be the test of vital wellbeing or illbeing to a generation, can we say that *these* generations are very first-rate ? And yet our heroic Men of Letters do teach, govern, are kings, priests, or what you like to call them ; intrinsically there is no preventing it by any means whatever. The world *has* to obey him who thinks and sees in the world. The world can alter the manner of that ; can either have it as blessed continuous summer sunshine, or as unblessed black thunder and tornado, — with unspeakable difference of profit for the world ! The manner of it is very alterable ; the matter and fact of it is not alterable by any power under the sky. Light; or, failing that, lightning : the world can take its choice. Not whether we call an Odin god, prophet, priest, or what we call him ; but whether we believe the word he tells us : there it all lies. If it be a true word, we shall have to believe it; believing it, we shall have to do it What *name* or welcome we give him or it, is a point that concerns ourselves mainly. *It*, the new Truth, new deeper revealing of the Secret of this Universe, is verily of the nature of a message from on high; and must and will have itself obeyed. —

My last remark is on that notablest phasis of Burns's history, — his visit to Edinburgh. Often it seems to me as if his demeanor there were the highest proof he gave of what a fund of worth and genuine manhood was in him. If we think of it, few heavier burdens could be laid on the strength of a man. So sudden; all common *Lionism*, which ruins innumerable men, was as nothing to this. It is as if Napoleon had been made a King of, not gradually, but at once from the Artillery Lieutenancy in the Regiment La Fère. Burns, still only in his twenty-seventh year, is no longer even a ploughman; he is flying to the West Indies to escape disgrace and a jail. This month he is a ruined peasant, his wages seven pounds a year, and these gone from him : next month he is in the blaze of rank and beauty, handing down jewelled Duchesses to dinner; the cynosure of all eyes! Adversity is sometimes hard upon a man; but for one man who can stand prosperity, there are a hundred that will stand adversity. I admire much the way in which Burns met all this. Perhaps no man one could point out, was ever so sorely tried, and so little forgot himself. Tranquil, unastonished; not abashed, not inflated, neither awkwardness nor affectation : he feels that *he* there is the man Robert

15

Burns; that the "rank is but the guinea-stamp;" that the celebrity is but the candle-light, which will show *what* man, not in the least make him a better or other man! Alas, it may readily, unless he look to it, make him a *worse* man; a wretched inflated windbag, — inflated till he *burst*, and become a *dead* lion; for whom, as some one has said, "there is no resurrection of the body;" worse than a living dog! — Burns is admirable here.

And yet, alas, as I have observed elsewhere, these Lion-hunters were the ruin and death of Burns. It was they that rendered it impossible for him to live! They gathered round him in his Farm; hindered his industry; no place was remote enough from them. He could not get his Lionism forgotten, honestly as he was disposed to do so. He falls into discontents, into miseries, faults; the world getting ever more desolate for him; health, character, peace of mind all gone; — solitary enough now. It is tragical to think of! These men came but to *see* him; it was out of no sympathy with him, nor no hatred to him. They came to get a little amusement: they got their amusement; — and the Hero's life went for it!

Richter says, in the Island of Sumatra there is a kind of "Light-chafers," large Fire-flies, which people stick upon spits, and illuminate the ways with at night. Persons of condition can thus travel with a pleasant radiance, which they much admire. Great honor to the Fire-flies! But! —

LECTURE VI.

THE HERO AS KING. — CROMWELL, NAPOLEON: MODERN REVOLUTIONISM.

WE come now to the last form of Heroism; that which we call Kingship. The Commander over Men; he to whose will our wills are to be subordinated, and loyally surrender themselves, and find their welfare in doing so, may be reckoned the most important of Great Men. He is practically the summary for us of *all* the various figures of Heroism; Priest, Teacher, whatsoever of earthly or of spiritual dignity we can fancy to reside in a man, embodies itself here, to *command* over us, to furnish us with constant practical teaching, to tell us for the day and hour what we are to *do*. He is called *Rex*, Regulator, *Roi:* our own name is still better; King, *Könning*, which means *Can*-ning, Able-man.

Numerous considerations, pointing towards deep, questionable, and indeed unfathomable regions, present themselves here: on the most of which we must resolutely for the present forbear to speak at all. As Burke said that perhaps fair *Trial by Jury* was the soul of Government, and that all legislation, administration, parliamentary debating, and the rest of it, went on, in "order to bring twelve impartial men into a jury-box;"—so, by much stronger reason, may I say here, that the finding of your *Ableman* and getting him invested with the *symbols of ability*, with dignity, worship (*worth*-ship), royalty, kinghood, or whatever we call it, so that *he* may actually have room to guide according to his faculty of doing it,—is the business, well or ill accomplished, of all social procedure whatsoever in this world! Hustings-speeches, Parliamentary motions, Reform Bills, French Revolutions, all mean at heart this; or else nothing. Find in any country the Ablest Man that exists there; raise *him* to the supreme place, and loyally reverence him: you have a perfect government for that country; no ballot-box, parliamentary eloquence, voting, constitution-building, or other machinery whatsoever can improve it a whit. It is in the perfect state; an ideal country. The Ablest Man; he means also the truest-hearted, justest, the Noblest Man: what he *tells us to do* must be precisely the wisest, fittest, that we could anywhere or anyhow learn;—the thing which it will in all ways behoove us, with right loyal thankfulness, and nothing doubting, to do! Our *doing* and life were then, so far as government could regulate it, well regulated; that were the ideal of constitutions.

Alas, we know very well that Ideals can never be completely embodied in practice. Ideals must ever lie a very great way off; and we will right thankfully content ourselves with any not intolerable approximation thereto! Let no man, as Schiller says, too querulously "measure by a scale of perfection the meagre product of reality" in this poor world of ours. We will esteem him no wise man; we will esteem him a sickly, discontented, foolish man. And yet, on the other hand, it is never to be forgotten that Ideals do exist; that if they be not approximated to at all, the whole matter goes to wreck! Infallibly. No brick-layer builds a wall *perfectly* perpendicular, mathematically this is not possible; a certain degree of perpendicularity suffices him; and he, like a good bricklayer, who must have done with his job, leaves it so. And yet if he sway *too much* from the perpendicular; above

all, if he throw plummet and level quite away from
him, and pile brick on brick heedless, just as it comes
to hand! — Such bricklayer, I think, is in a bad way.
He has forgotten himself: but the Law of Gravitation
does not forget to act on him; he and his wall rush-
down into confused welter of ruin! —

This is the history of all rebellions, French Revolutions, social explosions in ancient or modern times.
You have put the too *Un*able Man at the head of
affairs! The too ignoble, unvaliant, fatuous man.
You have forgotten that there is any rule, or natural
necessity whatever, of putting the Able Man there.
Brick must lie on brick as it may and can. Unable
Simulacrum of Ability, *quack*, in a word, must adjust
himself with quack, in all manner of administration of
human things; — which accordingly lie unadministered,
fermenting into unmeasured masses of failure, of in-
digent misery: in the outward, and in the inward or
spiritual, miserable millions stretch-out the hand for
their due supply, and it is not there. The "law of
gravitation" acts; Nature's laws do none of them
forget to act. The miserable millions burst-forth into
Sansculottism, or some other sort of madness: bricks
and bricklayer lie as a fatal chaos! —

Much sorry stuff, written some hundred years ago
or more, about the "Divine right of Kings," moulders
unread now in the Public Libraries of this country.
Far be it from us to disturb the calm process by
which it is disappearing harmlessly from the earth, in
those repositories! At the same time, not to let the
immense rubbish go without leaving us, as it ought,
some soul of it behind — I will say that it did mean
something; something true, which it is important for
us and all men to keep in mind. To assert that in
whatever man you chose to lay hold of (by this or the
other plan of clutching at him); and clapt a round

piece of metal on the head of, and called King, —
there straightway came to reside a divine virtue, so
that *he* became a kind of god, and a Divinity inspired
him with faculty and right to rule over you to all
lengths: this, — what can we do with this but leave
it to rot silently in the Public Libraries? But I will
say withal, and that is what these Divine right-men
meant, That in Kings, and in all human Authorities,
and relations that men god-created can form among
each other, there is verily either a Divine Right or
else a Diabolic Wrong; one or the other of these two!
For it is false altogether, what the last Sceptical Century taught us, that this world is a steamengine.
There is a God in this world; and a God's-sanction,
or else the violation of such, does look-out from all
ruling and obedience, from all moral acts of men.
There is no act more moral between men than that of
rule and obedience. Woe to him that claims obedience when it is not due; woe to him that refuses it
when it is! God's law is in that, I say, however the
Parchment-laws may run: there is a Divine Right or
else a Diabolic Wrong at the heart of every claim that
one man makes upon another.

It can do none of us harm to reflect on this: in all
the relations of life it will concern us; in Loyalty and
Royalty, the highest of these. I esteem the modern
error, That all goes by self-interest and the checking
and balancing of greedy knaveries, and that, in short,
there is nothing divine whatever in the association of
men, a still more despicable error, natural as it is to
an unbelieving century, than that of a " divine right "
in people *called* Kings. I say, Find me the true
Könning, King, or Able-man, and he *has* a divine
right over me. That we knew in some tolerable
measure how to find him, and that all men were ready
to acknowledge his divine right when found: this is

precisely the healing which a sick world is everywhere, in these ages, seeking after! The true King, as guide of the practical, has ever something of the Pontiff in him, — guide of the spiritual, from which all practice has its rise. This too is a true saying, That the *King* is head of the *Church*. But we will leave the Polemic stuff of a dead century to lie quiet on its bookshelves.

Certainly it is a fearful business, that of having your Able-man to *seek*, and not knowing in what manner to proceed about it! That is the world's sad predicament in these times of ours. They are times of revolution, and have long been. The bricklayer with his bricks, no longer heedful of plummet or the law of gravitation, have toppled, tumbled, and it all welters as we see! But the beginning of it was not the French Revolution; that is rather the *end*, we can hope. It were truer to say, the *beginning* was three centuries farther back: in the Reformation of Luther. That the thing which still called itself Christian Church had become a Falsehood, and brazenly went about pretending to pardon men's sins for metallic coined money, and to do much else which in the everlasting truth of Nature it did *not* now do: here lay the vital malady. The inward being wrong, all outward went ever more and more wrong. Belief died away; all was Doubt, Disbelief. The builder *cast away* his plummet; said to himself, "What is gravitation? Brick lies on brick there!" Alas, does it not still sound strange to many of us, the assertion that there *is* a God's-truth in the business of god-created men; that all is not a kind of grimace, an "expediency," diplomacy, one knows not what! —

From that first necessary assertion of Luther's, "You, self-styled *Papa*, you are no Father in God at all; you are — a Chimera, whom I know not how to name in polite language!" — from that onwards to the shout which rose round Camille Desmoulins in the Palais-Royal, "*Aux armes!*" when the people had burst-up against *all* manner of Chimeras, — I find a natural historical sequence. That shout too, so frightful, half-infernal, was a great matter. Once more the voice of awakened nations; — starting confusedly, as out of nightmare, as out of death-sleep, into some dim feeling that Life was real; that God's-world was not an expediency and diplomacy! Infernal; — yes, since they would not have it otherwise. Infernal, since not celestial or terrestrial! Hollow-ness, insincerity *has* to cease; sincerity of some sort has to begin. Cost what it may, reigns of terror, horrors of French Revolution or what else, we have to return to truth. Here is a Truth, as I said: a Truth clad in hellfire, since they would not but have it so! —

A common theory among considerable parties of men in England and elsewhere used to be, that the French Nation had, in those days, as it were gone *mad;* that the French Revolution was a general act of insanity, a temporary conversion of France and large sections of the world into a kind of Bedlam. The Event had risen and raged; but was a madness and nonentity, — gone now happily into the region of Dreams and the Picturesque! To such comfortable philosophers the Three Days of July 1830 must have been a surprising phenomenon. Here is the French Nation risen again, in musketry and death-struggle, out shooting and being shot, to make that same mad French Revolution good! The sons and grandsons of those men, it would seem, persist in the enterprise: they do not disown it; they will have it made good; **will have themselves shot, if it be not made good!**

To philosophers who had made-up their life-system on that "madness" quietus, no phenomenon could be more alarming. Poor Niebuhr, they say, the Prussian Professor and Historian, fell broken-hearted in consequence; sickened, if we can believe it, and died of the Three Days! It was surely not a very heroic death; — little better than Racine's, dying because Louis Fourteenth looked sternly on him once. The world had stood some considerable shocks, in its time; might have been expected to survive the Three Days too, and be found turning on its axis after even them! The Three Days told all mortals that the old French Revolution, mad as it might look, was not a transitory ebullition of Bedlam, but a genuine product of this Earth where we all live; that it was verily a Fact, and that the world in general would do well everywhere to regard it as such.

Truly, without the French Revolution, one would not know what to make of an age like this at all. We will hail the French Revolution, as shipwrecked mariners might the sternest rock, in a world otherwise all of baseless sea and waves. A true Apocalypse, though a terrible one, to this false withered artificial time; testifying once more that Nature is *preter*natural; if not divine, then diabolic; that Semblance is not Reality; that it has to become Reality, or the world will take-fire under it, — burn *it* into what it is, namely Nothing! Plausibility has ended; empty Routine has ended; much has ended. This, as with a Trump of Doom, has been proclaimed to all men. They are the wisest who will learn it soonest. Long confused generations before it be learned; peace impossible till it be! The earnest man, surrounded, as ever, with a world of inconsistencies, can await patiently, patiently strive to do *his* work, in the midst of that. Sentence of Death is written down in Heaven against all that ; sentence of Death is now proclaimed on the Earth against it : this he with his eyes may see. And surely, I should say, considering the other side of the matter, what enormous difficulties lie there, and how fast, fearfully fast, in all countries, the inexorable demand for solution of them is pressing on, — he may easily find other work to do than laboring in the Sansculottic province at this time of day !

To me, in these circumstances, that of "Hero-worship" becomes a fact inexpressibly precious ; the most solacing fact one sees in the world at present. There is an everlasting hope in it for the management of the world. Had all traditions, arrangements, creeds, societies that men ever instituted, sunk away, this would remain. The certainty of Heroes being sent us ; our faculty, our necessity, to reverence Heroes when sent : it shines like a polestar through smoke-clouds, dust-clouds, and all manner of down-rushing and conflagration.

Hero-worship would have sounded very strange to those workers and fighters in the French Revolution. Not reverence for Great Men ; not any hope or belief, or even wish, that Great Men could again appear in the world ! Nature, turned into a " Machine," was as if effete now ; could not any longer produce Great Men : — I can tell her, she may give-up the trade al-together, then ; we cannot do without Great Men ! — But neither have I any quarrel with that of " Liberty and Equality ;" with the faith that, wise great men being impossible, a level immensity of foolish small men would suffice. It was a natural faith then and there. " Liberty and Equality ; no Authority needed any longer. Hero-worship, reverence for *such* Au-thorities, has proved false, is itself a falsehood ; no more of it ! We have had such *forgeries*, we will now trust nothing. So many base plated coins passing in the market, the belief has now become common that no gold any longer exists, — and even that we can do very well without gold!" I find this, among other things, in that universal cry of Liberty and Equality; and find it very natural, as matters then stood.

And yet surely it is but the *transition* from false to true. Considered as the whole truth, it is false altogether; — the product of entire sceptical blindness, as yet only *struggling* to see. Hero-worship exists forever, and everywhere: not Loyalty alone; it extends from divine adoration down to the lowest practical regions of life. "Bending before men," if it is not to be a mere empty grimace, better dispensed with than practised, is Hero-worship, — a recognition that there does dwell in that presence of our brother something divine; that every created man, as Novalis said, is a "revelation in the Flesh." They were Poets too, that devised all those graceful courtesies which make life noble! Courtesy is not a falsehood or grimace; it need not be such. And Loyalty, religious Worship itself, are still possible; nay still inevitable.

May we not say, moreover, while so many of our late Heroes have worked rather as revolutionary men, that nevertheless every Great Man, every genuine man, is by the nature of him a son of Order, not of Disorder? It is a tragical position for a true man to work in revolutions. He seems an anarchist; and indeed a painful element of anarchy does encumber him at every step, — him to whose whole soul anarchy is hostile, hateful. His mission is Order; every man's is. He is here to make what was disorderly, chaotic, into a thing ruled, regular. He is the missionary of Order. Is not all work of man in this world a *making of Order?* The carpenter finds rough trees; shapes them, constrains them into square fitness, into purpose and use. We are all born enemies of Disorder:

it is tragical for us all to be concerned in image-breaking and down-pulling; for the Great Man, *more* a man than we, it is doubly tragical.

Thus too all human things, maddest French Sansculottisms, do and must work towards Order. I say, there is not a *man* in them, raging in the thickest of the madness, but is impelled withal, at all moments, towards Order. His very life means that; Disorder is dissolution, death. No chaos but it seeks a *centre* to revolve round. While man is man, some Cromwell or Napoleon is the necessary finish of a Sansculottism. Curious: in those days when Hero-worship was the most incredible thing to every one, how it does come-out nevertheless, and assert itself practically, in a way which all have to credit. Divine *right*, take it on the great scale, is found to mean divine *might* withal! While old false Formulas are getting trampled everywhere into destruction, new genuine Substances unexpectedly unfold themselves indestructible. In rebellious ages, when Kingship itself seems dead and abolished, Cromwell, Napoleon step-forth again as Kings. The history of these men is what we have now to look at, as our last phasis of Heroism. The old ages are brought back to us; the manner in which Kings were made, and Kingship itself first took rise, is again exhibited in the history of these Two.

We have had many civil-wars in England; wars of Red and White Roses, wars of Simon de Montfort; wars enough, which are not very memorable. But that war of the Puritans has a significance which belongs to no one of the others. Trusting to your candor, which will suggest on the other side what I have not room to say, I will call it a section once more of that great universal war which alone makes-up the true History of the World, — the war of Belief against

Unbelief! The struggle of men intent on the real essence of things, against men intent on the semblances and forms of things. The Puritans, to many, seem mere savage Iconoclasts, fierce destroyers of Forms; but it were more just to call them haters of *untrue* Forms. I hope we know how to respect Laud and his King as well as them. Poor Laud seems to me to have been weak and ill-starred, not dishonest; an unfortunate Pedant rather than anything worse. His "Dreams" and superstitions, at which they laugh so, have an affectionate, lovable kind of character. He is like a College-Tutor, whose whole world is forms, College-rules; whose notion is that these are the life and safety of the world. He is placed suddenly, with that unalterable luckless notion of his, at the head not of a College but of a Nation, to regulate the most complex deep-reaching interests of men. He thinks they ought to go by the old decent regulations; nay that their salvation will lie in extending and improving these. Like a weak man, he drives with spasmodic vehemence towards his purpose; cramps himself to it, heeding no voice of prudence, no cry of pity: He will have his College-rules obeyed by his Collegians; that first; and till that, nothing. He is an ill-starred Pedant, as I said. He would have it the world was a College of that kind, and the world *was not* that. Alas, was not his doom stern enough? Whatever wrongs he did, were they not all frightfully avenged on him?

It is meritorious to insist on forms; Religion and all else naturally clothes itself in forms. Everywhere the *formed* world is the only habitable one. The naked formlessness of Puritanism is not the thing I praise in the Puritans; it is the thing I pity, — praising only the spirit which had rendered that inevitable! All substances clothe themselves in forms: but there are suitable true forms, and then there are untrue unsuitable. As the briefest definition, one might say, Forms which *grow* round a substance, if we rightly understand that, will correspond to the real nature and purport of it, will be true, good ; forms which are consciously *put* round a substance, bad. I invite you to reflect on this. It distinguishes true from false in Ceremonial Form, earnest solemnity from empty pageant, in all human things.

There must be a veracity, a natural spontaneity in forms. In the commonest meeting of men, a person making, what we call, " set speeches," is not he an offence? In the mere drawing-room, whatsoever courtesies you see to be grimaces, prompted by no spontaneous reality within, are a thing you wish to get away from. But suppose now it were some matter of vital concernment, some transcendent matter (as Divine Worship is), about which your whole soul, struck dumb with its excess of feeling, knew not how to *form* itself into utterance at all, and preferred formless silence to any utterance there possible, — what should we say of a man coming forward to represent or utter it for you in the way of upholsterer-mummery? Such a man, — let him depart swiftly, if he love himself! You have lost your only son ; are mute, struck down, without even tears : an importunate man importunately offers to celebrate Funeral Games for him in the manner of the Greeks! Such mummery is not only not to be accepted, — it is hateful, unendurable. It is what the old Prophets called " Idolatry," worshipping of hollow *shows ;* what all earnest men do and will reject. We can partly understand what those poor Puritans meant. Laud dedicating that St. Catherine Creed's Church, in the manner we have it described ; with his multiplied ceremonial bowings, gesticulations, exclamations : surely it is rather the rigorous formal

Pedant, intent on his "College-rules," than the earnest Prophet, intent on the essence of the matter!

Puritanism found *such* forms insupportable; trampled on such forms; — we have to excuse it for saying, No form at all rather than such! It stood preaching in its bare pulpit, with nothing but the Bible in its hand. Nay, a man preaching from his earnest *soul* into the earnest *souls* of men: is not this virtually the essence of all Churches whatsoever? The nakedest, savagest reality, I say, is preferable to any semblance, however dignified. Besides, it will clothe itself with *due* semblance by and by, if it be real. No fear of that; actually no fear at all. Given the living *man*, there will be found *clothes* for him; he will find himself clothes. But the suit-of-clothes pretending that *it* is both clothes and man! — We cannot "fight the French" by three-hundred-thousand red uniforms; there must be *men* in the inside of them! Semblance, I assert, must actually *not* divorce itself from Reality. If Semblance do, — why then there must be men found to rebel against Semblance, for it has become a lie! These two Antagonisms at war here, in the case of Laud and the Puritans, are as old nearly as the world. They went to fierce battle over England in that age; and fought-out their confused controversy to a certain length, with many results for all of us.

In the age which directly followed that of the Puritans, their cause or themselves were little likely to have justice done them. Charles Second and his Rochesters were not the kind of men you would set to judge what the worth or meaning of such men might have been. That there could be any faith or truth in the life of a man, was what these poor Rochesters, and the age they ushered-in, had forgotten. Puritanism was hung on gibbets, — like the bones of the leading Puritans. Its work nevertheless went on accomplishing itself. All true work of a man, hang the author of it on what gibbet you like, must and will accomplish itself. We have our *Habeas-Corpus*, our free Representation of the People; acknowledgment, wide as the world, that all men are, or else must, shall, and will become, what we call *free* men; — men with their life grounded on reality and justice, not on tradition, which has become unjust and a chimera! This in part, and much besides this, was the work of the Puritans.

And indeed, as these things became gradually manifest, the character of the Puritans began to clear itself. Their memories were, one after another, taken *down* from the gibbet; nay a certain portion of them are now, in these days, as good as canonized. Eliot, Hampden, Pym, nay Ludlow, Hutchinson, Vane himself, are admitted to be a kind of Heroes; political Conscript Fathers, to whom in no small degree we owe what makes us a free England: it would not be safe for anybody to designate these men as wicked now. Few Puritans of note but find their apologists somewhere, and have a certain reverence paid them by earnest men. One Puritan, I think, and almost he alone, our poor Cromwell, seems to hang yet on the gibbet, and find no hearty apologist anywhere. Him neither saint nor sinner will acquit of great wickedness. A man of ability, infinite talent, courage, and so forth: but he betrayed the Cause. Selfish ambition, dishonesty, duplicity; a fierce, coarse, hypocritical *Tartufe;* turning all that noble Struggle for constitutional Liberty into a sorry farce played for his own benefit: this and worse is the character they give of Cromwell. And then there come contrasts with Washington and others; above all, with these noble

Pyms and Hampdens, whose noble work he stole for himself, and ruined into a futility and deformity.

This view of Cromwell seems to me the not unnatural product of a century like the Eighteenth. As we said of the Valet, so of the Sceptic: He does not know a Hero when he sees him! The Valet expected purple mantles, gilt sceptres, bodyguards and flourishes of trumpets: the Sceptic of the Eighteenth century looks for regulated respectable Formulas, "Principles," or what else he may call them; a style of speech and conduct which has got to seem "respectable," which can plead for itself in a handsome articulate manner, and gain the suffrages of an enlightened sceptical Eighteenth century! It is, at bottom, the same thing that both the Valet and he expect: the garnitures of some *acknowledged* royalty, which *then* they will acknowledge! The King coming to them in the rugged *un*formulistic state shall be no King.

For my own share, far be it from me to say or insinuate a word of disparagement against such characters as Hampden, Eliot, Pym; whom I believe to have been right worthy and useful men. I have read diligently what books and documents about them I could come at;—with the honestest wish to admire, to love and worship them like Heroes; but I am sorry to say, if the real truth must be told, with very indifferent success! At bottom, I found that it would not do. They are very noble men, these; step along in their stately way, with their measured euphemisms, philosophies, parliamentary eloquences, Ship-moneys, Monarchies of Man; a most constitutional, unblamable, dignified set of men. But the heart remains cold before them; the fancy alone endeavors to get-up some worship of them. What man's heart does, in reality, break-forth into any fire of brotherly love for these men? They are become dreadfully dull men!

16

One breaks-down often enough in the constitutional eloquence of the admirable Pym, with his " seventhly and lastly." You find that it may be the admirablest thing in the world, but that it is heavy, — heavy as lead, barren as brick-clay; that, in a word, for you there is little or nothing now surviving there! One leaves all these Nobilities standing in their niches of honor: the rugged outcast Cromwell, he is the man of them all in whom one still finds human stuff. The great savage *Baresark :* he could write no euphemistic " Monarchy of Man;" did not speak, did not work with glib regularity; had no straight story to tell for himself anywhere. But he stood bare, not cased in euphemistic coat-of-mail; he grappled like a giant, face to face, heart to heart, with the naked truth of things! That, after all, is the sort of man for one. I plead guilty to valuing such a man beyond all other sorts of men. Smooth-shaven Respectabilities not a few one finds, that are not good for much. Small thanks to a man for keeping his hands clean, who would not touch the work but with gloves on!

Neither, on the whole, does this constitutional tolerance of the Eighteenth century for the other happier Puritans seem to be a very great matter. One might say, it is but a piece of Formulism and Scepticism, like the rest. They tell us, It was a sorrowful thing to consider that the foundation of our English Liberties should have been laid by "Superstition." These Puritans came forward with Calvinistic incredible Creeds, Anti-Laudisms, Westminster Confessions; demanding, chiefly of all, that they should have liberty to *worship* in their own way. Liberty to *tax* themselves : that was the thing they should have demanded! It was Superstition, Fanaticism, disgraceful ignorance of Constitutional Philosophy to insist on the other thing! Liberty to *tax* oneself? Not to pay-out money from your pocket except on reason shown? No century, I think, but a rather barren one would have fixed on that as the first right of man! I should say, on the contrary, A just man will generally have better cause than *money* in what shape soever, before deciding to revolt against his Government. Ours is a most confused world; in which a good man will be thankful to see any kind of Government maintain itself in a not insupportable manner: and here in England, to this hour, if he is not ready to pay a great many taxes which *he* can see very small reason in, it will not go well with him, I think! He must try some other climate than this. Taxgatherer? Money? He will say: "Take my money, since you *can*, and it is so desirable to you; take it, — and take yourself away with it; and leave me alone to my work here. *I* am still here; can still work, after all the money you have taken from me!" But if they come to him, and say, "Acknowledge a Lie; pretend to say you are worshipping God, when you are not doing it: believe not the thing that *you* find true, but the thing that I find, or pretend to find true!" He will answer: "No; by God's help, no! You may take my purse; but I cannot have my moral Self annihilated. The purse is any Highwayman's who might meet me with a loaded pistol: but the Self is mine and God my Maker's; it is not yours; and I will resist you to the death, and revolt against you, and, on the whole, front all manner of extremities, accusations and confusions, in defence of that!"

Really, it seems to me the one reason which could justify revolting, this of the Puritans. It has been the soul of all just revolts among men. Not *Hunger* alone produced even the French Revolution; no, but the feeling of the insupportable all-pervading *Falsehood* which had now embodied itself in Hunger, in universal material Scarcity and Nonentity, and thereby become *indisputably* false in the eyes of all! We will leave the Eighteenth century with its "liberty to tax itself." We will not astonish ourselves that the meaning of such men as the Puritans remained dim to it. To men who believe in no reality at all, how shall a *real* human soul, the intensest of all realities, as it were the Voice of the world's Maker still speaking to *us*, — be intelligible? What it cannot reduce into constitutional doctrines relative to "taxing," or other the like material interest, gross, palpable to the sense, such a century will needs reject as an amorphous heap of rubbish. Hampdens, Pyms and Ship-money will be the theme of much constitutional eloquence, striving to be fervid; — which will glitter, if not as fire does, then as *ice* does: and the irreducible Cromwell will remain a chaotic mass of " madness," " hypocrisy," and much else.

From of old, I will confess, this theory of Cromwell's falsity has been incredible to me. Nay I cannot believe the like, of any Great Man whatever. Multitudes of Great Men figure in History as false selfish men; but if we will consider it, they are but *figures* for us, unintelligible shadows; we do not see into them as men that could have existed at all. A superficial unbelieving generation only, with no eye but for the surfaces and semblances of things, could form such notions of Great Men. Can a great soul be possible without a *conscience* in it, the essence of all *real* souls, great or small? No, we cannot figure Cromwell as a Falsity and Fatuity; the longer I study him and his career, I believe this the less. Why should we? There is no evidence of it. Is it not strange that, after all the mountains of calumny this man has been subject to, after being represented as the very prince of liars, who never, or hardly ever, spoke truth, but always some cunning counterfeit of truth, there should not yet have been one falsehood brought clearly home to him? A prince of liars, and no lie spoken by him. Not one that I could yet get sight of. It is like Pococke asking Grotius, Where is your *proof* of Mahomet's Pigeon? No proof! Let us leave all these calumnious chimeras, as chimeras ought to be left. They are not portraits of the man; they are distracted phantasms of him, the joint product of hatred and darkness.

Looking at the man's life with our own eyes, it seems to me, a very different hypothesis suggests itself. What little we know of his earlier obscure years, distorted as it has come down to us, does it not all betoken an earnest, affectionate, sincere kind of man? His nervous melancholic temperament indicates rather a seriousness *too* deep for him. Of those stories of "Spectres;" of the white Spectre in broad daylight predicting that he should be King of England, we are not bound to believe much;—probably no more than of the other black Spectre, or Devil in person, to whom the Officer *saw* him sell himself before Worcester Fight! But the mournful, over-sensitive, hypochondriac humor of Oliver, in his young years, is otherwise indisputably known. The Huntingdon Physician told Sir Philip Warwick himself, He had often been sent for at midnight; Mr. Cromwell was full of hypochondria, thought himself near dying, and "had fancies about the Town-cross." These things are significant. Such an excitable deep-feeling nature, in that rugged stubborn strength of his, is not the symptom of falsehood; it is the symptom and promise of quite other than falsehood!

The young Oliver is sent to study Law; falls, or is said to have fallen, for a little period, into some of the dissipations of youth; but if so, speedily repents, abandons all this: not much above twenty, he is married, settled as an altogether grave and quiet man. "He pays-back what money he had won at gambling," says the story; he does not think any gain of that kind could be really *his*. It is very interesting, very natural, this "conversion," as they well name it; this awakening of a great true soul from the worldly slough, to see into the awful *truth* of things;—to see that Time and its shows all rested on Eternity, and this poor Earth of ours was the threshold either of Heaven or of Hell! Oliver's life at St. Ives and Ely, as a sober industrious Farmer, is it not altogether as that of a true and devout man? He has renounced the world and its ways; *its* prizes are not the thing that can enrich him. He tills the earth; he reads his Bible; daily assembles his servants round him to worship God. He comforts persecuted ministers, is fond of preachers; nay can himself preach,—exhorts his neighbors to be wise, to redeem the time. In all this what "hypocrisy," "ambition," "cant," or other falsity? The man's hopes, I do believe, were fixed on the other Higher World; his aim to get well *thither* by walking well through his humble course in *this* world. He courts no notice: what could notice here do for him? "Ever in his great Taskmaster's eye."

It is striking, too, how he comes-out once into public view; he, since no other is willing to come: in resistance to a public grievance. I mean, in that matter of the Bedford Fens. No one else will go to law with Authority; therefore he will. That matter once settled, he returns back into obscurity, to his Bible and his Plough. "Gain influence"? His influence is the most legitimate; derived from personal knowledge of him, as a just, religious, reasonable and determined man. In this way he has lived till past forty; old age is now in view of him, and the earnest portal of Death and Eternity; it was at this point that he suddenly became "ambitious"! I do not interpret his Parliamentary mission in that way!

His successes in Parliament, his successes through the war, are honest successes of a brave man; who has more resolution in the heart of him, more light in the head of him than other men. His prayers to God; his spoken thanks to the God of Victory, who had preserved him safe, and carried him forward so far, through the furious clash of a world all set in conflict, through desperate-looking envelopments at Dunbar; through the death-hail of so many battles; mercy after mercy; to the "crowning mercy" of Worcester Fight: all this is good and genuine for a deep-hearted Calvinistic Cromwell. Only to vain unbelieving Cavaliers, worshipping not God but their own "lovelocks," frivolities and formalities, living quite apart from contemplations of God, living *without* God in the world, need it seem hypocritical.

Nor will his participation in the King's death involve him in condemnation with us. It is a stern business killing of a King! But if you once go to war with him, it lies *there;* this and all else lies there. Once at war, you have made wager of battle with him: it is he to die, or else you. Reconciliation is problematic; may be possible, or, far more likely, is impossible. It is now pretty generally admitted that the Parliament, having vanquished Charles First, had no way of making any tenable arrangement with him. The large Presbyterian party, apprehensive now of the Independents, were most anxious to do so; anxious indeed as for their own existence; but it could not be. The unhappy Charles, in those final Hampton-Court negotiations, shows himself as a man fatally incapable of being dealt with. A man who, once for all, could not and would not *understand:* — whose thought did not in any measure represent to him the real fact of the matter; nay worse, whose *word* did not at all represent his thought. We may say this of him without cruelty, with deep pity rather: but it is true and undeniable. Forsaken there of all but the *name* of Kingship, he still, finding himself treated with outward respect as a King, fancied that he might play-off party against party, and smuggle himself into his old power by deceiving both. Alas, they both *discovered* that he was deceiving them. A man whose *word* will not inform you at all what he means or will do, is not a man you can bargain with. You must get out of that man's way, or put him out of yours! The Presbyterians, in their despair, were still for believing Charles, though found false, unbelievable again and again. Not so Cromwell: "For all our fighting," says he, "we are to have a little bit of paper?" No! —

In fact, everywhere we have to note the decisive practical *eye* of this man; how he drives towards the practical and practicable; has a genuine insight into what *is* fact. Such an intellect, I maintain, does not belong to a false man: the false man sees false shows, plausibilities, expediences: the true man is needed to discern even practical truth. Cromwell's advice about the Parliament's Army, early in the contest, How they were to dismiss their city-tapsters, flimsy riotous persons, and choose substantial yeomen, whose heart was in the work, to be soldiers for them: this is advice by a man who *saw*. Fact answers, if you see into Fact! Cromwell's *Ironsides* were the embodiment of this insight of his; men fearing God; and without any other fear. No more conclusively genuine set of fighters ever trod the soil of England, or of any other land.

Neither will we blame greatly that word of Cromwell's to them; which was so blamed: "If the King should meet me in battle, I would kill the King." Why not? These words were spoken to men who stood as before a Higher than Kings. They had set more than their own lives on the cast. The Parliament may call it, in official language, a fighting "*for* the King;" but we, for our share, cannot understand that. To us it is no dilettante work, no sleek officiality; it is sheer rough death and earnest. They have brought it to the calling-forth of *War;* horrid internecine fight, man grappling with man in fire-eyed rage, — the *infernal* element in man called forth, to try it by that! *Do* that therefore; since that is the thing to be done. The successes of Cromwell seem to me a very natural thing! Since he was not shot in battle, they were an inevitable thing. That such a man, with the eye to see, with the heart to dare, should advance, from post to post, from victory to victory, till the Huntingdon Farmer became, by whatever name you might call him, the acknowledged Strongest Man in England, virtually the King of England, requires no magic to explain it! —

Truly it is a sad thing for a people, as for a man, to fall into Scepticism, into dilettantism, insincerity; not to know a Sincerity when they see it. For this world, and for all worlds, what curse is so fatal? The heart lying dead, the eye cannot see. What intellect remains is merely the *vulpine* intellect. That a true *King* be sent them is of small use; they do not know him when sent. They say scornfully, Is this your King? The Hero wastes his heroic faculty in bootless contradiction from the unworthy; and can accomplish little. For himself he does accomplish a heroic life, which is much, which is all; but for the world he accomplishes comparatively nothing. The wild rude Sincerity, direct from Nature, is not glib in answering from the witness-box : in your small-debt *pie-powder* court, he is scouted as a counterfeit. The vulpine intellect " detects " him. For being a man worth any thousand men, the response your Knox, your Cromwell gets, is an argument for two centuries whether he was a man at all. God's greatest gift to this Earth is sneeringly flung away. The miraculous talisman is a paltry plated coin, not fit to pass in the shops as a common guinea.

Lamentable this ! I say, this must be remedied. Till this be remedied in some measure, there is nothing remedied. " Detect quacks " ? Yes do, for Heaven's sake ; but know withal the men that are to be trusted ! Till we know that, what is all our knowledge ; how shall we even so much as " detect " ? For the vulpine sharpness, which considers itself to be knowledge, and " detects " in that fashion, is far mistaken. Dupes indeed are many : but, of all *dupes*, there is none so fatally situated as he who lives in undue terror of being duped. The world does exist ; the world has truth in it, or it would not exist ! First recognize what is true, we shall *then* discern what is false ; and properly never till then.

" Know the men that are to be trusted : " alas, this is yet, in these days, very far from us. The sincere alone can recognize sincerity. Not a Hero only is needed, but a world fit for him ; a world not of *Valets ;* — the Hero comes almost in vain to it otherwise ! Yes, it is far from us : but it must come ; thank God, it is visibly coming. Till it do come, what have we ? Ballot-boxes, suffrages, French Revolutions : — if we are as Valets, and do not know the Hero when we see him, what good are all these ? A heroic Cromwell comes ; and for a hundred-and-fifty years he cannot have a vote from us. Why, the insincere, unbelieving world is the *natural property* of the Quack, and of the

Father of quacks and quackeries! Misery, confusion, unveracity are alone possible there. By ballot-boxes we alter the *figure* of our Quack; but the substance of him continues. The Valet-World *has* to be governed by the Sham-Hero, by the King merely *dressed* in King-gear. It is his; he is its! In brief, one of two things: We shall either learn to know a Hero, a true Governor and Captain, somewhat better, when we see him; or else go on to be forever governed by the Unheroic; — had we ballot-boxes clattering at every street-corner, there were no remedy in these.

Poor Cromwell, — great Cromwell! The inarticulate Prophet; Prophet who could not *speak*. Rude, confused, struggling to utter himself, with his savage depth, with his wild sincerity; and he looked so strange, among the elegant Euphemisms, dainty little Falklands, didactic Chillingworths, diplomatic Clarendons! Consider him. An outer hull of chaotic confusion, visions of the Devil, nervous dreams, almost semi-madness; and yet such a clear determinate man's-energy working in the heart of that. A kind of chaotic man. The ray as of pure starlight and fire, working in such an element of boundless hypochondria, *un*-formed black of darkness! And yet withal this hypochondria, what was it but the very greatness of the man? The depth and tenderness of his wild affections: the quantity of *sympathy* he had with things, — the quantity of insight he would yet get into the heart of things, the mastery he would yet get over things: this was his hypochondria. The man's misery, as man's misery always does, came of his greatness. Samuel Johnson too is that kind of man. Sorrow-stricken, half-distracted; the wide element of mournful *black* enveloping him, — wide as the world. It is the character of a prophetic man; a man with his whole soul *seeing*, and struggling to see.

On this ground, too, I explain to myself Cromwell's reputed confusion of speech. To himself the internal meaning was sun-clear; but the material with which he was to clothe it in utterance was not there. He had *lived* silent; a great unnamed sea of Thought round him all his days; and in his way of life little call to attempt *naming* or uttering that. With his sharp power of vision, resolute power of action, I doubt not he could have learned to write Books withal, and speak fluently enough;—he did harder things than writing of Books. This kind of man is precisely he who is fit for doing manfully all things you will set him on doing. Intellect is not speaking and logicizing; it is seeing and ascertaining. Virtue, *Vir-tus*, manhood, *hero*hood, is not fair-spoken immaculate regularity; it is first of all, what the Germans well name it, *Tugend* (*Taugend, dow*-ing or *Dough*-tiness), Courage and the Faculty to *do*. This basis of the matter Cromwell had in him.

One understands moreover how, though he could not speak in Parliament, he might *preach*, rhapsodic preaching; above all, how he might be great in extempore prayer. These are the free outpouring utterances of what is in the heart: method is not required in them; warmth, depth, sincerity are all that is required. Cromwell's habit of prayer is a notable feature of him. All his great enterprises were commenced with prayer. In dark inextricable-looking difficulties, his Officers and he used to assemble, and pray alternately, for hours, for days, till some definite resolution rose among them, some "door of hope," as they would name it, disclosed itself. Consider that. In tears, in fervent prayers, and cries to the great God, to have pity on them, to make His light shine before them. They, armed Soldiers of Christ, as they felt themselves to be; a little band of Christian Brothers, who had drawn the sword against a great black devouring world not Christian, but Mammonish, Devilish, — they cried to God in their straits, in their extreme need, not to forsake the Cause that was His. The light which now rose upon them, — how could a human soul, by any means at all, get better light? Was not the purpose so formed like to be precisely the best, wisest, the one to be followed without hesitation any more? To them it was as the shining of Heaven's own Splendor in the waste-howling darkness; the Pillar of Fire by night, that was to guide them on their desolate perilous way. *Was* it not such? Can a man's soul, to this hour, get guidance by any other method than intrinsically by that same, — devout prostration of the earnest struggling soul before the Highest, the Giver of all Light; be such *prayer* a spoken, articulate, or be it a voiceless, inarticulate one? There is no other method. "Hypocrisy"? One begins to be weary of all that. They who call it so, have no right to speak on such matters. They never formed a purpose, what one can call a purpose. They went about balancing expediences, plausibilities; gathering votes, advices; they never were alone with the *truth* of a thing at all. Cromwell's prayers were likely to be "eloquent," and much more than that. His was the heart of a man who *could* pray.

But indeed his actual Speeches, I apprehend, were not nearly so ineloquent, incondite, as they look. We find he was, what all speakers aim to be, an impressive speaker, even in Parliament; one who, from the first, had weight. With that rude passionate voice of his, he was always understood to *mean* something, and men wished to know what. He disregarded eloquence, nay despised and disliked it; spoke always without premeditation of the words he was to use.

The Reporters, too, in those days seem to have been singularly candid; and to have given the Printer precisely what they found on their own note-paper. And withal, what a strange proof is it of Cromwell's being the premeditative ever-calculating hypocrite, acting a play before the world, That to the last he took no more charge of his Speeches! How came he not to study his words a little, before flinging them out to the public? If the words were true words, they could be left to shift for themselves.

But with regard to Cromwell's "lying," we will make one remark. This, I suppose, or something like this, to have been the nature of it. All parties found themselves deceived in him; each party understood him to be meaning *this*, heard him even say so, and behold he turns-out to have been meaning *that!* He was, cry they, the chief of liars. But now, intrinsically, is not all this the inevitable fortune, not of a false man in such times, but simply of a superior man? Such a man must have *reticences* in him. If he walk wearing his heart upon his sleeve for daws to peck at, his journey will not extend far! There is no use for any man's taking-up his abode in a house built of glass. A man always is to be himself the judge how much of his mind he will show to other men; even to those he would have work along with him. There are impertinent inquiries made: your rule is, to leave the inquirer *un*informed on that matter; not, if you can help it, *mis*informed, but precisely as dark as he was! This, could one hit the right phrase of response, is what the wise and faithful man would aim to answer in such a case.

Cromwell, no doubt of it, spoke often in the dialect of small subaltern parties; uttered to them a *part* of his mind. Each little party thought him all its own. Hence their rage, one and all, to find him not of their party, but of his own party! Was it his blame? At all seasons of his history he must have felt, among such people, how, if he explained to them the deeper insight he had, they must either have shuddered aghast at it, or believing it, their own little compact hypothesis must have gone wholly to wreck. They could not have worked in his province any more; nay perhaps they could not now have worked in their own province. It is the inevitable position of a great man among small men. Small men, most active, useful, are to be seen everywhere, whose whole activity depends on some conviction which to you is palpably a limited one; imperfect, what we call an *error*. But would it be a kindness always, is it a duty always or often, to disturb them in that? Many a man, doing loud work in the world, stands only on some thin traditionality, conventionality; to him indubitable, to you incredible: break that beneath him, he sinks to endless depths! "I might have my hand full of truth," said Fontenelle, "and open only my little finger."

And if this be the fact even in matters of doctrine, how much more in all departments of practice! He that cannot withal *keep his mind to himself* cannot practise any considerable thing whatever. And we call it "dissimulation," all this? What would you think of calling the general of an army a dissembler because he did not tell every corporal and private soldier, who pleased to put the question, what his thoughts were about everything? Cromwell, I should rather say, managed all this in a manner we must admire for its perfection. An endless vortex of such questioning "corporals" rolled confusedly round him through his whole course; whom he did answer. It must have been as a great true-seeing man that he managed this too. Not one proved falsehood, as I said; not one! Of what man that ever wound himself through such a coil of things will you say so much? —

But in fact there are two errors, widely prevalent, which pervert to the very basis our judgments formed about such men as Cromwell; about their "ambition," "falsity," and suchlike. The first is what I might call substituting the *goal* of their career for the course and starting-point of it. The vulgar Historian of a Cromwell fancies that he had determined on being Protector of England, at the time when he was ploughing the marsh lands of Cambridgeshire. His career lay all mapped-out: a program of the whole drama; which he then step by step dramatically unfolded, with all manner of cunning, deceptive dramaturgy, as he went on, — the hollow, scheming Ὑποκριτής, or Play-actor, that he was! This is a radical perversion; all but universal in such cases. And think for an instant how different the fact is! How much does one of *us* foresee of his own life? Short way ahead of us it is all dim; an *un*wound skein of possibilities, of apprehensions, attemptabilities, vague-looming hopes. This Cromwell had *not* his life lying all in that fashion of Program, which he needed then, with that unfathomable cunning of his, only to enact dramatically, scene after scene! Not so. We see it so; but to him it was in no measure so. What absurdities would fall-away of themselves, were this one undeniable fact kept honestly in view by History! Historians indeed will tell you that they do keep it in view; — but look whether such is practically the fact! Vulgar History, as in this Cromwell's case, omits it altogether; even the best kinds of History only remember it now and then. To remember it duly with rigorous perfection, as in the fact it *stood*, requires indeed a rare faculty; rare, nay impossible.

A very Shakspeare for faculty; or more than Shakspeare; who could *enact* a brother man's biography, see with the brother man's eyes at all points of his course what things *he* saw; in short, *know* his course and him, as few " Historians " are like to do. Half or more of all the thick-plied perversions which distort our image of Cromwell, will disappear, if we honestly so much as try to represent them so ; in sequence, as they *were;* not in the lump, as they are thrown-down before us.

But a second error, which I think the generality commit, refers to this same " ambition " itself. We exaggerate the ambition of Great Men; we mistake what the nature of it is. Great Men are not ambitious in that sense; he is a small poor man that is ambitious so. Examine the man who lives in misery because he does not shine above other men ; who goes about producing himself, pruriently anxious about his gifts and claims ; struggling to force everybody, as it were begging everybody for God's sake, to acknowledge him a great man, and set him over the heads of men ! Such a creature is among the wretchedest sights seen under this sun. A *great* man? A poor morbid prurient empty man; fitter for the ward of a hospital, than for a throne among men. I advise you to keep-out of his way. He cannot walk on quiet paths; unless you will look at him, wonder at him, write paragraphs about him, he cannot live. It is the *emptiness* of the man, not his greatness. Because there is nothing in himself, he hungers and thirsts that you would find something in him. In good truth, I believe no great man, not so much as a genuine man who had health and real substance in him of whatever magnitude, was ever much tormented in this way.

Your Cromwell, what good could it do him to be " noticed " by noisy crowds of people ? God his Maker already noticed him. He, Cromwell, was already there; no notice would make *him* other than he already was. Till his hair was grown gray; and Life from the downhill slope was all seen to be limited, not infinite but finite, and all a measurable matter *how* it went, — he had been content to plough the ground, and read his Bible. He in his old days could not support it any longer, without selling himself to Falsehood, that he might ride in gilt carriages to Whitehall, and have clerks with bundles of papers haunting him, "Decide this, decide that," which in utmost sorrow of heart no man can perfectly decide! What could gilt carriages do for this man? From of old, was there not in his life a weight of meaning, a terror and a splendor as of Heaven itself? His existence there as man set him beyond the need of gilding. Death, Judgment and Eternity: these already lay as the background of whatsoever he thought or did. All his life lay begirt as in a sea of nameless Thoughts, which no speech of a mortal could name. God's Word, as the Puritan prophets of that time had read it: this was great, and all else was little to him. To call such a man "ambitious," to figure him as the prurient windbag described above, seems to me the poorest solecism. Such a man will say: "Keep your gilt carriages and huzzaing mobs, keep your red-tape clerks, your influentialities, your important businesses. Leave me alone, leave me alone; there is *too much of life* in me already!" Old Samuel Johnson, the greatest soul in England in his day, was not ambitious. "Corsica Boswell" flaunted at public shows with printed ribbons round his hat; but the great old Samuel stayed at home. The world-wide soul wrapt-up in its thoughts, in its sorrows; — what could paradings, and ribbons in the hat, do for it?

Ah yes, I will say again: The great *silent* men!

Looking round on the noisy inanity of the world, words with little meaning, actions with little worth, one loves to reflect on the great Empire of *Silence.* The noble silent men, scattered here and there, each in his department; silently thinking, silently working; whom no Morning Newspaper makes mention of! They are the salt of the Earth. A country that has none or few of these is in a bad way. Like a forest which had no *roots;* which had all turned into leaves and boughs; — which must soon wither and be no forest. Woe for us if we had nothing but what we can *show,* or speak. Silence, the great Empire of Silence: higher than the stars; deeper than the Kingdoms of Death! It alone is great; all else is small. I hope we English will long maintain our *grand talent pour le silence.* Let others that cannot do without standing on barrel-heads, to spout, and be seen of all the market-place, cultivate speech exclusively, — become a most green forest without roots! Solomon says, There is a time to speak; but also a time to keep silence. Of some great silent Samuel, not urged to writing, as old Samuel Johnson says he was, by *want of money,* and nothing other, one might ask, "Why do not you too get up and speak; promulgate your system, found your sect?" "Truly," he will answer, "I am *continent* of my thought hitherto; happily I have yet had the ability to keep it in me, no compulsion strong enough to speak it. My 'system' is not for promulgation first of all; it is for serving myself to live by. That is the great purpose of it to me. And then the 'honor'? Alas, yes; — but as Cato said of the statue: So many statues in that Forum ot yours, may it not be better if they ask, Where is Cato's statue?" —

But now, by way of counterpoise to this of Silence, let me say that there are two kinds of ambition; one wholly blamable, the other laudable and inevitable. Nature has provided that the great silent Samuel shall not be silent too long. The selfish wish to shine over others, let it be accounted altogether poor and miserable. "Seekest thou great things, seek them not:" this is most true. And yet, I say, there is an irrepressible tendency in every man to develop himself according to the magnitude which Nature has made him of; to speak-out, to act-out, what Nature has laid in him. This is proper, fit, inevitable; nay it is a duty, and even the summary of duties for a man. The meaning of life here on earth might be defined as consisting in this: To unfold your *self*, to work what thing you have the faculty for. It is a necessity for the human being, the first law of our existence. Coleridge beautifully remarks that the infant learns to *speak* by this necessity it feels. We will say therefore: To decide about ambition, whether it is bad or not, you have two things to take into view. Not the coveting of the place alone, but the fitness of the man for the place withal: that is the question. Perhaps the place was *his;* perhaps he had a natural right, and even obligation to seek the place! Mirabeau's ambition to be Prime Minister, how shall we blame it, if he were "the only man in France that could have done any good there"? Hopefuler perhaps had he not so clearly *felt* how much good he could do! But a poor Necker, who could do no good, and had even felt that he could do none, yet sitting broken-hearted because they had flung him out, and he was now quit of it, well might Gibbon mourn over him. Nature, I say, has provided amply that the silent great man shall strive to speak withal; *too* amply, rather!

Fancy, for example, you had revealed to the brave old Samuel Johnson, in his shrouded-up existence, that it was possible for him to do priceless divine work for his country and the whole world. That the perfect Heavenly Law might be made Law on this Earth; that the prayer he prayed daily, " Thy kingdom come," was at length to be fulfilled! If you had convinced his judgment of this; that it was possible, practicable; that he the mournful silent Samuel was called to take a part in it! Would not the whole soul of the man have flamed-up into a divine clearness, into noble utterance and determination to act; casting all sorrows and misgivings under his feet, counting all affliction and contradiction small, — the whole dark element of his existence blazing into articulate radiance of light and lightning? It were a true ambition this! And think now how it actually was with Cromwell. From of old, the sufferings of God's Church, true zealous Preachers of the truth flung into dungeons, whipt, set on pillories, their ears cropt-off, God's Gospelcause trodden under foot of the unworthy: all this had lain heavy on his soul. Long years he had looked upon it, in silence, in prayer; seeing no remedy on Earth; trusting well that a remedy in Heaven's goodness would come, — that such a course was false, unjust, and could not last forever. And now behold the dawn of it; after twelve years silent waiting, all England stirs itself; there is to be once more a Parliament, the Right will get a voice for itself: inexpressible wellgrounded hope has come again into the Earth. Was not such a Parliament worth being a member of? Cromwell threw down his ploughs, and hastened thither.

He spoke there, — rugged bursts of earnestness, of a selfseen truth, where we get a glimpse of them. He worked there; he fought and strove, like a strong true giant of a man, through cannon-tumult and all else, — on and on, till the Cause *triumphed*, its once so formidable enemies all swept from before it, and the dawn of hope had become clear light of victory and certainty. That *he* stood there as the strongest soul of England, the undisputed Hero of all England, — what of this? It was possible that the Law of Christ's Gospel could now establish itself in the world! The Theocracy which John Knox in his pulpit might dream of as a "devout imagination," this practical man, experienced in the whole chaos of most rough practice, dared to consider as capable of being *realized*. Those that were highest in Christ's Church, the devoutest wisest men, were to rule the land : in some considerable degree, it might be so and should be so. Was it not *true*, God's truth? And if *true*, was it not then the very thing to do? The strongest practical intellect in England dared to answer, Yes! This I call a noble true purpose; is it not, in its own dialect, the noblest that could enter into the heart of Statesman or man? For a Knox to take it up was something : but for a Cromwell, with his great sound sense and experience of what our world *was*, — History, I think, shows it only this once in such a degree. I account it the culminating point of Protestantism; the most heroic phasis that "Faith in the Bible" was appointed to exhibit here below. Fancy it : that it were made manifest to one of us, how we could make the Right supremely victorious over Wrong, and all that we had longed and prayed for, as the highest good to England and all lands, an attainable fact!

Well, I must say, the *vulpine* intellect, with its knowingness, its alertness and expertness in "detecting hypocrites," seems to me a rather sorry business. We have had but one such Statesman in England; one man, that I can get sight of, who ever had in the heart of him any such purpose at all. One man, in the course of fifteen-hundred years; and this was his welcome. He had adherents by the hundred or the ten; opponents by the million. Had England rallied all round him, — why, then, England might have been a *Christian* land! As it is, vulpine knowingness sits yet at its hopeless problem, "Given a world of Knaves, to educe an Honesty from their united action;" — how cumbrous a problem, you may see in Chancery Law-Courts, and some other places! Till at length, by Heaven's just anger, but also by Heaven's great grace, the matter begins to stagnate; and this problem is becoming to all men a *palpably* hopeless one. —

But with regard to Cromwell and his purposes: Hume, and a multitude following him, come upon me here with an admission that Cromwell *was* sincere at first; a sincere "Fanatic" at first, but gradually became a "Hypocrite" as things opened round him. This of the Fanatic-Hypocrite is Hume's theory of it; extensively applied since, — to Mahomet and many others. Think of it seriously, you will find something in it; not much, not all, very far from all. Sincere hero hearts do not sink in this miserable manner. The Sun flings-forth impurities, gets balefully incrusted with spots; but it does not quench itself, and become no Sun at all, but a mass of Darkness! I will venture to say that such never befell a great deep Cromwell; I think, never. Nature's own lion-hearted Son; Antæus-like, his strength is got by *touching the Earth,* his Mother; lift him up from the Earth, lift him up into Hypocrisy, Inanity, his strength is gone. We will not assert that Cromwell was an immaculate man; that he fell into no faults, no insincerities among the rest. He was no dilettante professor of "perfections," "immaculate conducts." He was a rugged Orson, rending his rough way through actual true *work,* — doubtless with many a *fall* therein. Insincerities, faults, very many faults daily and hourly: it was too well known to him; known to God and him!

The Sun was dimmed many a time; but the Sun had not himself grown a Dimness. Cromwell's last words, as he lay waiting for death, are those of a Christian heroic man. Broken prayers to God, that He would judge him and this Cause, He since man could not, in justice yet in pity. They are most touching words. He breathed-out his wild great soul, its toils and sins all ended now, into the presence of his Maker, in this manner.

I, for one, will not call the man a Hypocrite! Hypocrite, mummer, the life of him a mere theatricality; empty barren quack, hungry for the shouts of mobs? The man had made obscurity do very well for him till his head was gray; and now he *was*, there as he stood recognized unblamed, the virtual King of England. Cannot a man do without King's Coaches and Cloaks? Is it such a blessedness to have clerks forever pestering you with bundles of papers in red tape? A simple Diocletian prefers planting of cabbages; a George Washington, no very immeasurable man, does the like. One would say, it is what any genuine man could do; and would do. The instant his real work were out in the matter of Kingship, — away with it!

Let us remark, meanwhile, how indispensable everywhere a *King* is, in all movements of men. It is strikingly shown, in this very War, what becomes of men when they cannot find a Chief Man, and their enemies can. The Scotch Nation was all but unanimous in Puritanism; zealous and of one mind about it, as in this English end of the Island was always far from being the case. But there was no great Cromwell among them; poor tremulous, hesitating, diplomatic Argyles and suchlike; none of them had a heart true enough for the truth, or durst commit himself to the truth. They had no leader; and the scattered Cavalier party in that country had one : Montrose, the noblest of all the Cavaliers ; an accomplished, gallant-hearted, splendid man ; what one may call the Hero-Cavalier. Well, look at it ; on the one hand subjects without a King ; on the other a King without subjects ! The subjects without King can do nothing ; the subject-less King can do something. This Montrose, with a handful of Irish or Highland savages, few of them so much as guns in their hands, dashes at the drilled Puritan armies like a wild whirlwind ; sweeps them, time after time, some five times over, from the field before him. He was at one period, for a short while, master of all Scotland. One man ; but he was a man : a million zealous men, but *without* the one ; they against him were powerless ! Perhaps of all the persons in that Puritan struggle, from first to last, the single indispensable one was verily Cromwell. To see and dare, and decide ; to be a fixed pillar in the welter of uncertainty ; — a King among them, whether they call him so or not.

Precisely here, however, lies the rub for Cromwell. His other proceedings have all found advocates, and stand generally justified ; but this dismissal of the Rump Parliament and assumption of the Protector-ship, is what no one can pardon him. He had fairly grown to be King in England ; Chief Man of the victorious party in England : but it seems he could not do without the King's Cloak, and sold himself to perdition in order to get it. Let us see a little how this was.

England, Scotland, Ireland, all lying now subdued at the feet of the Puritan Parliament, the practical question arose, What was to be done with it ? How will you govern these Nations, which Providence in a wondrous way has given-up to your disposal ? Clearly those hundred surviving members of the Long Parliament, who sit there as supreme authority, cannot continue forever to sit. What *is* to be done? It was a question which theoretical constitution-builders may find easy to answer; but to Cromwell, looking there into the real practical facts of it, there could be none more complicated. He asked of the Parliament, What it was they would decide upon? It was for the Parliament to say. Yet the Soldiers too, however contrary to Formula, they who had purchased this victory with their blood, it seemed to them that they also should have something to say in it! We will not "For all our fighting have nothing but a little piece of paper." We understand that the Law of God's Gospel, to which He through us has given the victory, shall establish itself, or try to establish itself, in this land!

For three years, Cromwell says, this question had been sounded in the ears of the Parliament. They could make no answer; nothing but talk, talk. Perhaps it lies in the nature of Parliamentary bodies; perhaps no Parliament could in such case make any answer but even that of talk, talk! Nevertheless the question must and shall be answered. You sixty men there, becoming fast odious, even despicable, to the whole nation, whom the nation already calls Rump Parliament, *you* cannot continue to sit there : who or what then is to follow? "Free Parliament," right of Election, Constitutional Formulas of one sort or the other, — the thing is a hungry Fact coming on us, which we must answer or be devoured by it! And who are you that prate of Constitutional Formulas, rights of Parliament? You have had to kill your King, to make Pride's Purges, to expel and banish by the law of the stronger whosoever would not let your Cause prosper: there are but fifty or three-score of you left there, debating in these days. Tell us what we shall do; not in the way of Formula, but of practicable Fact!

How they did finally answer, remains obscure to this day. The diligent Godwin himself admits that he cannot make it out. The likeliest is, that this poor Parliament still would not, and indeed could not dissolve and disperse; that when it came to the point of actually dispersing, they, again, for the tenth or twentieth time, adjourned it, — and Cromwell's patience failed him. But we will take the favorablest hypothesis ever started for the Parliament; the favorablest, though I believe it is not the true one, but too favorable.

According to this version: At the uttermost crisis, when Cromwell and his Officers were met on the one hand, and the fifty or sixty Rump Members on the other, it was suddenly told Cromwell that the Rump in its despair *was* answering in a very singular way; that in their splenetic envious despair to keep-out the Army at least, these men were hurrying through the House a kind of Reform Bill, — Parliament to be chosen by the whole of England; equable electoral division into districts; free suffrage, and the rest of it! A very questionable, or indeed for *them* an unquestionable thing. Reform Bill, free suffrage of Englishmen? Why, the Royalists themselves, silenced indeed but not exterminated, perhaps out*number* us; the great numerical majority of England was always indifferent to our Cause, merely looked at it and submitted to it. It is in weight and force, not by counting of heads, that we are the majority! And now with your Formulas and Reform Bills, the whole matter, sorely won by our swords, shall again launch itself to sea; become a mere hope, and likelihood, *small* even as a likelihood? And it is not a likelihood; it is a certainty, which we have won, by God's strength and our own right hands, and do now hold *here.* Cromwell walked down to these refractory Members; interrupted them in that rapid speed of their Reform Bill; — ordered them to begone, and talk there no more. Can we not forgive him? Can we not understand him? John Milton, who looked on it all near at hand, could applaud him. The Reality had swept the Formulas away before it. I fancy, most men who were realities in England might see into the necessity of that.

The strong daring man, therefore, has set all manner of Formulas and logical superficialities against him; has dared appeal to the genuine Fact of this England, Whether it will support him or not? It is curious to see how he struggles to govern in some constitutional way; find some Parliament to support him; but cannot. His first Parliament, the one they call Barebones's Parliament, is, so to speak, a *Convocation of the Notables.* From all quarters of England the leading Ministers and chief Puritan Officials nominate the men most distinguished by religious reputation, influence and attachment to the true Cause : these are assembled to shape-out a plan. They sanctioned what was past; shaped as they could what was to come. They were scornfully called *Barebones's Parliament :* the man's name, it seems, was not *Barebones,* but Barbone, — a good enough man. Nor was it a jest, their work; it was a most serious reality, — a trial on the part of these Puritan Notables how far the Law of Christ could become the Law of this England. There were men of sense among them, men of some quality; men of deep piety I suppose the most of them were. They failed, it seems, and broke-down, endeavoring to reform the Court of Chancery! They dissolved themselves, as incompetent; delivered-up their power again into the hands of the Lord General Cromwell, to do with it what he liked and could.

What *will* he do with it? The Lord General Cromwell, "Commander-in-chief of all the Forces raised and to be raised;" he hereby sees himself, at this unexampled juncture, as it were the one available Authority left in England, nothing between England and utter Anarchy but him alone. Such is the undeniable Fact of his position and England's, there and then. What will he do with it? After deliberation, he decides that he will *accept* it; will formally, with public solemnity, say and vow before God and men, "Yes, the Fact is so, and I will do the best I can with it!" Protectorship, Instrument of Government, — these are the external forms of the thing; worked out and sanctioned as they could in the circumstances be, by the Judges, by the leading Official people, "Council of Officers and Persons of interest in the Nation:" and as for the thing itself, undeniably enough, at the pass matters had now come to, there *was* no alternative but Anarchy or that. Puritan England might accept it or not; but Puritan England was, in real truth, saved from suicide thereby! I believe the Puritan People did, in an inarticulate, grumbling, yet on the whole grateful and real way, accept this anomalous act of Oliver's; at least, he and they together made it good, and always better to the last. But in their Parliamentary *articulate* way, they had their difficulties, and never knew fully what to say to it! —

Oliver's second Parliament, properly his *first* regular Parliament, chosen by the rule laid-down in the Instrument of Government, did assemble, and worked; — but got, before long, into bottomless questions as to the Protector's *right*, as to "usurpation," and so forth; and had at the earliest legal day to be dismissed. Cromwell's concluding Speech to these men is a remarkable one. So likewise to his third Parliament, in similar rebuke for their pedantries and obstinacies. Most rude, chaotic, all these Speeches are; but most earnest-looking. You would say, it was a sincere helpless man; not used to *speak* the great inorganic thought of him, but to act it rather! A helplessness of utterance, in such bursting fulness of meaning. He talks much about "births of Providence": All these changes, so many victories and events, were not forethoughts, and theatrical contrivances of men, of *me* or of men; it is blind blasphemers that will persist in calling them so! He insists with a heavy sulphurous wrathful emphasis on this. As he well might. As if a Cromwell in that dark huge game he had been playing, the world wholly thrown into chaos round him, had *foreseen* it all, and played it all off like a precontrived puppetshow by wood and wire! These things were foreseen by no man, he says; no man could tell what a day would bring forth: they were "births of Providence," God's finger guided us on, and we came at last to clear height of victory, God's Cause triumphant in these Nations; and you as a Parliament could assemble together, and say in what manner all this could be *organized*, reduced into rational feasibility among the affairs of men. You were to help with your wise counsel in doing that. "You have had such an opportunity as no Parliament in England ever had." Christ's Law, the Right and True, was to be in some measure made the Law of this land. In place of that, you have got into your idle pedantries, constitutionalities, bottomless cavillings and questionings about written laws for *my* coming here;—and would send the whole matter in Chaos again, because I have no Notary's parchment, but only God's voice from the battle-whirlwind, for being President among you! That opportunity is gone; and we know not when it will return. You have had your constitutional Logic; and Mammon's Law, not Christ's Law, rules yet in this land. "God be judge between you and me!" These are his final words to them: Take you your constitution-formulas in your hand; and I my *in-formal* struggles, purposes, realities and acts; and "God be judge between you and me!"—

We said above what shapeless, involved chaotic things the printed Speeches of Cromwell are. *Wilfully* ambiguous, unintelligible, say the most: a hypocrite shrouding himself in confused Jesuitic jargon! To me they do not seem so. I will say rather, they afforded the first glimpses I could ever get into the reality of this Cromwell, nay into the possibility of him. Try to believe that he means something, search lovingly what that may be: you will find a real *speech* lying imprisoned in these broken rude tortuous utterances; a meaning in the great heart of this inarticulate man! You will, for the first time, begin to see that he was a man; not an enigmatic chimera, unintelligible to you, incredible to you. The Histories and Biographies written of this Cromwell, written in shallow sceptical generations that could not know or conceive of a deep believing man, are far more *obscure* than Cromwell's Speeches. You look through them only into the infinite vague of Black and the Inane. "Heats and jealousies," says Lord Clarendon himself: "heats and jealousies," mere crabbed whims, theories and crotchets; these induced slow sober quiet Englishmen to lay down their ploughs and work; and fly into red fury of confused war against the best-conditioned of Kings! *Try* if you can find that true. Scepticism writing about Belief may have great gifts; but it is really *ultra vires* there. It is Blindness laying-down the Laws of Optics.—

Cromwell's third Parliament split on the same rock

as his second. Ever the constitutional Formula: How came *you* there? Show us some Notary parchment! Blind pedants : — " Why, surely the same power which makes you a Parliament, that, and something more, made me a Protector!" If my Protectorship is nothing, what in the name of wonder is your Parliamenteership, a reflex and creation of that?

Parliaments having failed, there remained nothing but the way of Despotism. Military Dictators, each with his district, to *coerce* the Royalist and other gainsayers, to govern them, if not by act of Parliament, then by the sword. Formula shall *not* carry it, while the Reality is here ! I will go on, protecting oppressed Protestants abroad, appointing just judges, wise managers, at home, cherishing true Gospel ministers ; doing the best I can to make England a Christian England, greater than old Rome, the Queen of Protestant Christianity; I, since you will not help me; I while God leaves me life ! Why did he not give it up; retire into obscurity again, since the Law would not acknowledge him? cry several. That is where they mistake. For him there was no giving of it up ! Prime Ministers have governed countries, Pitt, Pombal, Choiseul; and their word was a law while it held : but this Prime Minister was one that *could not get resigned*. Let him once resign, Charles Stuart and the Cavaliers waited to kill him ; to kill the Cause *and* him. Once embarked, there is no retreat, no return. This Prime Minister could *retire* no-whither except into his tomb.

One is sorry for Cromwell in his old days. His complaint is incessant of the heavy burden Providence has laid on him. Heavy; which he must bear till death. Old Colonel Hutchinson, as his wife relates it, Hutchinson, his old battle-mate, coming to see him on some indispensable business, much against his will,

— Cromwell " follows him to the door," in a most fraternal, domestic, conciliatory style ; begs that he would be reconciled to him, his old brother in arms ; says how much it grieves him to be misunderstood, deserted by true fellow-soldiers, dear to him from of old : the rigorous Hutchinson, cased in his Republican formula, sullenly goes his way. And the man's head now white ; his strong arm growing weary with its long work ! I think always too of his poor Mother, now very old, living in that Palace of his ; a right brave woman ; as indeed they lived all an honest God-fearing Household there : if she heard a shot go-off, she thought it was her son killed. He had to come to her at least once a day, that she might see with her own eyes that he was yet living. The poor old Mother ! — What had this man gained ; what had he gained ? He had a life of sore strife and toil, to his last day. Fame, ambition, place in History ? His dead body was hung in chains ; his " place in History," — place in History forsooth ! — has been a place of ignominy, accusation, blackness and disgrace ; and here, this day, who knows if it is not rash in me to be among the first that ever ventured to pronounce him not a knave and liar, but a genuinely honest man ! Peace to him. Did he not, in spite of all, accomplish much for us ? *We* walk smoothly over his great rough heroic life ; step-over his body sunk in the ditch there. We need not *spurn* it, as we step on it ! Let the Hero rest. It was not to *men's* judgment that he appealed : nor have men judged him very well.

Precisely a century and a year after this of Puritanism had got itself hushed-up into decent composure, and its results made smooth, in 1688, there broke-out a far deeper explosion, much more difficult to hush-up, known to all mortals, and like to be long known, by the name of French Revolution. It is properly the

18

third and final act of Protestantism; the explosive confused return of mankind to Reality and Fact, now that they were perishing of Semblance and Sham. We call our English Puritanism the second act: "Well then, the Bible is true; let us go by the Bible!" "In Church," said Luther; "In Church and State," said Cromwell, "let us go by what actually *is* God's Truth." Men have to return to reality; they cannot live on semblance. The French Revolution, or third act, we may well call the final one; for lower than that savage *Sansculottism* men cannot go. They stand there on the nakedest haggard Fact, undeniable in all seasons and circumstances; and may and must begin again confidently to build-up from that. The French explosion, like the English one, got its King, — who had no Notary parchment to show for himself. We have still to glance for a moment at Napoleon, our second modern King.

Napoleon does by no means seem to me so great a man as Cromwell. His enormous victories which reached over all Europe, while Cromwell abode mainly in our little England, are but as the high *stilts* on which the man is seen standing; the stature of the man is not altered thereby. I find in him no such *sincerity* as in Cromwell; only a far inferior sort. No silent walking, through long years, with the Awful Unnamable of this Universe; "walking with God," as he called it; and faith and strength in that alone: *latent* thought and valor, content to lie latent, then burst out as in blaze of Heaven's lightning! Napoleon lived in an age when God was no longer believed; the meaning of all Silence, Latency, was thought to be Nonentity: he had to begin not out of the Puritan Bible, but out of poor Sceptical *Encyclopédies*. This was the length the man carried it. Meritorious to get so far. His compact, prompt, everyway articulate character is in itself perhaps small, compared with our great chaotic *in*articulate Cromwell's. Instead of "*dumb* Prophet struggling to speak," we have a protentous mixture of the Quack withal! Hume's notion of the Fanatic-Hypocrite, with such truth as it has, will apply much better to Napoleon than it did to Cromwell, to Mahomet or the like, — where indeed taken strictly it has hardly any truth at all. An element of blamable ambition shows itself, from the first, in this man; gets the victory over him at last, and involves him and his work in ruin.

"False as a bulletin" became a proverb in Napoleon's time. He makes what excuse he could for it: that it was necessary to mislead the enemy, to keep-up his own men's courage, and so forth. On the whole, there are no excuses. A man in no case has liberty to tell lies. It had been, in the long-run, *better* for Napoleon too if he had not told any. In fact, if a man have any purpose reaching beyond the hour and day, meant to be found extant *next* day, what good can it ever be to promulgate lies? The lies are found-out; ruinous penalty is exacted for them. No man will believe the liar next time even when he speaks truth, when it is of the last importance that he be believed. The old cry of wolf! A Lie is *no*-thing; you cannot of nothing make something; you make *nothing* at last, and lose your labor into the bargain.

Yet Napoleon *had* a sincerity: we are to distinguish between what is superficial and what is fundamental in insincerity. Across these outer manœuverings and quackeries of his, which were many and most blamable, let us discern withal that the man had a certain instinctive ineradicable feeling for reality; and did base himself upon fact, so long as he had any basis. He has an instinct of Nature better than his culture was. His *savans*, Bourrienne tells us, in that voyage

to Egypt were one evening busily occupied arguing
that there could be no God. They had proved it, to
their satisfaction, by all manner of logic. Napoleon
looking up into the stars, answers, "Very ingenious,
Messieurs: but *who made* all that?" The Atheistic
logic runs-off from him like water; the great Fact
stares him in the face: "Who made all that?" So
too in Practice: he, as every man that can be great,
or have victory in this world, sees, through all entan-
glements, the practical heart of the matter; drives
straight towards that. When the steward of his Tuil-
eries Palace was exhibiting the new upholstery, with
praises, and demonstration how glorious it was, and
how cheap withal, Napoleon, making little answer,
asked for a pair of scissors, clipt one of the gold tas-
sels from a window-curtain, put it in his pocket, and
walked on. Some days afterwards, he produced it at
the right moment, to the horror of his upholstery
functionary; it was not gold but tinsel! In St.
Helena, it is notable how he still, to his last days, insists on the practical, the real. "Why talk and complain; above all, why quarrel with one another?
There is no *result* in it; it comes to nothing that one
can *do*. Say nothing, if one can do nothing!" He
speaks often so, to his poor discontented followers; he
is like a piece of silent strength in the middle of their
morbid querulousness there.

And accordingly was there not what we can call a
faith in him, genuine so far as it went? That this
new enormous Democracy asserting itself here in the
French Revolution is an insuppressible Fact, which
the whole world, with its old forces and institutions,
cannot put down; this was a true insight of his, and
took his conscience and enthusiasm along with it, — a
faith. And did he not interpret the dim purport of it
well? "*La carrière ouverte aux talens*, The imple-

ments to him who can handle them:" this actually is the truth and even the whole truth; it includes whatever the French Revolution, or any Revolution, could mean. Napoleon, in his first period, was a true Democrat. And yet by the nature of him, fostered too by his military trade, he knew that Democracy, if it were a true thing at all, could not be an anarchy: the man had a heart-hatred for anarchy. On that Twentieth of June (1792), Bourrienne and he sat in a coffee-house, as the mob rolled by: Napoleon expresses the deepest contempt for persons in authority that they do not restrain this rabble. On the Tenth of August he wonders why there is no man to command these poor Swiss; they would conquer if there were. Such a faith in Democracy, yet hatred of anarchy, it is that carries Napoleon through all his great work. Through his brilliant Italian Campaigns, onwards to the Peace of Leoben, one would say, his inspiration is: " Triumph to the French Revolution; assertion of it against these Austrian Simulacra that pretend to call it a Simulacrum!" Withal, however, he feels, and has a right to feel, how necessary a strong Authority is; how the Revolution cannot prosper or last without such. To bridle-in that great devouring, self-devouring French Revolution; to *tame* it, so that its intrinsic purpose can be made good, that it may become *organic*, and be able to live among other organisms and *formed* things, not as a wasting destruction alone : is not this still what he partly aimed at, as the true purport of his life; nay what he actually managed to do? Through Wagrams, Austerlitzes; triumph after triumph, — he triumphed so far. There was an eye to see in this man, a soul to dare and do. He rose naturally to be the King. All men saw that he *was* such. The common soldiers used to say on the march : " These babbling *Avocats*, up at Paris; all talk and no work! What wonder it runs all wrong? We shall have to go and put our *Petit Caporal* there!" They went, and put him there; they and France at large. Chief-consulship, Emperorship, victory over Europe; — till the poor Lieutenant of *La Fère*, not unnaturally, might seem to himself the greatest of all men that had been in the world for some ages.

But at this point, I think, the fatal charlatan-element got the upper hand. He apostatized from his old faith in Facts, took to believing in Semblances; strove to connect himself with Austrian Dynasties, Popedoms, with the old false Feudalities which he once saw clearly to be false; — considered that *he* would found "his Dynasty" and so forth; that the enormous French Revolution meant only that! The man was "given-up to strong delusion, that he should believe a lie;" a fearful but most sure thing. He did not know true from false now when he looked at them, — the fearfulest penalty a man pays for yielding to untruth of heart. *Self* and false ambition had now become his god: *self*-deception once yielded to, *all* other deceptions follow naturally more and more. What a paltry patchwork of theatrical paper-mantles, tinsel and mummery, had this man wrapt his own great reality in, thinking to make it more real thereby! His hollow Pope's-*Concordat*, pretending to be a re-establishment of Catholicism, felt by himself to be the method of extirpating it, "*la vaccine de la religion:*" his ceremonial Coronations, consecrations by the old Italian Chimera in Notre-Dame, — "wanting nothing to complete the pomp of it," as Augereau said, "nothing but the half-million of men who had died to put an end to all that"! Cromwell's Inauguration was by the Sword and Bible; what we must call a genuinely *true* one. Sword and Bible were borne before him, without any chimera : were not these the *real* emblems of Puritanism ; its true decoration and insignia ? It had used them both in a very real manner, and pretended to stand by them now ! But this poor Napoleon mistook : he believed too much in the *Dupe-ability* of men; saw no fact deeper in man than Hunger and this ! He was mistaken. Like a man that should build upon cloud ; his house and he fall down in confused wreck, and depart out of the world.

Alas, in all of us this charlatan-element exists ; and *might* be developed, were the temptation strong enough. " Lead us not into temptation " ! But it is fatal, I say, that it *be* developed. The thing into which it enters as a cognizable ingredient is doomed to be altogether transitory ; and, however huge it may *look*, is in itself small. Napoleon's working, accordingly, what was it with all the noise it made ? A flash as of gunpowder wide-spread ; a blazing-up as of dry heath. For an hour the whole Universe seems wrapt in smoke and flame ; but only for an hour. It goes out : the Universe with its old mountains and streams, its stars above and kind soil beneath, is still there.

The Duke of Weimar told his friends always, To be of courage ; this Napoleonism was *unjust*, a falsehood, and could not last. It is true doctrine. The heavier this Napoleon trampled on the world, holding it tyrannously down, the fiercer would the world's recoil against him be, one day. Injustice pays itself with frightful compound-interest. I am not sure but he had better have lost his best park of artillery, or had his best regiment drowned in the sea, than shot that poor German Bookseller, Palm ! It was a palpable tyrannous murderous injustice, which no man, let him paint an inch thick, could make-out to be other. It burnt deep into the hearts of men, it and the like of it ; suppressed fire flashed in the eyes of men, as they thought of it, — waiting their day ! Which day *came :* Germany rose round him. What Napoleon *did* will in the long-run amount to what he did *justly ;* what Nature with her laws will sanction. To what of reality was in him ; to that and nothing more. The rest was all smoke and waste. *La carrière ouverte aux talens :* that great true Message, which has yet to articulate and fulfil itself everywhere, he left in a most inarticulate state. He was a great *ébauche,* a rude-draught never completed ; as indeed what great man is other ? Left in *too* rude a state, alas !

His notions of the world, as he expresses them there at St. Helena, are almost tragical to consider. He seems to feel the most unaffected surprise that it has all gone so ; that he is flung-out on the rock here, and the World is still moving on its axis. France is great, and all-great ; and at bottom, he is France. England itself, he says, is by Nature only an appendage of France ; "another Isle of Oleron to France." So it was *by Nature,* by Napoleon-Nature ; and yet look how in fact — HERE AM I ! He cannot understand it : inconceivable that the reality has not corresponded to his program of it ; that France was not all-great, that he was not France. "Strong delusion," that he should believe the thing to be which *is* not ! The compact, clear-seeing, decisive Italian nature of him, strong, genuine, which he once had, has enveloped itself, half-dissolved itself, in a turbid atmosphere of French fanfaronade. The world was not disposed to be trodden-down underfoot ; to be bound into masses, and built together, as *he* liked, for a pedestal to France and him : the world had quite other purposes in view ! Napoleon's astonishment is extreme. But alas, what help now ? He had gone that way of his ; and Nature also had gone her way. Having once parted with Reality, he tumbles helpless in Vacuity ; no rescue for him.   He had to sink there, mournfully as man seldom did; and break his great heart, and die, — this poor Napoleon: a great implement too soon wasted, till it was useless: our last Great Man!

Our last, in a double sense.   For here finally these wide roamings of ours through so many times and places, in search and study of Heroes, are to terminate. I am sorry for it: there was pleasure for me in this business, if also much pain.   It is a great subject, and a most grave and wide one, this which, not to be too grave about it, I have named *Hero-worship*.   It enters deeply, as I think, into the secret of Mankind's ways and vitalest interests in this world, and is well worth explaining at present.   With six months, instead of six days, we might have done better.   I promised to break-ground on it; I know not whether I have even managed to do that.   I have had to tear it up in the rudest manner in order to get into it at all.   Often enough, with these abrupt utterances thrown-out isolated, unexplained, has your tolerance been put to the trial. Tolerance, patient candor, all-hoping favor and kindness, which I will not speak of at present.   The accomplished and distinguished, the beautiful, the wise, something of what is best in England, have listened patiently to my rude words.   With many feelings, I heartily thank you all; and say, Good be with you all!

INDEX.

86; the infinite nature of Duty, 90.

Mary, Queen, and Knox, 173.

Mayflower, sailing of the, 168.

Mecca, 61, 62.

Middle Ages, represented by Dante and Shakspeare, 115, 116, 120.

Montrose, the Hero-Cavalier, 265.

Musical, all deep things, 99, 100.

Napoleon, a portentous mixture of Quack and Hero, 274; his instinct for the practical, 276; his democratic *faith*, and heart-hatred for anarchy, 277; apostatised from his old faith in Facts, and took to believing in Semblances, 278; this Napoleonism was *unjust*, and could not last, 279.

Nature all one great Miracle, 14, 82, 83, 165; a righteous umpire, 75.

Novalis, on Man, 18; Belief, 70; Shakspeare, 128.

Odin, the first Norse "man of genius," 30; historic rumors and guesses, 31; how he came to be deified, 34; invented "runes," 36; Hero, Prophet, God, 38.

Olaf, King, and Thor, 51.

Original man the *sincere* man, 57, 148.

Paganism, Scandinavian, 10; not mere Allegory, 12; Nature-worship, 14, 40; Hero-worship, 22; creed of our fathers, 24, 46, 50; Impersonation of the visible workings of Nature, 25; contrasted with Greek Paganism, 28; the first Norse Thinker, 30; main practical Belief; indispensable to be brave, 41; hearty, homely, rugged Mythology; Balder, Thor, 45; Consecration of Valor, 52.

Parliaments superseded by Books, 191; Cromwell's Parliaments, 265.

Past, the whole, the possession of the Present, 52.

Poet, the, and Prophet, 96, 119, 131.

Poetry and Prose, distinction of, 99, 108.

Popery, 160, 161.

Poverty, advantages of, 129.

Priest, the true, a kind of Prophet, 136.

Printing, consequences of, 191.

Private judgment, 146.

Progress of the Species, 139.

Prose. See Poetry.

Protestantism, the root of Modern European History, 145, 146; not dead yet, 161; its living fruit, 167, 231.

Purgatory, noble Catholic conception of, 114.

Puritanism, founded by Knox, 168; true beginning of America, 168; the one epoch of Scotland, 169; Theocracy, 177-179; Puritanism in England, 236, 237.

Quackery originates nothing, 11, 55; age of, 203; Quacks and Dupes, 250.

Ragnarök, 50.

Reformer, the true, 136.

Religion, a man's, the chief fact with regard to him, 8; based on Hero-worship, 18; propagating, by the sword, 74; cannot succeed by being "easy," 85.

Revolution, 227; the French, 231, 273.

Richter, 163.

Right and Wrong, 90, 115.

Rousseau, not a strong man; his Portrait; egoism, 214; his passionate appeals, 216; his Books, like himself, unhealthy; the

MONK AND KNIGHT.

An Historical Study in Fiction.

BY THE REV. DR. F. W. GUNSAULUS.

Two Vols. 12mo, 707 pages. Price, $2.00.

This work is one that challenges attention for its ambitious character and its high aim. It is an historical novel, — or, rather, as the author prefers to call it, " An Historical Study in Fiction." It is the result of long and careful study of the period of which it treats, and hence is the product of genuine sympathies and a freshly-fired imagination. The field is Europe, and the period is the beginning of the sixteenth century, — a time when the fading glow of the later Renaissance is giving place to the brighter glories of the dawning Reformation.

The book deals, in a broad sense, with the grand theme of the progress of intellectual liberty. Many of its characters are well-known historical personages, — such as Erasmus, Sir Thomas More, Cardinal Wolsey, Henry VIII. of England, Francis I. of France, the disturbing monk Martin Luther, and the magnificent Pope Leo X.; other characters are of course fictitious, introduced to give proper play to the author's fancy and to form a suitable framework for the story.

Interwoven with the more solid fabric are gleaming threads of romance; and bright bits of description and glows of sentiment relieve the more sombre coloring. The memorable meeting of the French and English monarchs on the Field of the Cloth of Gold, with its gorgeous pageantry of knights and steeds and silken banners, and all the glitter and charm of chivalry, furnish material for several chapters, in which the author's descriptive powers are put to the severest test; while the Waldensian heroes in their mountain homes, resisting the persecutions of their religious foes, afford some thrilling and dramatic situations.

Sold by all booksellers, or mailed, on receipt of price, by

A. C. McCLURG & CO., PUBLISHERS,

COR. WABASH AVE. AND MADISON ST., CHICAGO.

Printed in the United Kingdom
 by Lightning Source UK Ltd.
116428UKS00001B/26